FROM 0 TO 260+ PROPERTIES IN 7 YEARS

100% SATISFACTION GUARANTEED!

If you read this book and you don't think the knowledge you gain will increase your property profits by at least 10 times the book's cost, then post it back to me for a full refund!*

It's simple — you either profit or you don't pay. You can't lose!

(*See pages xiv to xv for the full terms and conditions of this offer.)

FROM 0 TO 260+ PROPERTIES IN 7 YEARS

Steve McKnight

#1 Best-Selling Author and Professional Investor

Wrightbooks

BICENTENNIAL
1807
WILEY
2007
BICENTENNIAL

WHAT PEOPLE ARE SAYING ABOUT
FROM 0 TO 260+ PROPERTIES IN 7 YEARS

'It might sound clichéd, but Steve McKnight has done it again. This book takes investing to the next level and introduces strategies I've not seen or heard anywhere else ever before.'

— **Allan Rawack (NSW)**

'Read this book! It's a toolkit of "How-to" information that's relevant to every current and aspiring investor.'

— **Ryan Minster (Vic.)**

'While the whole book is great, chapter 11 is a real cracker! The content is new, powerful and challenging.'

— **Craig Sutherland-Muir (NSW)**

'This is just about the best investing book I've ever read, and that's saying something because I've read lots of them.'

— **Greg Brierley (ACT)**

'The information in this book is priceless! It's clear, practical and provides confidence. For example Steve's "Three Second Solution" (chapter 15) is like a secret weapon!'

— **Tammy Bolch (Qld)**

'If you're serious and want to increase your property portfolio then this book is a must have! It's not only entertaining, it provides insights that all property investors should consider regardless of their skills and experience.'

— **Rachel Bobrowski (NSW)**

'If you're hungry for new and exciting concepts then this book is for you. It's practical without being complicated, and entertaining while also packed with analytical and sensible information. It's well worth buying.'

— **Tamsin Young (WA)**

'I'm only up to chapter 12 and I can't put it down! I like the way it contains income and growth strategies, and how it's full of real-life deals that show you how to make money in the current market.'

— **Cassie Buono (NSW)**

'This book sets a new standard of excellence when it comes to investing books! It's worth many times the asking price.'

— **Luke Abnett (Qld)**

'The content of "0 to 260+" is real and relevant to today's property market. I now have a number of new ideas on how to create additional value, whether at purchase, during ownership/ tenancy, renovation or sale. This is recommended reading.'

— **Mark Milkos (NSW)**

'There isn't another property book around like it! It's certainly investing "brain food" as it will help you to create a winning investing mindset at the same time as delivering unique and practical tools and concepts.'

— **Jo Bourke (NSW)**

'I couldn't put this book down! Where other investment books can be dry and boring, Steve's conversational style makes it interesting and enjoyable. I found many new "a-ha" moments. Thanks!'

— **Richard Muhling (Qld)**

First published 2007 by Wrightbooks
an imprint of John Wiley & Sons Australia, Ltd
42 McDougall Street, Milton Qld 4064

Offices also in Sydney and Melbourne

Typeset in AGaramond 12/14.4 pt

National Library of Australia Cataloguing-in-Publication data:

McKnight, Steve.

     From 0 to 260+ Properties in 7 Years.

     Includes index.

     ISBN 9780731405770.

     ISBN 0 731405 77 3

     1. Real estate investment. 2. Real estate business.
     I. Title.

     332.6324

Cover design by Alister Cameron

Front cover photograph © iStockphoto.com (photograph by Colin McKie)

Edited and typeset by Damian Alway <www.PublishingServices.com.au>

Printed in Australia by McPherson's Printing Group

10 9 8 7 6 5 4 3 2 1

Disclaimer

Contents

Part III — Real Estate 'Steve Style'

Part IV — Deal Time

Part V — What Next?

ACKNOWLEDGEMENTS

'Don't hoard treasure down here where it gets eaten by moths
and corroded by rust or worse, stolen by burglars! Stockpile
treasure in heaven, where it's safe from moth and rust and
burglars. It's obvious, isn't it? The place where your treasure is,
is the place you will most want to be, and end up being.'

— Matthew 6:19-21

While this is a book about wealth creation, my life has become far richer
than I could ever have imagined since accepting Jesus as my Lord and
Saviour in 2001. It's God, not me, who deserves the complete credit
for this book! All the thoughts and information I've included reflect
the ideas and inspiration He provided through prayer.

This book was written in eight weeks and, as such, is a bona
fide miracle. It was only possible with the assistance of many more
people than I could list on one page, so a special thank you to all who
helped. Specifically, I'd like to acknowledge the following:

➲ my wife and children for accepting the sacrifices that were
made to write this book

➲ the office team: Eugene, Jeremy, Brendan, Simon, Lisa,
David G. and Elise

➲ Katrina for listening to the ramblings of an exhausted author

➲ the generous contributors: Juliet, Jan, Dale, Vanessa, Cam
and Lisa, Troy and Bec, Tammy, Katrina and Suzanne,
Anna, Simon and Melissa

➲ the many parties who were gracious enough to allow my
publishers permission to reproduce the photos and graphs
that appear in this book (see overleaf for a full listing)

➲ the support team, including Alister and Damian, and those who
helped to proofread the book and provided feedback.

More than merely enjoying this book, my sincerest hope and prayer
is that you will apply the information herein and, when it works, start
teaching it to others. Thank you for your trust in buying this book.

IMAGE CREDITS
(More Acknowledgements!)

Chapter 2. Extracts from a conversation with Brendan Nichols are reproduced with Brendan's kind permission.

Chapter 5. Two graphs constructed using statistics sourced from the Reserve Bank of Australia (RBA) have been reprinted with the bank's permission.

Chapter 15. Photograph of a house in Ballarat is reproduced with the kind permission of Dean Parker.

Chapter 16. Two photos from contributor Troy Harris, reproduced with his permission.

Chapter 17. Two photos by contributor Tammy Reid, reproduced with her permission.

Chapter 18. Photo from contributors Suzanne Davis and Katrina Maes, reproduced with the permission of Katrina Maes.

Chapter 19. Before renovation images reproduced with kind permission of Dee McCleay. After renovation images reproduced with the permission of Terry Tompkin.

Chapter 21. Two photos from contributor Melissa Lowe, reproduced with Melissa's kind permission.

Chapter 22. Two photos from contributor Kate Gilbert, reproduced with her permission.

IN ADDITION, all graphs and charts created using Microsoft Excel have been reprinted with the kind permission of the Microsoft Corporation.

Bad Advice in a Fish and Chip Shop

Being a chubby kid at primary school, I wasn't blessed with much popularity, so the people that I did manage to form friendships with in those early years will always have a special place in my heart. You'll understand then that a chance run-in with Dean Maloney, an old primary school mate, in a local fish and chip shop a few years back, resulted in more than the usual swap of pleasantries.

As the chips were cooking Dean and I filled each other in on all that we'd done over the past 15 or so years since we'd last met. It turned out that Dean had become a successful plumber, and when he discovered that I was a qualified chartered accountant, he said, 'Steve, I pay a fortune in income tax, is there any way I can invest some money and lower the amount the government stings me at the same time?' Happy to help, I told Dean about an investing strategy called negative gearing.

'It works like this', I said, 'you buy a property that has more expenses than income (one that makes a loss). You then offset your loss against the money you earn from your job, so overall you'll end up paying less tax. In the meantime, you'll make a profit as your property goes up in value, but you won't pay any tax on that profit until you sell'.

As we paid for our take away Dean asked, 'Is it legal?'

'Absolutely', I said. 'Stacks of people are doing it, and I hope to do it too when I have more money'.

While I haven't seen Dean since, I often think back to that conversation and hope, with all my heart, that he didn't take my advice. Although I answered accurately and truthfully, any argument for blindly following the strategy I suggested would contain a massive flaw. The name of the wealth-creation game isn't to save tax, it's to make money.

Dean's question touches on two key investing truths:

1. if you make money, then you must expect to pay tax, and

2. making a loss is never a good idea.

Sadly, today, even right this very second, there will be people like Dean wondering whether or not right now is a good time to buy real estate. Since the first question they'll ask themselves is, 'How do I save tax?', their choices about which properties to buy and which strategies to use will make it very difficult to ever achieve financial independence.

Like lotto, there are far more losers than there are winners in the property game, and far more dreamers than people achieving and living the dream of owning enough property to fund their chosen lifestyles. An inescapable truth of wealth creation is that you must buy assets that make money. If you own property, shares or businesses that are currently losing money, then you'll be burning wealth, rather than building it.

As someone who's bought (in conjunction with my former business partner Dave Bradley) more than 260 properties in the past seven years, my advice is this: use a competent accountant for tax advice, and find a successful investor to teach you about profitable investing. (And don't take advice you hear in fish and chip shops.)

Steve's Investing Tip

It's simple. Sustainable wealth creation demands that you buy properties that make money, *all* the time.

IN A NUTSHELL

Are your properties making money? Is the strategy that you're using providing the results you desire? Success is no fluke. The more you do of what you've done, the more you'll get of what you've got. In a nutshell, I've written this book to share with you the exact same information that I'm giving my family and closest friends concerning the following two areas.

1. The Interest Rate Squeeze

If you're not fully confident and skilled at property investing then you'll find the current property market a treacherous and dangerous place to invest in. The inflation genie has escaped its bottle, and interest rates are now trending up in an attempt to catch and control it.

Higher interest rates will result in decreased home loan affordability, especially for Aussies who have gorged themselves silly at the 'borrow as much as you like' debt buffet. The consequence will be more houses put up for sale and, in turn, this will cause housing supply to exceed buyer demand, resulting in pressure for property prices to soften.

Sophisticated investors always maintain control and there's much you can do to protect yourself. This book contains detailed strategies revealing many options that will safeguard your property portfolio in the event of a real estate meltdown.

2. Bargains Are There to Be Bought

If a property is to be sold, someone must buy it. As unfortunate as it may be for unsuspecting property owners who are being squeezed by market forces, for prepared and competent investors there will be some super bargains hitting the market in the coming weeks, months and years.

There's a popular saying — 'buy your straw hats in the winter' — and it applies just as well to property investing. Opportunities abound in the 'off season' when prices are low. It was hard to buy a bargain when the market was booming, but changing times bring with them new opportunities. Once you've bullet-proofed your property empire, it would be worthwhile to sniff around and see what deals are available. In this book I'll share with you the choice opportunities that I, and other investors, are buying right now. In doing so, I'll reveal how you can get in on the action too.

A GUARANTEE

This book is certainly not a rehash of concepts outlined in my previous two best-selling titles. Sure, there will need to be some minor (and I mean minor) mention of important points, but this will only be to show that the principles remain the same with only the context changing.

In fact, if having read the entire book, you're not completely convinced that the tips and insights I've included have the power to help you earn investment income worth at least 10 times what you paid for the book, then I'll personally send you a cheque for the cost of buying it. My legal team has suggested that a few simple conditions ought to be included to protect all parties. Accordingly, this incredible refund offer is subject to the following:

- ➲ You must send a written refund request to PropertyInvesting.com, PO Box 92, Blackburn, Vic 3130. Include the book and your original purchase receipt, together with your name, address and daytime contact phone number.

- ➲ The book must be returned in a good condition with no writing in it or damage to the pages.

- ➲ PropertyInvesting.com must receive your refund request within 40 days from the date of your purchase (as shown on your original receipt)

- ➲ Only one refund will be granted per customer.

All in all, if you don't agree that the book is everything I've promised and more, then provided you meet the above conditions, I'll swiftly refund every cent. In short, I don't want your money if you can't profit from the information I've shared. I'm certain you won't be disappointed!

Right then! With the formalities over let's get started because the market is changing quickly and there's not a second to lose.

Sincerely,

Steve McKnight
Melbourne
November, 2006

Making a Start

The Real Steve McKnight

The third year of my RMIT accounting degree (which was called a 'co-op' year) required that I find 12 months of relevant paid work experience. This was no easy task as back in 1991 the economy was in the grips of a recession and accounting jobs were pretty tough to land. Unlike some of my less fortunate peers, of the maximum 10 resumes that I was allowed to submit, I managed to secure three first-round interviews. One was at the massive accounting firm Price Waterhouse, another at The Herald and Weekly Times, and a third at a small accounting practice called Boyd Partners.

My job interview at Price Waterhouse was a disaster. First up, when they rang to arrange an interview I wasn't home and my brother answered the phone. When the lady provided her return contact number it started with 666, to which my brother quipped, 'You're not the devil, are you?' As you can imagine, I nearly died when he told me!

Still, despite my brother's best intentions, I was granted an interview a couple of days later, and I turned up full of confidence dressed in a lovely new black suit, white shirt and pink, swirly floral tie. Sadly though, the interview didn't last very long. I bombed out badly when asked, 'So, what would be your dream job?' Having no experience in interview politics, I answered truthfully when I said, 'I really enjoy basketball coaching and I can see myself finishing my degree and going into sports management.'

Well, the interview basically ended there and then! Later my uni friends advised me of the 'correct' answer: 'I'd really like to work long hours for you as I can't imagine anything better than a long and fulfilling career here at <insert organisation name>'.

Oh well, one interview down and two more to go.

The Herald and Weekly Times interview went much better, and I believe I would have been in the running for the job had the organisation not needed to cut back staff. After the interview I received a letter. It began by thanking me for my interest (not what you want to read at the start of such a letter), and advising me that the company had decided to withdraw from the RMIT co-op program for cost-saving reasons.

Things were becoming desperate. I only had one shot left — Boyd Partners. Whilst this firm was offering two places, one of them had already been snapped up by a fellow student named Andrew. Later I would learn that Andrew did some clever extracurricular groundwork and had sewn up the position well before the interview process even began. Nevertheless, walking into the interview, I had my mum's wise words ringing in my ears: 'Just be yourself, and it'll happen if it's meant to be'.

I had the interview with Sue, one of the partners, and it was the best of the three. We seemed to click and I liked the sound of working in a small team. Later Sue told me that the last position was a two-horse race — a choice between myself and another. Luckily, I was offered (and subsequently accepted) the job, which came with the kingly starting salary of $20,000! It's a little quirky, but to this day I'll divide the profit I make from a property deal into $20,000 lots. I then equate each lot to a year of blood, sweat, tears and timesheets that I've saved myself.

SAD SUNDAY NIGHTS

Sue was merciful in granting me that job; my university marks certainly didn't warrant the position. I was mainly a passes and credits student. I did manage to get a distinction for the first year subject 'Generation and Distribution of Wealth', but that didn't count for much since the subject was completely assessed based on assignments and class participation, so all you had to do was turn up and you would at least score a credit!

It's not that I wasn't extremely grateful for the job, but within a few months of starting I began to feel like a fish out of water. It was a great place to work — everything that was promised and more. My problem was that I came to the conclusion that I didn't want to be an accountant. Slowly over time my feelings of being unsettled turned into despair at having to work in a job that I didn't like. I hated Sunday afternoons as I started to think about having to go to work the following day. Sunday nights were even worse, as I'd have to spend an hour of precious time ironing five shirts for the week ahead. While I may sound like a sook, sometimes I'd even cry!

Even now, from time to time on a Sunday afternoon I'll look down at my watch and be gripped with a small glimpse of sudden dread. Should I be running a Sunday seminar, I'll tell the audience about it and see knowing looks on a lot of faces. Looks that say, 'I know what you mean! I have to go home after this seminar and iron shirts for the week ahead myself'.

As a child, what did you want to do when you were grown up? I wonder then, and particularly so if you're unhappy, how did you end up where you are right now?

Something powerful that I've come to learn is that our life (and investment) positions are the direct results of the choices we make. If you want a different outcome, then you need to make different choices.

A SLOW LEARNER

My wife, Julie, will tell you that I'm a slow learner. Although I'd love to dispute this, it really must be true because I persisted as an accountant for 10 and a half years before finally turning my back on the profession once and for all.

Looking back, I was always conscious of being unhappy deep down, but what I lacked was the courage to take action that would address the situation. I failed to take control or ownership of my circumstances and to pursue a different direction rather than merely accepting what was dished up.

I challenge you to stop reading for a moment and to spend a minute or two thinking about times in your life when you've achieved substantial success — perhaps a sporting achievement, a time when you landed the job of your dreams, or a date with someone you liked. Go on — stop reading for a moment and think …

Now, with one or two particularly happy moments in mind, did you get into these situations through random luck or did you plan for a certain outcome and then work hard to achieve it? Sustained success is no fluke — it's a result. It's the culmination of the expertise and planning invested into the process you employed to reach the outcome. This being the case, I just can't understand why so many people live a minority of their lives (say 10%) in a zone or mindset they know (from previous results) will deliver an above-average outcome, and spend the rest of their time (say 90%) living in passive ignorance by allowing their lives to drift by around them.

Sure, life isn't solely about achievement after achievement, but studies have been done and the conclusions are alarming. I'm told a research analyst once visited a series of aged care centres and surveyed a sample of residents. They were asked, 'If you had your life over again, what would you do differently?'

The top two answers were:

1. take more risks, and

2. spend more time with family.

Do you recognise these basic desires? Maybe they're the same two points that you want to take action on in your life. Don't be deaf to the wisdom of those who have gone before us, take action while you still have the time and inclination to do something about it!

ESTABLISHING A NEW DIRECTION

Having decided to prematurely retire from my accounting career, you might be surprised to learn that I didn't have much of an idea of what I wanted to do next. No doubt some of you more sensible readers would regard this as crazy. You might believe it's dangerous to leave a job with no certainty, and no new income arranged. Ordinarily, I'd agree with you, but you have to understand how unhappy I was and how desperate I'd become for a change in circumstances.

Irrespective of commonsense, once I opened myself up to a new opportunity it transpired that destiny found me, rather than the other way around. Don't get me wrong though, I wasn't expecting the opportunity of a lifetime to simply land in my lap. However, given that I'd achieved success before (both personally and in my career), I had the firm belief that provided I could identify what had worked well for me in the past, all I needed to do was to find a new context in which to apply those same skills, and success would not be far away.

In my case, I looked into the world of investing and wealth creation. In no particular order I spent time analysing the merits of share investing, share trading, options trading, futures trading, network marketing, franchises, negative gearing, time share investments, positive gearing, and many others. As you'd expect, each held the promise of massive riches and each had its share of success stories. I remember one in particular, which was the incredible tale of how someone had made a fortune trading the US market in the middle of the night, wearing only underwear!

Steve's Investing Tip

If you can identify the skills behind your past successes and then apply them in an investing context, a profitable result won't be far away.

One thing I noticed was that the higher the buy-in cost, the bigger the promise of instant and significant wealth. Hmmm. I may have been new to the industry, but I wasn't stupid. Using my audit training (I had been promised that my auditing experience would be good for something one day!) I tested the assertions of each of the methods. Let's have a look at the conclusions I came up with.

Shares

It certainly wasn't hard to find stock market success stories, as the print media was full of ads with bold and punchy headlines declaring how so-and-so had made a quick fortune. However, even assuming that these were true, the result seemed uncontrollable. That is, you could profit from taking a stand in the market, but you could never directly control that result yourself. To me, this meant that the stock market was, at best, going to be a rollercoaster ride.

Going one step further, not only was the investment outcome largely uncontrollable, it also required that you regularly monitor the market. I'd seen this firsthand with some of my friends who had become permanently glued to their computer screens, or other gizmos, as they watched their investments go up and down in value. Yes, there were stories of quick profits, but I couldn't find anyone who had funded their lifestyle from share investing for five or more years. My conclusion was that you could make money from shares, but it was not going to be a source of income that you could rely on to substitute for a salary.

Network Marketing

I doubt there will be a single person reading this who hasn't had a negative experience with network marketing. It seems everyone I know has been dubiously invited to attend a 'business opportunity' meeting. This almost always leads to a lecture about the money-making possibilities of selling dog wash or magic pills to family and friends.

I tried to find people who had achieved the upper echelons of network marketing and who could move away from that business and still draw an income. What I found was that the most successful achievers earned a fabulous salary, but they had to work the model hard and burned many friends along the way.

It didn't seem like a model that felt right for me.

Franchises

Franchises seemed interesting, however I quickly concluded that there was more money in selling franchises than buying them. In most cases, franchises are business solutions — systems in a box — where the labour is provided (by the franchisee) and the product and procedures bought from the franchisor.

My conclusion was that you could make good money from a franchise, but you needed to work long hours at the same time as being confined to the franchise way of doing business. For example, you couldn't buy a McDonald's store and then come up with your own McBurger. In my case, if I wanted to work long hours in a job, I could earn more money from accounting.

Property

Having never owned any property before, I started off my examination of real estate from an accounting perspective. At first glance there seemed good potential as statistically, property values increase over time. Upon further investigation, I found there were two options when investing in real estate. The first and most popular was negative gearing.

Negative Gearing

This was a growth-based strategy where you'd profit from unrealised gains (as the property appreciated in value) at the same time as making a tax-deductible realised loss (as a result of the property's expenses being more than its rental income).

Positive gearing (or positive cashflow) was the alternative option. This was more of a cashflow-focused strategy, in which the property's cash receipts were higher than its associated cash costs. The surplus would then be taxable (as a realised or cash gain). There was also the potential for capital appreciation too.

Upon assessing the merits of the two possibilities there was one critical problem with negative gearing that I couldn't resolve: where did the money come from to pay for the losses associated with the expenses being higher than the income? Friends and colleagues who used the technique were using their salaries to fund their losses. That was okay, but I didn't want to go back to an unsatisfying job for the sake of earning money to pay for a property portfolio.

As I completed more research, other phenomenon surfaced — those who did have negatively geared portfolios could only manage to acquire two or three properties. This was because a salary could only soak up so many losses before it was impossible to afford to buy any more deals. In my mind, I started to have serious doubts about negative gearing as an investing strategy — it seemed that the more properties you owned, the poorer you became!

Positive Gearing

Next, I turned my focus to positively geared property and immediately hit a significant stumbling block — I couldn't find anyone to use as a success story. Not wanting to give up easily,

I tried to find a positively geared property for myself within the Melbourne metropolitan area, and couldn't.

It was only after I attended a Robert Kiyosaki seminar that I gained the critical snippet of missing information: positive cashflow (residential) properties tended to only exist in outlying or regional areas. I canvassed the idea of investing in regional areas with some of my accounting colleagues. They all looked at me like I had two heads and said that I'd be mad because, 'you'll never get capital growth in the country'.

Just as there was uncertainty in my mind back in 1999, so I see the same uncertainty in the minds of investors today.

Steve's Investing Tip

Your chosen investment strategy needs to do more than simply provide the prospect of making money. It has to logically meet your needs.

Pushing all the noise of other people's opinions aside, I was left with a simple realisation: I had to match the needs of my own personal circumstances with the objectives of my long-term goals, and then choose the investment strategy that met the requirements of both in the best possible way. The decision was made: I needed to invest my working capital to buy real estate that earned a net cashflow surplus first, and any capital appreciation would be a bonus. In other words, I needed to *make* money, not *lose* money.

I was full of enthusiasm as I packed up the car and headed off to Ballarat. Within a few weeks I had bought my first property and was well on the road to property investing success.

OVERCOMING UNCERTAINTY

While the real estate market has changed substantially since 1999, I continue to apply a simple benchmark to all my investment decisions: each asset must make a minimum amount of money within an identified timeframe.

Steve's Investing Tip

A key difference between investors and speculators is the existence of a written plan.

Do you have a written plan or budget for the minimum amount of money that your properties must make, and a timeframe in which that profit must be made? It's never too late to make one. Successful investors avoid making risky decisions, so rather than throwing caution to the wind, when I started my investing I sought to take a calculated risk, rather than an uncontrolled gamble. I did this by identifying my 'team', and then enlisting their support and assistance.

At home, my wife and I made the decision to live humbly (to put it nicely), and to pay for our lifestyle expenses from her salary. At work, my business partner at the time, Dave Bradley, agreed to keep working as an accountant to bring in enough investment capital so that we could keep buying property.

I make this point as I see quite a number of eager investors trying to be property Han Solos — that is, trying to do everything themselves. This is usually a critical error in judgement, because real estate is all about the 'we', and little about the 'me'. It's okay to be ambitious, but don't be foolish. If you're a one-person investing unit and you want to free up more time to invest, try cutting down your work week one day at a time, rather than quitting altogether.

Investing always contains an element of uncertainty, and this can never be entirely removed. The best you can do is to take a calculated risk, and then work hard to mitigate the possibility of things going wrong.

First Deal and Changing Times

Having decided to go full steam into real estate investing, Dave and I bought our first investment property in May 1999: an ex-commission house in Wendouree West for $44,000 with a rental income of $120 per week. At the time of writing, the same house would sell for between $110,000 and $120,000, and would attract a market rent of $150 per week.

I have crunched the numbers for you below, and as you can see, the property would no longer generate a positive cashflow result because of the higher interest cost associated with borrowing more money.

Steve's First Deal Revisited		
	In 2006	In 1999
Purchase price	$120,000	$44,000
Deposit (20%)	$24,000	$8,800
Closing costs (5%)	$6,000	$2,200
My cash needed	$30,000	$11,000
Rent	$7,800	$6,240
Loan payment[1]	–$8,909	–$3,267
Rental management (8%)	–$624	–$500
Council rates	–$850	–$690
Insurance	–$300	–$200
Repairs budget	–$300	–$200
Cashflow	–$3,183	$1,383
Investment return	–10.61%	12.57%

[1] 80% loan, 25-year term, assumed same interest rate of 8.05% with weekly repayments.

If I wanted to stick to a 'buy and hold' positive cashflow rental strategy, I would have two options in the current market.

Option #1: Borrow Less

I could buy the same property but contribute more cash and therefore borrow less. This option might result in a positive cashflow outcome, but it would lower my investment return. For example, I have presented the numbers again below on the basis of keeping the loan payments roughly the same as in 1999. To do this would require a 70% deposit.

Steve's First Deal Revisited with Similar Repayments	
	In 2006
Purchase price	$120,000
Deposit (70%)	$84,000
Closing costs (5%)	$6,000
My cash needed	$90,000
Rent	$7,800
Loan payment[1]	−$3,341
Rental management (8%)	−$624
Council rates	−$850
Insurance	−$300
Repairs budget	−$300
Cashflow	$2,385
Investment return	2.65%

[1] 80% loan, 25-year term, interest rate of 8.05%, weekly repayments.

Unless there was significant growth potential, you'd probably be better off with the return achieved by leaving your money in an interest-bearing deposit account, and you'd have none of the associated real estate risk.

Option #2: Look Around

I could look for a different property with higher rent, and a cheaper price, within the same area or look for a similarly priced property on a similar rental return in a different area.

Changing with the Market

This example shows how the market has changed, and how we need to change with the market or risk our investment strategy becoming irrelevant or obsolete.

As prices rose and the market changed, Dave and I varied our investment strategy accordingly. When the Ballarat market boomed, we went to the La Trobe Valley. When prices went up there we went to Tassie. Once Tassie took off, we went to New Zealand, and then to the United States. Along the way we changed from residential homes to blocks of units, and then to commercial property. It's funny because, over 260 properties and millions of dollars in profit later, I'm back in the Ballarat market buying residential properties again.

THE REAL STEVE MCKNIGHT

Some may find it hard to believe, but those who have come to know me by attending my seminars or participating in my mentoring program quickly conclude that I'm just a normal person who has big visions, and a determination to do the things I say.

As you have read, it took a while for me to find my niche, and to develop a successful model. However, once I found a winning system, I applied it over and over again in multiple markets.

I believe I'm an investor who uses real estate, not a real estate buyer who dabbles in investing. This means that I'm always seeking to maximise my return and don't hold a bias, beyond being ethical, as to the method I use.

I am not secretive about the way I invest — I freely share the information. Some people don't understand this approach, but I feel that there are more than enough deals for all of us to do. While it's likely we will both be looking to make a profit, our motives and needs behind the profit are likely to differ.

Since successful methods are widely available, achieving the results you desire often comes down to constructing a written plan and committing yourself to stick to it. Finding the ongoing motivation to follow through is the challenge. In the next chapter we'll explore that in more detail and talk about the importance of attributing significance to your actions.

Chapter 1 Insights

Insight #1:

Real estate is all about the 'we' and little about the 'me'. Be sure to build a good team around you.

Insight #2:

You don't need to be super smart — just committed to your goals and determined to achieve a better life.

Insight #3:

The way to acquire 260 plus properties in seven years is one deal at a time.

Insight #4:

The property market has changed and you must adjust your investing approach or risk becoming obsolete.

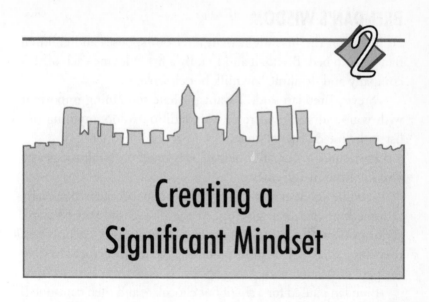

Creating a
Significant Mindset

Brendan Nichols had been coaching people for a long time, so he only needed a second or two to look me over in order to conclude that I was tired to the point of physical and emotional exhaustion. It was July 2006 and I'd just been through one of the most demanding periods of my life. Not only had I just completed a gruelling seminar schedule that saw me run several events and give various speeches but I'd also come from the funeral of my father-in-law, Kevin.

While Brendan and I had only met 10 months earlier, we quickly formed a friendship, seeing each other as wealth-creation brethren rather than competitors. Brendan's forte is businesses, mine is property. More importantly though, our young daughters took an instant liking to each other and went skipping down the road like they'd been best friends forever. As Brendan and I were both busy people, we set a date a few months beforehand when we decided to hook up at Coffs Harbour to enjoy a combined family holiday.

BRENDAN'S WISDOM

So it was on the first night that, after our spouses and children had gone to bed, Brendan and I sat by a fire enjoying each other's company and drinking soy milk hot chocolates.

'Steve', Brendan said, 'I want to share something important with you, and since you're in no condition to do anything but listen, let me do the talking'.

I was so worn out, all I could do was gratefully blink and gently nod my head in agreement.

'A while ago you asked me why so many people make a start at something and then give up. At the time I told you I'd think about it. Now I have the answer. Here it is: People give up when they think there will be more pain involved in going forward than the pain associated with going back'.

Brendan paused for a sip of hot chocolate and then continued. 'The critical observation here is that either way there is pain, the issue becomes weighing up which delivers the lesser amount. For example, while you and I don't do this, it's not unusual for participants to come out of seminars feeling all revved up and believing that anything is possible. I call that the "Seminar Sugar Rush" because it's fleeting, and when it wears off, it can leave you feeling worse than before. In order to achieve a lasting impact there needs to be a connection back to a person's "Source of Significance".'

Brendan, sensing that I was hearing but not listening, was gracious in saying, 'I can see you're getting tired mate, so let me just add one more thing and then we'll call it a night. Everyone has an ego, and this means we're all on a crusade to achieve meaning from the things we fill our lives with. In your case, you probably think you run seminars because you like to teach, but I suspect that you draw meaning from having an impact on people's lives, and it's this influence that sees you agree to do silly things like crazy speaking schedules.

'The problem, though, is that unless you can directly connect to your source of significance, you'll find the tasks physically and emotionally draining rather than enriching. You see it all the time, and especially on public transport, people who live in what I call "The Dead Zone". What happens is that, apart from a few hours each night, and on the weekend, these people live their lives like they're already dead. It's hard, but the way to escape the "The Dead Zone" is to identify your "Sources of Significance", and then spend more time pursuing these activities than the ones that are causing you to look and to act like a zombie'.

Sensing that I was almost totally emotionally spent, Brendan gulped down the rest of his hot chocolate and concluded. 'Okay, that's enough. Let's call it a night'.

Are You in the Dead Zone?

Do you currently feel like some, most, or all of your time is spent in what Brendan calls 'The Dead Zone'? What can you do to reconnect with the things that bring you lasting enjoyment and a sense of accomplishment in your life?

In their daily journal, the people whom I mentor are required to make a note of how much of their day's activities will make the highlight reels of their lives. How much of what you do each day is worthy enough for you to really feel a sense of accomplishment, like you've achieved something important?

THE PROPERTY INVESTING MOUNTAIN

It's amazing what a good night's sleep can do, because the following morning I began to feel and look a lot more like my normal cheerful and thoughtful self. My subconscious must have been processing Brendan's comments overnight because when I awoke in the morning, I'd reached several of my own 'significant' conclusions. In particular, I'd constructed a mental picture of how my mindset had grown, changed and evolved over the past seven or so years.

Basking in the warmth of fresh morning sunlight, I munched my way through a bowl of cereal and tried to sketch out what was in my head. After some tweaking and refinement, the illustration below is basically what I came up with.

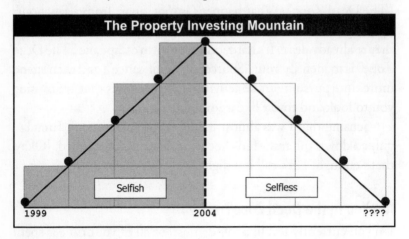

The Start: 1999

I'm not ashamed to say that I wanted to use real estate to become financially independent. For this to happen, I had to buy enough property to generate enough income to ensure that I never had to work as an accountant again. This meant that my investing became a numbers game — I had to find enough money for deposits to buy enough property, whilst making enough profit to fund the family budget for my desired lifestyle.

Dave and I set an initial goal of $250,000 per annum ($125,000 each). Assuming each property generated $50 per week in net income, this meant that we had to acquire slightly less than 100 houses.

The Journey: 1999 to 2004

For a long time I really struggled to explain to people what I did for a job. Then one day I came up with a novel idea — I began to tell people that I played the game of Monopoly in real life. This was always a great conversation starter at parties, because most people have played and enjoyed the game of Monopoly.

Digressing slightly for a minute, I can remember a particular Monopoly game I played with three uni mates. I seemed to have the luck of the dice that day and I quickly established a portfolio of properties. In fact, I seem to remember landing on Park Lane and Mayfair on the first lap. Anyway, it became apparent that I was going to win the game, so the other guys ganged up against me and did sweetheart deals to swap titles. When this didn't work they merged and forced me out of the game. In a fit of rage, I stormed out and left them with slightly stunned looks on their faces as they were at my house!

I must have learned my lesson, though, because today I have come to realise that forming teams and building alliances is the quickest way to get ahead. Trying to do it all yourself is the slow way around the board and the least effective strategy you can use.

Steve's Investing Tip

If you're trying to do everything yourself then you're doing it the hard way!

So it was then, that between 1999 and 2004, Dave Bradley and I joined forces and moved our pieces around in a real life game of Monopoly. Sometimes other investors would beat us to the best deals, and sometimes we'd beat them. On rare occasions we'd team up with other investors along the way, and other times we would be happy going it alone. All in all we made excellent progress, and we were greatly encouraged as we passed key milestones. In the context of the Property Investing Mountain diagram, these milestones are shown by the series of dots leading up to the summit.

Please don't think that it was easy or without difficulty — there were challenges and setbacks, and there was always the issue of trying to secure enough finance for the deals we wanted to buy.

Steve's Investing Tip

While we didn't know exactly how we were going to achieve our goal, that didn't stop us from stepping out and doing our best.

Are you looking for certainty before making a life-changing decision? I can only say that, having achieved my dreams, my encouragement would be to give it a red hot go, as you can always go back if things don't work out.

Mission Accomplished: May 2004

We only varied our original goal once — in October 2003 — as I sensed a major change in the mood of the property market. Pessimism had replaced optimism, and I felt that real estate values had peaked. In response, Dave and I changed our goal to $200,000 of passive income per annum, and $1,000,000 in cash.

On May 9, 2004, without any fanfare or fireworks, Dave and I shook hands to celebrate achieving this milestone.

The Descent: 2004 to 2006

Brendan Nichols once told me that, 'Money doesn't buy happiness, but everyone has the right to figure this out for themselves'. Well, in 1999 I would have believed that money could buy happiness, but having reached the top of my wealth-creation mountain, I'd have to now agree with Brendan. Don't get me wrong — it's great to be able to do what you want, when you want to, but there's only so far a self-based agenda will take you. For example, let's say that you acquire every property on the Monopoly board and clean the bank out of money. What next? Would you keep moving your piece around the board admiring everything that you've achieved?

Sitting at that table with my now empty cereal bowl, I came to the conclusion that the best thing money can buy is the ability and capacity to contribute to the lives of others. Therefore, if the ascent up the property mountain was all about selfish ambition (setting yourself up), the descent should be all about using your wealth to help others. In a nutshell, I've come to realise that the best and most fulfilling source of significance comes from using your money to benefit others, rather than hoarding it up for the betterment of yourself.

Bill Gates and Warren Buffett

A while ago I read with interest that Bill Gates had decided to walk away from his job as CEO of Microsoft. It seems he had decided to devote his time to managing his charitable foundation and, in doing so, further impact on the lives of those less fortunate in the world. Inspired by Gate's vision, fellow billionaire Warren Buffett declared that he would give away 85% of his Berkshire Hathaway holding to charities — a donation in the vicinity of US$36 billion!

Surely we can learn from these leads and read between the lines: at some point, enough money has to be enough, then it's time to find a new focus.

The 'A-ha!' Moment

Brendan's wisdom about significance helped me to unlock a massive personal 'A-ha!' moment. It allowed me to see that my physical and mental tiredness was a response to my inability to draw further significance from my investing or business pursuits. If I wanted to re-energise myself, then I had to take a different approach — one that had a 'contribution' focus, as this would help me find new meaning in my investing and give me renewed motivation.

2006 and Beyond ...

In July 2006, Dave Bradley and I decided to shake hands and to head in different directions. There weren't any fights or fisticuffs, nor was there any anger or arguments. Perhaps the best way I can describe what happened is that the movie ended. Yes, it was a great movie, an epic, but the time had come for closure since this was required to begin the next phases of our lives.

As part of our agreed and amicable settlement, Dave assumed control over the property portfolio and I took over the reins of the PropertyInvesting.com business and our charitable foundation. This was an outcome in which we both received what we wanted and valued most from the business. In the wash up, this has effectively seen me go from 130 plus properties, back to zero in 3.5 seconds!

STARTING FROM SCRATCH

So, here I am again — back at the base camp of the property investing mountain. Looking around, I see there's a few of us saying our teary goodbyes and checking our equipment prior to heading up the long and winding trail. First time around I was doing it for myself, but now I have enough money to last me for a few lifetimes. This time I'm doing it for the benefit of others. This will be the best of both worlds as I'll derive greater significance from the contribution that I am able to make.

Hey, how about we tackle the property investing mountain together? If you're up for the challenge then I should warn you that there are some tough conditions up on those slopes and even though the journey and the rewards are amazing, you'll have to dig deep at times to find the motivation to stick to your plans and meet your goals. You'll remember Brendan Nichol's words, that people turn back when they associate more pain with continuing than with retreating. Of course, the reverse is also true — if you understand the pain associated with not taking action, it can help you to stick to your goals. With this in mind, if you need any further motivation, we're going to time warp forward in the next chapter, to meet the ghosts of your unaltered potential financial futures. Hang on!

Chapter 2 Insights

Insight #1:

People who have lost their passion in life start to live in 'The Dead Zone'. Once there, the only way to escape is to reconnect to things that make you feel alive.

Insight #2:

Money obtains its value from what you do with it, not how much of it you have. Even if you die with a million-dollar bank balance, you're still dead.

Insight #3:

There are lots of sources of potential significance: your job, your family, your ambition and so on. The more sources of significance you have, the happier and more rewarding you'll find your investing will be.

Insight #4:

Investing to fund financial freedom is great, but what will you do after you've won the money game?

Insight #5:

The ultimate source of significance is a positive contribution to the lives of other people.

BRENDAN NICHOLS

I've learned a lot from Brendan Nichols and can highly recommend him as a source of wisdom and inspiration. To find out more about Brendan, visit:

<www.BrendanNichols.com/FreeGift>

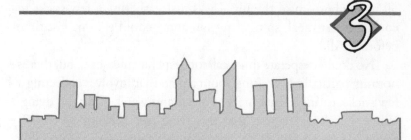

Don't Rely on a Government Aged Pension

Times were tough. Very tough. A severe drought had gripped the land, and people were literally starving to death. While her name is not recorded, what we do know is that she was a widow, that she had a son, and that she had only enough food to cook one last meal.

With all the strength she could manage she decided to venture outside to collect the firewood needed to bake some bread, and in her cooking, use up the tiny amount of flour and oil that was left. Imagine her inconvenience then when a total stranger appeared asking for a glass of water. Forgetting her own needs, she turned to fetch his request, only to be stopped in her tracks as the stranger also called out for a bite of bread too.

Well, a glass of water was one thing, but to ask for her last morsel of food, that was another. In desperation she decided to plead her case.

'I have only a handful of flour left in the jar and a little cooking oil in the bottom of the jug. I was just gathering a few sticks to cook this last meal, so that my son and I could eat one last time before we die'.

No doubt desperate times call for desperate measures, but there's nothing particularly exciting about a plan that involves collecting a few sticks, eating a final meal of bread and water, and then dying. While *The Bible* suggests that this event (see 1 Kings 17:10–12) occurred around 500 BC, there's a lot that remains uncomfortably familiar about the widow's hopeless plan, and the bare-bones prospects for those approaching modern-day retirement.

AN ALTOGETHER NASTY PICTURE

Do you have a picture of what your life will look like when you retire from the workforce? Will you be hand-in-hand with your partner walking along the beach as the sun slips below the horizon? Perhaps you have visions similar to those portrayed on the glossy brochures produced by retirement villages — the ones that show senior citizens having the times of their lives as they laugh and lap up their golden years?

Sadly, for the average retiree, there will be no Disney ending — no happily ever after. Instead, something similar to the widow's plan for survival — collecting a few pension cheques, eating a few basic meals and then dying — will become a bleak reality.

According to Australian Bureau of Statistics (ABS) information, the gross average household income of a lone person aged 65 and over was just $396 per week in 2003–04[1]. Equating that back to a 40-hour working week, it's equivalent to getting paid $9.90 per hour. Perhaps more alarmingly, 69.4% of those aged 65 and over said that a government pension or allowance was their principal source of income, and less than two in 10 people said they were totally self-sufficient — meaning that they didn't rely on any government handout support at all.

---

[1] Cat. No. 6523.0 *Household Income and Income Distribution, Australia*, 2003–04.

I don't know about you, but relying on the government to look after my welfare in retirement isn't a plan that I would choose as my first option. At the time of writing, the aged pension payment was a mere $512.10 per fortnight for a single, and $427.70 per person per fortnight for a couple.

Ageing Population

To add to the misery, it's doubtful whether the payment of an aged pension even as low as that outlined above will be possible for many more generations. Given Australia's ageing population, it is difficult to see how the workers of the future will be able to pay enough tax to support ongoing aged pensions.

Steve's Investing Tip

If you plan to rely on the aged pension to fund your retirement, think again.

I'm not just some crazed author who has drunk far too much coffee — these are very real facts I'm presenting. As you can see by the graphs on the next page, ABS projected population figures over the next 60 years will see senior citizens take over the Australian population.

To prove the point, let's try to build a crude but effective forecast for the future. According to the ABS projections, in 2064 there will be 10.4 million people aged over 65. If we assumed that 69.4% of these people required the aged pension, half were couples and half were singles, and the amount of the aged pension remained the same, then the government's annual spending on the aged pension would be $86.2 billion!

That's more than four times the estimated spend at the time of writing ($20.7 billion) on aged pensions.

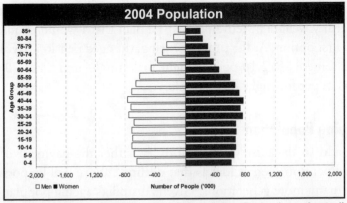

Based on ABS data, Cat No. 3222.0 Population Projections, Australia

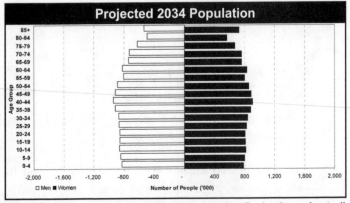

Based on ABS data, Cat No. 3222.0 Population Projections, Australia

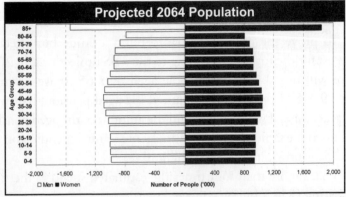

Based on ABS data, Cat No. 3222.0 Population Projections, Australia

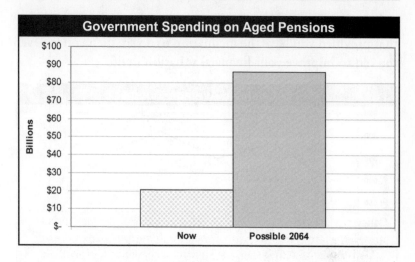

Where is all this money going to come from? Will it be greater taxation, less spending, or perhaps a combination of both?

Retirement: A Time to Earn More, Not Less

Retirement is traditionally the stage of life where a person earns the least amount of income.[2] In other words, history shows that average people work their entire lives and then retire on less than they ever earned before. Is that a situation you want to subscribe to?

The graph and table overleaf are constructed using data from the Reserve Bank of Australia. They show that our earning peaks in the 45 to 54 age bracket, and falls sharply from then on. The government hasn't been ignorant to this crisis. Its response has been to introduce compulsory retirement savings in the form of superannuation, and to require employers to pay a minimum percentage of each employee's pay into the employee's chosen superannuation fund.

YOU'RE NEVER TOO OLD

A question that I'm often asked is, 'When is it too late to make a start?' While I think that the longer you leave it, the harder it will

---

[2] Cat. No. 6523.0 *Household Income and Income Distribution, Australia*, 2003–04.

be to achieve a good quality of financial independence, I think that provided you have the inclination to do so, then you're never too old to improve your financial situation in life.

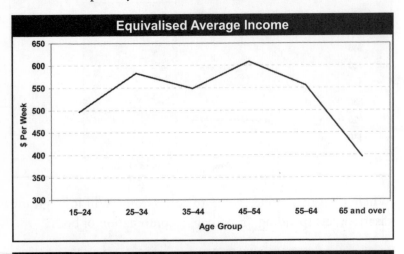

Equivalised Average Income

Average Household Incomes By Age			
Age group	Average (Mean) Equivalised Household Income		% Increase or decrease on previous group
	Per week	Per annum	
15 to 24	$497	$25,844	NA
25 to 34	$583	$30,316	+17.38%
35 to 44	$549	$28,548	−5.8%
45 to 54	$609	$31,668	+10.98%
55 to 64	$556	$28,912	−8.7%
65+	$396	$20,592	−28.8%

Steve's Investing Tip

You're only too old to make a start when you think you're beyond trying!

I'm greatly encouraged by two of the people I've been mentoring through the R.E.S.U.L.T.S. program[3]. Let me share with you some of their stories and their successes.

Jan Dawson

Jan is accustomed to hard work. Married at 16, she held down three jobs just to make ends meet and to be able to piggybank whatever little was left over for her future. Her savings came in handy when, at 23, she incredibly bought a Chinese restaurant without knowing a thing about Chinese cooking, and being about as Chinese as I am.

When I expressed amazement at her lateral thinking, Jan said, 'Steve, I saw an opportunity and went for it! At the time there was massive demand for Chinese food, but not enough restaurants. I knew there was a solution if I looked and thought hard enough about it'.

Jan went to school as a mature-age student and gained her business degree. It took her five years to complete (part time) while also holding down a full-time job together with being there for her family too. Nowadays, at age 64, Jan works as an accountant. It's the job of her dreams since she's passionate about number crunching and helping people with their tax problems. There's no secret to Jan's youthful outlook. She says that she picks her age and then lives it. 'Currently I'm somewhere between 28 and 42!' she jokes. Besides liking Jan a lot, I admire her for her tenacity and her willingness to keep trying in difficult circumstances. This positive mindset and willingness to work hard paid off recently when she banked a great property profit in quick time.

Towards the end of 2005, Jan decided that she wanted to give renovating properties a go. After some research, she found a deal in Sunnybank Hills, Queensland — a highset, brick, three-bedroom

---

[3] R.E.S.U.L.T.S is a powerful mentoring program that I run from time to time. The acronym stands for Real Estate Success Using Leverage Tenacity and Strategy. Find out more by visiting <www.PropertyInvesting.com/RESULTS>.

home that was in serious cosmetic decline. Her rough numbers were that she could buy it for around $180,000, spend about $45,000 doing it up, and then put it back on the market for around $350,000. She bought the property on a six-week settlement for $175,000 and then immediately went to work renovating it.

'The roof had those ugly white acoustic ceiling tiles that had long ago turned brown from cigarette smoke. When I told the painter to spruce it up, he looked dubious and said, "It's going to take a few coats of paint"'.

Two weeks into the project and things were going well — the painting was progressing as planned and the kitchen had been ripped out and a new one ordered. Then, one afternoon, there was a knock at the door and in walked a man seeking the details of the painter. Looking over the house, he was impressed by its size and asked, 'What are you going to do with it?' Jan replied that she was going to renovate it and then put it back on the market. On hearing this news, the mysterious visitor replied, 'Can I make you an offer for it right now, as is?' Jan said, 'Sure', and when he said '$250,000', it took her less than a minute of thinking time before they shook hands and the deal was done.

While not a typical result that everyone should expect, Jan's story teaches us:

➲ about the importance of research in order to identify opportunity

➲ that great profits can be made quickly, and

➲ that you're never too old to invest successfully.

In explaining her biggest learning outcome, Jan said, 'At the price the buyer paid, there was money in it for him and money in it for me. There's nothing to be gained by being greedy'.

When I asked Jan if she'd like to contribute any wisdom for inclusion in this book she smiled warmly and said, 'Well, I tell people who ask that you wouldn't build a house without a plan, so why would you go through life without a life plan either?'

Jan is currently assessing more renovation opportunities. There's no stopping her. The table below shows an outline of her profit from the project.

Jan's Dawson's Profit		
Sale price		$250,000
— Purchase and closing costs		
Purchase price	$175,000	
Closing costs	$2,708	$177,708
— Other costs		
Renovation costs	$1,000	
Holding costs*	$222	
Sale costs	$420	$1,642
Profit		$70,650
Time		33 days

* Jan paid cash so there was no interest.

Juliet Kitchen

Juliet isn't letting her age, or a lack of computer skills, stand in the way of her building a profitable investment portfolio either. Being in her late 60s, some of her peers would have well and truly given up the hope of starting a property empire. However, with her son as her business partner, and her daughter offering IT support, Juliet is keen to expand her financial horizons.

Not long ago I received the following email. With Juliet's permission I've included it here for you:

```
Dear Steve,

Just a note to tell you that I've achieved my
first goal — to buy a property before August 27.
I planned my work, and I worked my plan, and
succeed I did! I've just bought a two-bedroom
```

house in need of updating, and I'm confident about moving through the next stage.

Thank you and the R.E.S.U.L.T.S. gang so much for your enormous help, encouragement and for just 'being there' for me. My jigsaw puzzle is progressing very nicely and I'm becoming more confident by the minute.

My larger goal is to complete at least three of these renos and to sell them by July 31st next year. The only slight variable is how long the properties will take to sell. Otherwise, I'll be right on target.

Steve, I know that this is only a fairly small achievement, but to me, what is so great, is not actually buying or making money on a property, but rather attaining a personal sense of worth, and taking charge and responsibility for my life. I am grabbing life with both hands and I know now that the sky's the limit — not for the money, but for me.

I have realised that I'd never been truly accountable to myself before. Instead, I tended to live in 'my story' and did not relate to the highest discipline and accountability of which I was capable, thereby always paddling very hard around in circles and wondering why I never got anywhere. I feel so excited for my future now. It's taken me so long to grow up. Thank you for giving me the tools, your assistance and mostly the insight needed.

I can't wait for Sydney and I would love to catch up with you there.

All the best,

Juliet Kitchen

Wow, what an inspiring email! Juliet's case is a perfect example to demonstrate how investing can be as much about significance as it is about making money. Did you notice the sense of satisfaction and thrill that Juliet writes with now that she's taken responsibility for her financial future? The same is on offer for you too.

In case you're curious, the table below shows an outline of the numbers in Juliet's deal.

An Outline of Juliet's Deal	
Expected sale price	$255,000
— **Purchase and closing costs**	
Purchase price	$199,000
Closing costs	$8,600
— **Other costs**	
Renovation costs	$10,000
Holding costs	$5,496
Sale costs	$7,650
Expected profit	$24,254
Expected time	4 months

Juliet is a total inspiration! Here's some of what I learned from her story:

➲ Investing can deliver far more than just a profitable return. It can be a rewarding and empowering experience when you challenge your comfort zones.

➲ It's wise to partner with others to help overcome shortfalls in finance and experience. Juliet has joined with her son. While this can be dangerous, so long as it's treated as a business deal rather than a family relationship, it can still work.

CHOOSE YOUR FUTURE NOW

Some people will have no option but to rely on the government to provide an aged pension. This is both appropriate and necessary as we live in a country where those less fortunate should be supported in their need. However, just because the government currently provides an aged pension does not guarantee that it will continue to do so for generations to come.

Since the introduction of compulsory superannuation, the politicians at head office have telegraphed their intention to make average mums and dads more accountable for their own financial futures. Will you heed their call? Can you accept the responsibility for securing enough assets to provide income for the retirement you desire?

In the next chapter you'll find a challenging but fun, 20-question survey that will provide you with a good assessment of how you're tracking financially. Completing the survey will also leave you with great clarity by quantifying how much money you need in retirement, and also the required balance of total assets needed to generate your desired income return.

A HAPPY ENDING

In case you're wondering how things turned out for the starving widow we met at the start of this chapter, *The Bible* tells us that, because of her faith, God miraculously prevented her flour jar and oil jug from ever running out. I'm not expecting the same miracle from the Australian Government though. My aim in providing you with a glimpse into the future has been to give you a massive reality check, and to shock you into action.

You will never have a better opportunity and more time on your side than you have right now. Don't delay another day. Choose right now to take action and to accept responsibility for crafting your own financial future.

Chapter 3 Insights

Insight #1:

The aged pension does not provide enough money for anything more than basic survival.

Insight #2:

Australia has an ageing population. This means that it will be harder for the government to provide the same amount to aged pensioners in the future, as it does today.

Insight #3:

As you approach retirement, your ability to earn money from a job generally decreases. It is critical that you make hay while the sun shines and use your best income-earning years to provide for those times when your pay will drop. Everyone ages — you will too.

Insight #4:

No-one has more riding on your financial future than you do. When will you accept full responsibility for planning and implementing an investment strategy that provides for an adequate lifestyle when you no longer work?

Insight #5:

You're only too old to give financial independence a go if you've lost the inclination to try.

Take the
Steve McKnight Challenge!

Okay, now for a change of pace and something fun. While we can certainly share stories from our journeys as property investors and provide support, the reality is that we're all starting from different positions. Before you can map out a course, you need to pinpoint where you stand in relation to your target destination. To help you to clarify where you stand financially at the moment, and how far you are from your goals, I've devised a 20-question survey that will not only test how you're tracking, but it'll also help you to start planning for your financial future. It's more of a guide than a guarantee, but I think you'll enjoy giving it a go and seeing how the results come out. Before you start you'll need access to a calculator, as well as the following accurate information:

➲ figures for the amounts of money you earn and owe, and

➲ the current estimated value of your investment assets.

When you're ready, grab a calculator and pencil and let's get going. It's better to do the quiz as an individual, however you can also do it as a family unit, but you will need to tailor some of the questions that I ask to your own circumstances. If you're confused about any of the questions, then see the explanatory notes and scoring section, which begins on page 45.

Once you've written down all your answers, read the summary and award yourself a score. If it's easier, or if you'd like to get your friends and family to take the test too, then you can do it online as many times as you like (and have the scores tallied for you) at: <www.PropertyInvesting.com/financialquiz>.

The Steve McKnight Challenge		
Question	Answer	Score
Question 1 How old are you now?		
Question 2 At what age do you plan to achieve your definition of financial independence?		
Question 3 How many more years do you plan to have to work? *(For most people it's the answer to Question 2 less the answer to Question 1.)*		
Question 4 How much **per annum** (before-tax) do you currently earn from employment?		
Question 5 How much **per month** (before-tax) do you currently earn from your employment activities? *(Divide the answer to Question 4 by 12.)*		

The Steve McKnight Challenge *(cont'd)*		
Question	Answer	Score
Question 6 What is 70% of your (before-tax) monthly employment-related income? This converts the before-tax dollars into after-tax dollars. *(Multiply the answer to Question 5 by 70%.)*		
Question 7 How much income per annum (after tax) do you think you'll need to **survive**?		
Question 8 How much income per annum (after tax) do you think you'll need to live **comfortably**?		
Question 9 How much income per annum (after tax) do you think you'll need to live an **extravagant** lifestyle?		
Question 10 At the moment, how many hours are you working each week in paid employment?		
Question 11 Ideally, how many hours would you like to work (in paid employment) each week when you become financially independent?		
Question 12 How many hours are you allocating to managing your private (non-business) money each week?		

The Steve McKnight Challenge *(cont'd)*		
Question	Answer	Score
Question 13 At the moment, how much money do you have saved and available in cash? *(See the notes that follow for a list of items to include.)*		
Question 14 How many months of after-tax income do you currently have in savings? *(The answer to Question 13 ÷ the answer to Question 6.)*		
Question 15 In total, how much personal (non-investment) debt do you have at the moment? *(See the notes that follow for a list of items to include.)*		
Question 16 Assuming a 30% tax rate, how many months would you have to work to repay your current personal debt? *(The answer to Question 15 ÷ the answer to Question 6.)*		
Question 17 What is the current value of your total investment (non-personal) assets? *(See the notes that follow for a list of items to include.)*		
Question 18 What is your total net asset investment position? That is, total investment assets less total investment liabilities?		

The Steve McKnight Challenge *(cont'd)*		
Question	Answer	Score
Question 19 How many months of after-tax income does your net investment asset position represent? *(Question 18 ÷ Question 6.)*		
Question 20 How would you rate your overall financial position? Poor, Average, Good or Exceptional?		
Total Score		

Phew! Well done, you've made it through! Let's see how you went.

NOTES AND SCORING

Question 1: Your Age

The two biggest factors determining your wealth-building capabilities are:

1. your investing horizon — the amount of time over which you plan to invest, and

2. the financial returns you'll achieve on your investments.

The longer you can give your assets to multiply, the less aggressive you need to be in finding and buying high-return investments. On the other hand, if you're on a crusade to fast-track your wealth creation then you'll need to acquire assets that offer high returns, and this often means that the risk associated with the investments can increase dramatically.

Steve's Investing Tip

The more time you give your assets to compound in value, the easier it'll be for you to achieve financial independence.

Question 1 Survey Score: Your Current Age	
15 to 29 years	Score: 4
30 to 44 years	Score: 3
45 to 59 years	Score: 2
60 plus years	Score: 1

Question 2: Age at Financial Independence

The ABS publishes official life expectancy tables based on your current age. For example, a baby boy born in 2003 is expected to live until age 77.8, while a baby girl born in the same year is expected to live until age 82.8.[1]

As a general rule, the older you are when you retire from your job, the less income-producing assets you should need, due to the shorter retirement period. Conversely, the earlier you retire, the more assets you will need to fund your longer retirement.

Question 2 Survey Score: Your Age When You Plan to Be Financially Independent	
15 to 29 years	Score: −4
30 to 44 years	Score: −3
45 to 59 years	Score: −1
60 plus years	Score: 0

[1] Cat 1301.0 *Year Book Australia* 2006.

Question 3: Years of Work

The longer you plan to work the easier it'll be for you to achieve financial independence. This is because you will continue to receive an income that you can use to purchase investments and to borrow against.

Furthermore, the fewer the years that you plan to continue paid employment, the harder you'll have to work to accumulate enough income-generating investments to supply your retirement needs.

Question 3 Survey Score: Years Left of Work	
Less than 1	Score: 0
1 to 9 years	Score: 1
10 to 19 years	Score: 2
20 years plus	Score: 3

Question 4: Current Annual Earnings

Theoretically, the more you earn:

- ⊃ the more you should be able to save, and

- ⊃ the more you should be able to borrow, and therefore

- ⊃ the easier it should be for you to become financially independent.

However, higher paid individuals will normally have more extravagant retirement requirements and so they'll need to accumulate a lot more assets to provide the income needed to live their desired lifestyles. Obviously, those with more modest expectations don't require as many assets.

Note, your current annual earnings should be calculated using your ordinary earnings. If you are paid commission or overtime then include a conservative amount. If you're self-employed then try to come up with an average payment amount that you think is fair.

If you're not working at the moment then include your last salary. If you're still unable to come up with an approximate figure then use what you think you'd be paid provided you could find a suitable job.

Question 4 Survey Score: Current Annual Earnings	
$0 to $19,000	Score: 0
$20,000 to $49,999	Score: 2
$50,000 to $89,999	Score: 3
$90,000 to $149,999	Score: 4
$150,000 plus	Score: 5

Question 5: Monthly Earnings

Divide your annual salary by 12 to recalculate it on a monthly basis. There is no score for this item as it has been derived from Question 4, for which you've already been scored.

Question 6: 70% of Monthly Earnings

Next, to calculate 70% of your monthly salary, simply multiply this amount by 0.7. (This assumes that you pay an average of 30% in income tax.) Again, there is no score for this item as it has been derived from Question 4.

Questions 7, 8 and 9:
Income for Survival, Comfort or Extravagance

The higher the income you need to survive, the harder it is to purchase enough assets to pay for your financial independence.

Question 7 Survey Score: Income to Survive	
$0 to $29,999	Score: 2
$30,000 to $59,999	Score: 1
$60,000 to $89,999	Score: 0
$90,000 plus	Score: -2

Question 8 Survey Score: Income for Comfortable Lifestyle	
$0 to $29,999	Score: 4
$30,000 to $59,999	Score: 3
$60,000 to $89,999	Score: 2
$90,000 plus	Score: 1

Question 9 Survey Score: Income for Extravagant Lifestyle	
$0 to $29,999	Score: 4
$30,000 to $59,999	Score: 3
$60,000 to $89,999	Score: 2
$90,000 plus	Score: 1

Question 10: Hours Currently Worked in Paid Employment

The more hours you're working, the less time you'll have available for investing and managing your money, and the harder it'll be to find and to buy great deals. On the flip side though, the more hours you work, the more you'll be paid. Nevertheless, the most important asset investors have is time, because they can always use someone else's money.

Question 10 Survey Score: Hours Worked Per Week	
0 to 19	Score: 2
20 to 29	Score: 3
30 to 39	Score: 2
40 to 49	Score: 1
50 to 69	Score: 0
70 plus	Score: −1

Question 11: Ideal Hours Worked in Paid Employment

Not everyone wants to quit work forever when they become financially free. Some people would like to remain in paid employment, and this can help them to continue to borrow money and to gain extra cash to invest with.

Question 11 Survey Score: Planned Weekly Work Hours When Financially Free	
0 hours	Score: 0
1 to 9 hours	Score: 2
10 to 19 hours	Score: 3
20 to 39 hours	Score: 2
40 hours plus	Score: 1

Question 12: Weekly Hours Spent on Money Management

The person who retains the biggest vested interest in your financial success will always be you. The more time you spend planning, recording and managing your money, the more frequent and better the opportunities that will become available for you to maximise your investment returns.

Question 12 Survey Score: Weekly Hours Spent on Money Management	
0 hours	Score: −1
1 to 3 hours	Score: 0
4 to 7 hours	Score: 1
7 to 12 hours	Score: 2
13 hours plus	Score: 3

Question 13: Money in the Bank

Money in the bank includes:

- ✓ cash
- ✓ term deposits
- ✓ savings
- ✓ at call accounts.

Strange as it may sound, any investment expert will tell you that savings are one of the least effective ways to build wealth. This is because the returns are so low — often barely above inflation. However, savings are important for three reasons:

1. they provide a pool of funds for you to use when buying investment assets

2. they provide a safety buffer should you fall on hard financial times

3. they demonstrate that you have the ability to spend less than you earn.

It is this last point that is really important, because as outlined in the next chapter, if you can't spend less than you earn, then you'll never be financially independent.

Steve's Investing Tip

If you have too much hoarded in cash then you run the risk of not maximising your wealth-building opportunities, as you won't be using the power of compounding returns.

Question 13 Survey Score: Amount of Cash Savings	
$0	Score: 0
$1 to $9,999	Score: 1
$10,000 to $39,999	Score: 2
$40,000 to $99,000	Score: 3
$100,000 plus	Score: 4

Question 14: Savings as Months of Pre-Tax Income

Savings represents security, so the more money you have in the bank the greater your margin for peace of mind because you have access to cash in the event of an emergency.

If you live on the financial red line then it's reasonable to expect a crisis from time to time. Let's just hope that the crisis doesn't wipe you out!

Question 14 Survey Score: Savings in Months	
Less than 1 month	Score: 0
1 month to 5 months	Score: 1
6 to 12 months	Score: 2
13 to 18 months	Score: 3
19 months or more	Score: 4

Question 15: Total Personal Debt

Included in personal debt are the following:

- ✓ Home loans
- ✓ HECS (student debt)
- ✓ Car loans
- ✓ Personal loans
- ✓ Credit cards
- ✓ Family loans
- ✓ Consumer finance (no deposit easy payments).

The more personal debt you have, the harder it'll be for you to build a strong financial position on the basis that more of your income will be swallowed up in debt repayments and interest costs.

When you borrow money, you're essentially gaining early access to future earnings. To repay the loan you must then 'pay back' those work hours that you've borrowed against.

Steve's Investing Tip

Borrowing money is like getting an advance on your future wages. It handcuffs you to your job.

As a general rule, it's wise to keep your personal debt as low as you possibly can, particularly in an environment of increasing interest rates or economic uncertainty.

Question 15 Survey Score: Total Personal Debt	
$0	Score: 3
$1 to $4,999	Score: 1
$5,000 to $14,999	Score: 0
$15,000 to $99,999	Score: –2
$100,000 plus	Score: –3

Question 16: Months Worked to Pay Off Debt

Given a few minutes, most people can quickly add up how much they owe. However, many don't go the extra step of then equating their total debt back to the number of months worth of work it represents. To do so often calls for a tricky calculation, because you'll need to use after-tax dollars to repay the debt (see chapter 8).

For example, if you owed $2,500 on your credit card then you'd have to earn $2,500 plus the income tax applicable on $2,500 in order to have enough money to repay the debt.

For simplicity, I've assumed that your income and salary attracts an average income tax rate of 30%. If you're aware of a more accurate amount then by all means use it.[2] Chapter 5 talks about the dangers of debt in a lot more detail, so for the time being, it's enough to say that the more months you need to work to pay off your current personal debt, the longer it will take to establish a solid foundation from which to build a stronger financial future.

Question 16 Survey Score: Months of Work to Repay Debt	
0	Score: 3
1 to 3	Score: 1
4 to 12	Score: 0
13 to 36	Score: –1
36 plus	Score: –2

---

[2] The formula to calculate your after-tax pay is: your gross pay × (1 – your average income tax rate).

Question 17: Total Investment Assets

Included in total investment assets are the following:

- ✓ Savings as per Question 13
- ✓ Shares
- ✓ Property (not own home)
- ✓ Business equity
- ✓ Other assets.

If you've already managed to build up a savings and/or investment portfolio then you can use it to fast track your property-based wealth creation. For example, you'll find it easier to borrow money, and you'll have access to capital to pay for deposits and closing costs.

Question 17 Survey Score: Current Total Investment Assets	
$0	Score: 0
$1 to $49,999	Score: 1
$50,000 to $99,999	Score: 2
$100,000 to $249,999	Score: 3
$250,000 plus	Score: 4

Question 18: Net Investment Assets

Your net investment asset position is the sum of all your investment assets less all your investment liabilities. Your current net asset position is a great way to judge the effectiveness of your existing wealth-creation plan. If it's working well for you then that's great, if not then perhaps now is a good time to have a serious rethink.

Question 18 Survey Score: Current Total Net Investment Assets	
$0 or less	Score: −2
$1 to $39,999	Score: 1
$40,000 to $79,999	Score: 2
$80,000 to $139,999	Score: 3
$140,000 to $199,999	Score: 4
$200,000 plus	Score: 5

Question 19: Months of Net Investment Assets

Back in Question 14 you calculated the number of months of work 'saved' on the basis of your current savings. Let's now expand out this calculation to include your total net investment assets and see how the situation improves.

Note: If the majority of your total investment assets include significant unrealised gains (such as properties or shares that have boomed in value), then you'll be better off using your before-tax salary (i.e. Question 5) on the basis that you have a future tax liability that will come into existence when you sell these assets.

Question 19 Survey Score: Months of Net Investment Assets	
Less than 0	Score: –2
0 to 3	Score: 0
4 to 11	Score: 1
12 to 23	Score: 2
24 to 35	Score: 3
36 plus	Score: 4

Question 20: Your Assessment

Okay, time for some honesty! Considering all the factors that make up your current financial position, how would you rate your wealth-building efforts to date: Poor, Average, Good or Exceptional?

Note: This is not your opinion of the *effort* you've contributed — it's your opinion of the *results* you've achieved.

Question 20 Survey Score: Your Assessment	
Poor	Score: 0
Average	Score: 1
Good	Score: 2
Exceptional	Score: 3

STEVE'S ASSESSMENT

There's not really a maximum score possible. For example, your answer to Questions 1 and 2 largely offset each other to demonstrate that any age has its benefits and whilst young people have more time, older investors often have more maturity. As such, I've provided you with the scoring scale that follows.

Scoring Scale	
<10	**Help Needed, Quick!**
	You've got some serious work to do as your financial position is probably quite desperate. You are where you are as a result of the decisions you have made, so it's my suggestion that you see a qualified and experienced adviser to help you with money management and financial planning issues. Pay particular attention to debt management and work out a strategy to repay what you owe in personal debt quickly.
	How many hours a week do you devote to managing your money? Is it any fluke you are in this position? Seek help as you need it. In the meantime, you'll be able to locate your weakest points by looking back over your answers and identifying those questions where you scored less than two.
10 to 22	**Could Do Better**
	You've demonstrated that you have a grasp of the basics of good money management, however you probably haven't made the most of the financial opportunities that have come your way. For example, over your lifetime you'll probably earn well in excess of $1,500,000. My encouragement is to concentrate on developing strong money habits that see you spend less than you earn, and then to use your savings to invest with.
	Remember that cash savings are not generally considered a strong long-term investment option. You should seek some professional help when considering other assets such as shares and property.

Scoring Scale *(cont'd)*	
23 to 32	**A Pass, But Nothing To Write Home About**
	While you've passed the test, you should be hoping for much better. You've probably read a lot of books, and attended a few investment seminars, however, for one reason or another, you haven't hit the big time yet. My expectation is that you would have capitalised on a few good opportunities that have come your way, but at the same time you will be able to outline several 'big financial fishes' that got away too. The result is that you probably have an asset portfolio that includes a mix of solid performers, as well as a few duds. I wonder, what has to happen for those duds to come good?
	Clearly you're able to manage your money, so the best way forward is to pinpoint your weaknesses and to devise strategies to turn them around. If a deal you owned underperformed during the boom, how much harder will it be for that investment to make money in a weaker economic climate? Provided you are wise with your money, you may be ready for some more sophisticated or creative deals that provide higher returns but also carry greater risks.
33 to 39	**Impressive, Thus Far**
	Congratulations! You've made excellent progress towards achieving financial independence. No doubt you're aware of your less effective money habits, so the only question is, 'When are you going to become serious enough to do something about them?' An important point to remember is that investors maximise their money, and this means that you need to continually monitor and evaluate the returns your investments are generating.
	If you have a lot of equity in your investments, then this may be a weak point as you may have a lot of 'lazy money' (see chapter 6). The best way forward for you is to take a look at what's worked well for you in the past, and then to simply look to undertake similar projects in the future.

Scoring Scale *(cont'd)*	
40+	**Wow!**
	Tell me your secrets. What are you reading this book for? You should write your own success story as there are plenty of people who could learn a lot from your approach to wealth creation!
	If you are not there already, you're probably very close to achieving financial independence. I would encourage you to start looking to non-monetary pursuits that will help you gain a sense of significance from the contribution you can make. From an investment perspective, if you are not already looking at it, a possible way to broaden your wealth is to consider providing venture capital for other projects, as well as continuing to invest in your own right.
	Finally, remember this: shrouds don't have pockets, so be sure to enjoy and share your wealth rather than hoarding it away.

FORWARD PLANNING

I hope you've enjoyed completing this survey, and that it's helped you to identify areas in which you can improve your financial performance. Now that you've done all the hard work, the last part of this chapter pulls together the information you've already supplied in order to give you a concrete plan for achieving financial freedom. All you need to do is fill in the gaps.

Beware of Unrealistic Goals

When we road-tested this survey in the office, the overwhelming response was, 'Gee, I have a lot of hard work to do!' In fact, there was almost a feeling that the road ahead was too hard.

Over the past seven years, I've had extensive experience with helping investors set and achieve their wealth-creation goals. Drawing upon this knowledge, I'd have to say that setting unrealistic objectives is one of the biggest inhibitors of success.

A Forward Plan	
Question A How many more years are you planning to work in full-time employment? *(See Question 3.)*	Years
Question B How much annual after-tax income do you need in order to live the retirement lifestyle you desire? *(Depending on whether you are planning basic survival, comfort or an extravagant lifestyle, choose the total from either Questions 7, 8 or 9.)*	$
Question C Assuming your investments earned an 8% per annum after-tax return, how much in total net investment assets do you need to generate enough income for you to fund your retirement? *(Question B ÷ 0.08)*	$
Question D How much in total net investment assets do you have at the moment? *(See Question 18.)*	$
Question E What is the current surplus or shortfall in your net investment assets needed to generate an 8% return (after tax)?* *(Question C – Question D.)*	$
Question F Assuming that you acquire the shortfall in net investment assets evenly, what net value of investment assets do you need to acquire each year over your remaining working life? *(Question E ÷ Question A.)*	$ per year

* If you have a surplus then it's possible that you are not maximising the wealth-building power of your assets.

Be totally honest with yourself, and if you feel that the objectives in your forward plan are only remotely possible then you'd be well advised to reconsider the key parameters that drive the numbers.

For example, you could:

- ⊃ extend the age that you're planning to achieve financial independence by a few years
- ⊃ choose to work in paid employment a little longer
- ⊃ reduce your desired after-employment income.

Steve's Investing Tip

It is better to set realistic goals rather than pie-in-the-sky goals.

Note: There are two big assumptions behind this survey:

1. You pay an average of 30% income tax. If you pay less then you will need less income and assets as the government will take a smaller slice of the profit pie. The reverse is also true for those who pay an average income tax rate of more than 30%.

2. You can invest in assets that provide an after-tax return of 8%. This book contains plenty of deals that reveal how others have achieved returns far in excess of that percentage, however your ability to source and acquire similar examples will depend on your available time and your investing skill.

THE CRITICAL QUESTION

In wrapping up, the critical question becomes, 'What do you need to do to make the final figure in your forward plan (the answer to Question F) a reality?'

This book can open your eyes to what's possible, however I'm not going to do the investing for you — that's your responsibility. The results you've been achieving are a by-product of the strategy and approach you've applied to your wealth creation and money management thus far.

In chapter 3 we learned that less than two in 10 retirees over 65 were able to self-fund their retirement. This means that around eight out of 10 retirees lack, for one reason or another, the skills to manage their money so that they can retire with more than a pension-funded existence.

Your future is your responsibility. Don't waste another day. Get educated and get serious about creating enough wealth to provide for your life after work.

ADDITIONAL BONUS

Jeremy from the office has created a 'Focus Board' to help you to turn the information you've outlined in this chapter into an effective goal. You can get this for free by going to:

<www.PropertyInvesting.com/focusboard>

Chapter 4 Insights

Insight #1:

The survey I've provided is only a guide — it's like a chat about tomorrow's weather rather than a seminar on how to read a barometric chart. My aim is to get you thinking, which is the first step in creating wealth.

Insight #2:

Your score is representative of the plan you have been implementing thus far. If you are unhappy with your progress then either the plan is flawed, or else your application has been faulty.

Insight #3:

There's not a lot of science needed to plan for financial independence: work out how much income you need in retirement, work backwards to how many assets this represents, and then get busy acquiring them!

Insight #4:

The responsibility for providing you with anything more than a bare-bones survival in retirement is solely yours. Don't leave it too late before you accept it.

PART I SUMMARY

The financial journey from where you are today to where you want to be tomorrow is one that you don't want to spend on cruise control. It's vital that you take action and control of your situation.

My own journey to financial independence was triggered by a dislike for the work-a-day world of accounting. What is your trigger? What will be your source of motivation and how will you attribute significance to your actions?

We all have skills and abilities that have driven us to success in our lives before. Our challenge is to put these to use in an investing context. A brief glimpse into the financial future reveals that a pension-based retirement existence is a risky bet and an uncomfortable result at best. The government can't be expected to look after us in the style we'd prefer. The responsibility for our financial futures rests in our own hands.

If you've taken my Quiz Challenge then right now you have a good idea of how far away you are from reaching your goals and just how challenging some of the milestones that you'll need to meet along the way might be. Rest assured, there are plenty of people in the same boat, and there's plenty of support available. We're all starting out on our own journeys towards our own definition of the property investing summit.

In Part II we're going to begin with some safety lessons as we examine some common mistakes and the disasterous consequences these can have.

PART II:

A Recipe for Disaster

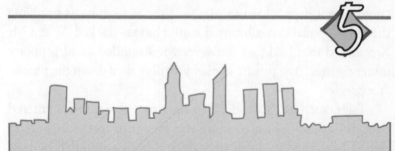

The Dreadful Dangers
of Personal Debt

I recently received a phone call from an investing associate (we'll call him Mr X) who was busting to tell me about a conversation he'd just had with his private banker. So excited was my friend that he said he had to pinch himself to make sure he wasn't dreaming. Over the past few years, Mr X and I have had long chats about our experiences when dealing with lenders: phone calls going unanswered, suffering long delays, waiting while lenders are tied up in red tape and not being able to settle on time causing us to pay penalties, and feeling like we had to get down on both knees and beg just to get a loan approval across the line.

Today though, it seemed that Mr X had hit the lending jackpot. Recounting the incredible story, Mr X said that he'd received an unusual phone call from his private banker who said that he was under his lending target, and that he needed to sign-up some loans as soon as possible in order to secure an upcoming bonus.

Accordingly, the private banker wanted to know how much he could pencil in as a loan to Mr X, at the same time as implying that any applications submitted would be fast-tracked. When Mr X outlined that he'd just put several million dollars of property under contract, the private banker literally yelled down the phone, 'Yeesssss!'

Tales, such as this can mean only one thing: we've entered dangerous financial times. Have you ever tried to cancel a credit card? I have tried to do so recently and been astounded by how hard it was. To start with, the bank tried to talk me out of it, attempting to convince me that what I needed was a higher credit card limit instead of a cancellation. Next, the form I had to fill in was far more complicated than the one required to obtain the credit card in the first place. Finally, because I had to go into a branch and wait in line, I eventually gave up after standing there for 20 minutes and getting nowhere.

Steve's Investing Tip

You know we're in strange times when it's harder to discharge a debt than it is to take one out in the first place.

It's now far easier to obtain a loan than ever before. The days of needing an established savings history and a relationship with the lender are well and truly over. Today, all you have to do to be treated like a movie star is to approach a lender and say that you want to borrow money. However, just because a financier welcomes you with open arms and offers to lend you a very flattering amount, it doesn't mean that it's in your best interests to take the money. Financial institutions will often tempt you with a little debt, and unless you're diligent and careful, before you know it you can be hooked for life.

ADDICTED TO SPENDING

Judging by the graphs below, Australians love to use their credit cards. Ten years ago the average amount owing per account holder was $965. This amount restated in 2006 dollars (assuming an average inflation rate of 4%) is $1,428. According to Reserve Bank of Australia (RBA) data, the actual average balance owing in May 2006 was $2,808.

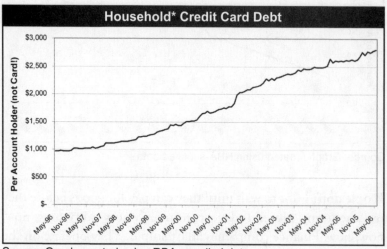

Source: Graph created using RBA-supplied data.

* This is the average balance per account holder, not per card issued. For example, some accounts have multiple cards attached to them. This does not include business credit cards. The same applies to the table overleaf.

The conclusion we reach is that credit card account holders now owe roughly twice as much on their credit cards as they did 10 years ago (in inflation-adjusted dollars). Not only do we owe more, there are far more account holders as the graph overleaf shows.

It's not just credit cards that are the problem though. The days of old-fashioned laybuys — where you'd put a deposit on a purchase and then pay it off before taking possession of the item — are coming to a gradual end. Instead, attend any homemaker centre on a Saturday and you'll see people queuing up to buy goods on 24 months 'interest free'.

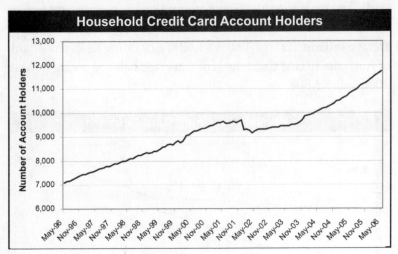

Source: Graph created using RBA-supplied data.

People don't want to wait until they can pay for goods before they use them any more. Today's consumer wants everything now, now, now. Finance companies aren't stupid. They operate on the understanding that most people will only pay the bare minimum (which is sometimes nothing) along the way and then be unable to afford the lump sum owing at the conclusion. That's when the interest, at a whopping 27% plus, kicks in.

A NEW ERA

If I had told you 10 years ago that people would happily pay over $5,000 for a TV set, what would you have said? It seems that our buying behaviour has changed dramatically, and with it the way we think about debt. Whereas once the idea of carrying an outstanding amount on a credit card was seen as foolish, it's now normal to maintain a balance of at least a few hundred, if not a few thousand.

This is seen with the increase in average limits on credit card accounts. In May 1996, an average card had a limit of $2,951. In May 2006 this had increased by 267% to $7,890.

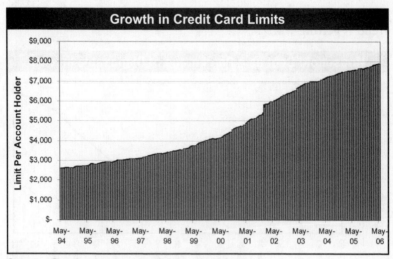

Growth in Credit Card Limits

Source: Graph created using RBA-supplied data.

Instead of debt being seen as temporary — something you get into and then out of — many now see owing money as a natural part of life. Sometime recently we've been conned into accepting that consumer debt is typical and okay. Instead of thinking about the pain associated with repaying what's owed, consumers happily whip out the plastic and have the positive association of earning rewards for spending. Gotchya! With the marketing geniuses high-fiving each other at the water coolers, a new generation of slaves is created — those who are convinced that it's a good idea to spend tens of thousands of dollars to earn enough loyalty points to redeem a 'free' trinket worth a few hundred dollars. Sadly, as they redeem their prizes they forget that the balance owing is attracting interest at over 16% per annum.

In August 2006, the *Herald Sun* reported that each Australian household had about $155 worth of debt for every $100 it cleared in its pay packet.[1] This disastrous financial outcome didn't just happen overnight, it's the consequence of a long period of financial abuse. The graph below tracks total household debt as a percentage of household income. Today, the average household will need to work one and a half years just to repay existing debt — and this trend is getting worse.

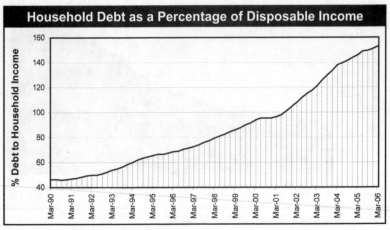

Source: Graph created using RBA-supplied data.

As a nation we've become addicted to the equivalent of financial fast food and now we're starting to feel the accompanying health risks. We need to start doing things differently or else we risk being owned by the executives and bean counters of large corporations who will stop at nothing to drive shareholder value higher.

DALE'S DEBTS

Dale, one of my R.E.S.U.L.T.S. mentoring participants, was in deep trouble. Her three Visa cards, together with her two American Express cards, were maxed out to the tune of $60,000. Not only was she struggling to repay what she owed, finding the money to

---

[1] Belt Tighter than 17% Days, Scott Murdoch, the *Herald Sun*, 03/08/2006.

just afford the interest (approximately $10,000 per annum) was a daily worry.

Dale's not silly. She's an educated and well-respected professional who has earned an annual salary of well over $100,000 in the past. In her case it was just a couple of disastrous financial choices that led to her demise. To start with, Dale turned to credit to fund her lifestyle in the belief that her period of unemployment would be temporary. That is, her income dropped but her lifestyle expenses remained on par with when she earned a professional salary. Sadly, the field in which she works is highly specialised and she has now suffered a prolonged period without regular employment. Without enough money to repay her debt, Dale committed a deadly financial sin: using a credit card to obtain a cash advance to repay another debt.

The other error she made was that she thought she'd be able to clear the debt through the sale of her home. She had hoped to find a buyer willing to pay $500,000, but due to a market correction, she only received $460,000.

Dale turned to me to get some advice about how to invest her way out of the situation. That is, how to do some quick property deals to earn enough money to repay what was owed and to then start again. When I said that I couldn't help her, Dale asked me 'why not?' My answer was this: until you can prove that you can manage money, your investing will only add to your problems rather than solve them.

Steve's Investing Tip

Having more money treats the symptoms of poor money management, but it doesn't address the root cause.

My advice to Dale wasn't sexy or glamorous, and it wasn't a quick fix. I encouraged her to approach her creditors and to work out a repayment plan. I then said that there would be pain, anguish and hard work, but that until she could demonstrate an ability to handle her money more appropriately, property investing needed to be off the cards.

Steve's Investing Tip

Escaping debt requires the same essential skill as successful investing: making sacrifices and delaying gratification.

I'm pleased to report that, after just four months, Dale's debt is down to $47,000. Her plan shows that she will repay everything by the end of 2007.

In seeking permission to use her story as a case study for this book, I asked Dale if there was anything that she would like to say to readers. Here's what she said:

```
Don't ever spend more than you earn. If you
find yourself out of control then pull back
immediately — don't wait or believe that
everything will be okay. And whatever you do,
never ever rely on credit cards to get you
over the line.
```

Dale's advice is timely given the spending trends outlined so far. Will you heed her warning? Will you tell others you know who are in deep financial trouble in time to save them? Please don't gloss over this knowledge — use and implement it.

Proving that Dale is experiencing an impressive change in mindset, last month she received a letter from the bank asking if she would like an increase on her credit card limit. She tells me that she ripped up the letter and filed it in the bin.

Do you need to manage your money better? Things are the way they are until you decide to change them. While I doubt we can do much to change the system, we can certainly do a lot to ensure that we don't become entangled in a debt trap. I am trying to spread the message to all who'll listen, that great money management is as simple as saying, 'Y – E = S'!

Y – E = S

I've said this before and I'll say it again: all wealth creation begins with the principle of spending less than you earn. To get the message across, I've come up with the following formula:

$$Y - E = S$$

If you break it down, it stands for:

Income – Expenses = Savings

Let's take a quick look at each of the components:

Y = Income

'Y' is the letter that economists assign to the term 'income' — the money you earn from your job(s) and also your investments (rent, interest, dividends, capital gains, and so on).

E = Expenses

Expenses are the funds that flow out of your wallet (or purse) to pay for your life. Expenses include taxes, home loan repayments, groceries, holidays, and so on. It's important to understand that, for the majority of people, a lot of spending is discretionary rather than essential. This means that they have a choice about whether or not to spend the excess over and above the cost of paying for essentials such as groceries, heating, health care and so on.

The decision to own a home rather than rent one is a good illustration of this point. In financial terms, renting usually makes a lot more sense than owning. However, because we price a large amount of emotion into the decision (it's the great Australian dream), it's normal to buy a home using mostly borrowed money rather than choosing to go without as a form of delayed gratification, and instead using the deposit money for investing purposes.

If you can happily choose not to spend, then you'll be a long way advanced in your quest for financial success.

S = Savings

Savings represents the surplus of your income over your expenses. As such, your ability to save is one of the quickest and easiest ways to tell how well you're handling your money. As a nation, we're not great savers, with the savings trend deteriorating from 16.75% of disposable income in 1979 to –2.39% in March 2006. In case you missed it, this means that the average Aussie household now spends 102.39% of what it earns.

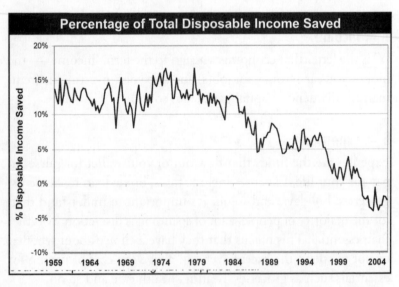

As I mentioned in the last chapter, long-term savings are usually a poor wealth-creation option. This is because the returns are so low when compared to inflation. However, the big benefit of savings is that they represent your mastery of the most important wealth-creation habit of all: spending less than you earn.

How much of your earnings do you spend? If you've never worked it out then you may be in for a rude shock.

Steve's Investing Tip

Conventionally, as a minimum you should save at least 10% of your total gross income.

Borrowings

When you have more expenses than income, you have the choice to either run down your savings or else to borrow from others in order to pay for the shortfall. When you borrow money, what is it that the financier is lending against?

Your first answer may be the security offered (such as the first mortgage over a property), but no, that's not quite right as the mortgage represents the collateral the lender takes to protect itself in the event you default.

What you're really borrowing against is your future income. Therefore, when you borrow you use tomorrow's income to pay for today's consumption. So the more you use debt to pay for today's consumption, the harder you'll have to work tomorrow just to break even.

IMPROVING YOUR FINANCIAL POSITION

Here are five ways that you can use the Y − E = S formula to get ahead financially.

1. Increase Income While Controlling Expenses

This is the first choice almost everyone makes, as earning more money is seen as a better approach than taking a lifestyle cut by decreasing spending. There's a significant danger though — as your income rises, so too does the temptation to spend the extra dollars earned as opposed to investing them, or else reducing debt.

Another issue to be aware of is that each extra dollar of income you earn will be subject to income tax. This means that a pay rise of $5,000 won't equate to an extra $5,000 that you can put towards your savings. (It will be $5,000 less income tax.)

2. Increase Income By More Than You Increase Expenses

Even if you do indulge in some occasional 'retail therapy', provided you spend less than the after-tax amount of the extra money you've earned then you'll still be building wealth.

3. Decrease Expenses While Controlling Income

You don't necessarily need to be earning more money in order to improve your financial position. In fact, controlling and reducing expenses is often a more effective option because your savings account will receive the full benefit of every dollar you don't spend. That is, you are not taxed again if you choose to keep a dollar, but if you spend it and try to earn another instead, the new dollar will be reduced by tax.

4. Decrease Expenses By More Than You Decrease Income

Even if your income suffers a hit, provided you can reduce your expenses by more than the drop in your pay packet then you'll keep building wealth.

5. Increase Income While Decreasing Expenses

Should you be able to earn more money at the same time as limiting non-essential spending then you'll be going gangbusters! What is non-essential spending? Well, spending money on anything that you don't absolutely need.

UNLOCKING THE DOOR TO FINANCIAL FREEDOM

Have you ever tried to unlock a door using the wrong key? I do it regularly when trying to open my front door since there are many keys that fit but only one that actually works and opens it. I must look like a dill because I'll often be wriggling keys into the lock for several minutes before I find the right one.

Everyday I see people standing at the door to financial freedom while trying to unlock it with the wrong key. If you learn anything from this chapter then understand that average Australians are programmed to fail at long-term wealth creation because they're inclined to spend more than they earn. Doing things differently is not just an option, it's a total necessity.

The key that the majority of people use is so well worn that the only door it unlocks is one that can be easily pushed open anyway — the door to financial mediocrity. Debt is like quicksand — it's easy to get into but extremely hard to get out of. On the other hand, with a little more effort and a commitment to working hard, you can get your hands on a shiny gold key that unlocks a much brighter financial future. The keys are illustrated below.

No doubt you'll observe that they're very different. The key to financial failure has more expenses than income, leading to little savings and next to no investment assets. The key to financial freedom has higher income since it's boosted by investment returns. It also has less expenses because the owner has good money habits, has substantial savings from the surplus of earnings over spending, and has a significant amount of investment assets.

As we wind up this chapter, to get you actively thinking about the points we've covered, I'd like you to draw the teeth (for income, expenses, savings, personal debt and net investment assets) on your own wealth-creation keys — shown opposite — as they are now, and also as you would like them to be in the future.

Once you've done that then compare your keys with the model Financial Failure and Financial Freedom keys given. Which future financial door will your key unlock? It's your choice.

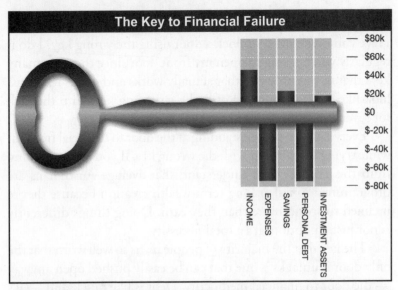

The Key to Financial Failure

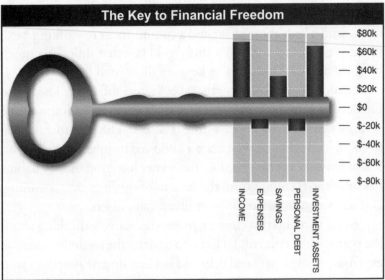

The Key to Financial Freedom

DON'T GIVE IN TO DEBT

Hopefully I've been able to show you that personal debt is a dangerous thing and in today's society the temptation has never been greater. Lenders are falling over themselves to give us money because they want to hit us with interest and are banking on our poor money-management skills. When it comes to fighting off personal debt, we all have to wage our own wars and face our own temptations. We must never give in.

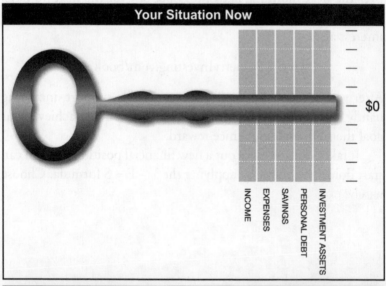

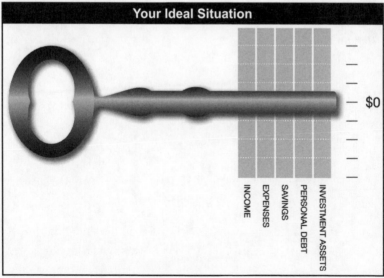

THE 33:30 CHALLENGE

Are you up for a challenge? If the answer is, 'Yes', then I'm throwing down the gauntlet to see if you can use one (or more) of the five money-saving options listed in this chapter to save at least $1,000 over the next month. That is, $33 per day for the next 30 days. If you'd like to join in then all you need to do is register your interest at:

<www.PropertyInvesting.com/book3>

After you've registered you'll receive valuable support, including handy tools, to help you along the way. Also, if you achieve your goal then I'll send you a nice reward.

It takes time to carve out a new financial position but you can start doing this today by applying the $Y - E = S$ formula. Choose wisely!

Chapter 5 Insights

Insight #1:

Massive commissions and bonuses on loans written is setting the financial system up for a big crash. In years to come, academics will look back on this practice and wonder how unlicensed lending was ever allowed.

Insight #2:

Australians now owe far more on their credit cards than they did a decade ago. Average credit limits are 167% higher. This worrying trend indicates that consumers are more willing to use debt, and less inclined to pay it off.

Insight #3:

When borrowing money you're effectively taking tomorrow's earnings and using them to pay for today's consumption. The way to get out of debt is to earn without over consuming.

Insight #4:

If you follow the normal pattern of consumption then you'll get the same outcome as everyone else. Don't aspire to this. Dare to be different and choose to spend well within your earning capacity.

Insight #5:

The best wealth-creation tip that I can give you is $Y - E = S$.

Insight #6:

Make sure your wealth-creation key unlocks the door to financial independence. The building blocks are sustained earnings, controlled spending, regular savings and an ever increasing net asset portfolio.

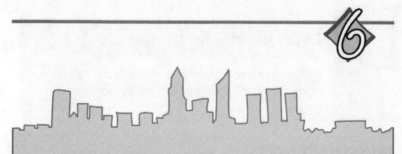

There Are Only Two Types of Debt: Bad and Worse

You may have heard it said that there are two types of debt: good debt (which is a loan that someone else repays on your behalf) and bad debt (which is a loan you have to repay yourself). Personally, I think this distinction is a big pile of hogwash! Don't ever forget that the responsibility for repaying your borrowings always rests on your own head. I've heard of plenty of investors who have been made bankrupt for failing to make loan repayments, but I'm yet to read about tenants being sued for failing to pay their rent and causing loan defaults. In my mind all debt is bad, the only question open to debate is exactly how nasty each particular debt might be.

As the property market becomes increasingly uncertain, I'm absolutely convinced that your ability to survive and flourish during the down times will rest fairly and squarely on your ability to manage and control debt.

Steve's Investing Tip

All forms of debt have nasty side effects, ranging from mild inconvenience right up to financial death.

INVESTMENT DEBT

In the last chapter I went to great lengths to help you see and understand the perils of personal debt and how it can quickly trap you into having to work tomorrow in order to repay money that you've borrowed and spent today. While still dangerous, investment debt is different. If you like, it's akin to fire in that a little is critical for survival, but too much can quickly get out of control and burn the house down.

Steve's Investing Tip

Investment debt makes a good servant but a terrible master.

Put simply, if you're planning to purchase real estate then you're going to need access to someone's cash in order to pay out the seller and to receive the title to the property. Your three financing options are to:

1. use entirely your own money

2. borrow someone else's money, or

3. use a combination of your money and someone else's money.

Let's look at each option in more detail.

1. Using Your Own Money

Using your own money may appear to be the least risky option because you'll be avoiding the need to borrow. Accordingly, when interest rates rise you won't suffer from higher mortgage repayments. However, there are two issues that pretty much eliminate the option of putting 100% of the cash down from your own pocket.

You Only Have a Limited Amount of Cash

Unless you're blessed with owning a tree that flowers $100 notes (that would make a nice present!) the size of your property portfolio will be limited by the amount of your cash reserves. This would keep most people to a maximum of one or two properties.

The underlying motto behind my achievements is that success comes from doing things differently. One manifestation of this principle is my belief that property investing is most profitable when you own multiple dwellings. Seriously, what's the use of a money-making strategy if you can only implement it once or twice and then you conk out? Surely, if you can find a winning strategy then you'll want to implement it over, and over, and over again!

Lack of Asset Diversification

Since the number of properties you can afford without debt will be limited, the risk you eliminate from having zero debt re-emerges in a different form — all your property investing eggs will be sitting in the one basket, under one or two roofs. In this situation the risk of vacancy and market exposure become serious threats. For example, consider the dangerous impact of having no income if you only owned one higher-value property that sat vacant for a long period of time. Alternatively, what if your one investment property suffered a sudden drop in value?

Owning multiple properties, or a diversified property portfolio, provides some natural 'insurance' against these risks. For example, if you owned 10 properties then all 10 would need to be vacant, and all 10 would need to fall in value for you to be in the same risk position. Clearly, that's unlikely.

2. Borrowing 100% of the Money

The second option when financing a purchase lies at the other extreme — it's borrowing the entire purchase price. In theory, there's no limit to the number of properties you can accumulate in your portfolio if you continue borrowing 100% of the purchase price and closing costs. Sadly, like most theories, this one doesn't work too well in real life for the following reasons.

Glass Lending Ceiling

Traditional lenders have maximum limits on the amount of money they'll be willing to lend. The amount lenders will make available will generally depend on:

➲ *Your Ability to Manage Money and Debt*
This will be assessed by reviewing your personal asset statements and doing a credit check.

➲ *Your Ability to Afford the Repayments*
Most lenders will happily provide a loan of up to a '30% Serviceability Ratio'. That is, where the total annual repayments represent 30% of the borrower's total income.

➲ *The Quality of the Investment Asset*
While lenders don't want to repossess properties, if they have to do so then they want to feel sure they can quickly sell them to recover the amount owing. As a rule, lenders don't have any qualms about lending up to 80% of a property's value. Anything higher and you'll probably be slapped with mortgage insurance and may need to put up extra loan collateral too.

Even if you were able to gain 100% finance, the fact that you'd be so highly geared would add to the bank's nervousness in lending a high amount on future projects.

Investing-Based Limitations

Ignoring lending limitations for a moment, the money-making strategy employed by many real estate investors strangles their prospects of acquiring a multiple property portfolio. How many property investors do you know who own five or more negatively geared properties? I can't think of one. There's a simple explanation though — an investor's income can only soak up so much in losses before owning more property becomes unaffordable.

Consider this example. Let's say that you're a growth-focused investor who earns an annual salary of $100,000. You don't have a lot of savings, but you can access up to $400,000 of equity from other investments to help pay for the purchase price. You come across what you think is a good investment property — a three-bedroom townhouse in a superior location with good growth prospects. The numbers on the deal are as shown in the following table.

The Numbers on Your Investment	
Purchase price (after closing costs)	$400,000
Weekly rent	$500
Rental management	9% of the rent
Annual costs	
Rates	$2,000
Insurance	$500
Repairs	$300
Other	$250
Annual interest	
80% LVR mortgage at 8% interest-only	$ 25,600
20% Line of credit against equity at 7% interest-only	$5,600
Expected annual growth	$30,000

Grab a pen and have a go at working out the profitability of this investment using the table overleaf.

Investment Profitability	
Annual rent	$
– Rental management	$
– Annual costs	$
– Interest	$
= Cashflow	$
+ Expected annual growth	$
= Net profit	$

A solution is outlined at the end of the chapter.

My answer was a cashflow loss of $10,590 and a net after-growth profit of $19,410. In theory, if it makes sense to own one property then it must also make sense to own 10 of the same kind. Let's see what happens now as we scale up the number and imagine that you bought multiples of this same deal.

Scalability Illustrated				
Number of Properties	1	3	5	10
Cashflow loss	($10,590)	($31,770)	($52,950)	($105,900)
+ Expected annual growth	$30,000	$90,000	$150,000	$300,000
= Net profit	$19,410	$58,230	$97,050	$194,100

If you struggle to understand the numbers, I've supplied a graph of the above table (opposite) to illustrate the point.

Theoretically, owning 10 of these properties would seem like a great investment since the annual profit would be $194,100. However, a salary of $100,000 can only support so many annual cashflow losses. With a salary of $100,000 your available cash would probably support one negatively geared property comfortably, two properties with some difficulty, and three properties with a lot of pain and stress. Let's do some very quick numbers.

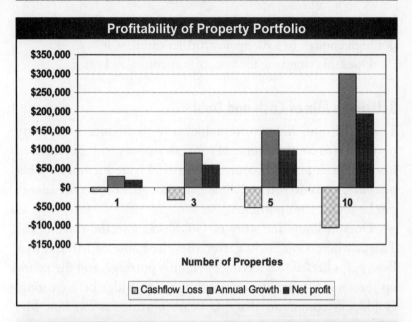

Some Quick Numbers	
Annual salary	$100,000
– Income tax	$30,550[1]
– Medicare levy	$1,500[1]
– Living costs	$31,200[2]
= Available cash	$36,750

[1] As per the Australian Tax Office website for the 2006 income year.
[2] Assumed to be $600 per week.

I've presented this financial model to illustrate that although a property portfolio may be profitable overall, a cashflow loss will limit the maximum number of dwellings that you can afford to own. I believe this example is a fair illustration of why the Australian Bureau of Statistics (ABS) survey of property investors revealed that 92% only owned one or two dwellings.[1] That is, investors couldn't

---

[1] Cat No. 8711.0, *Household Investors in Rental Dwellings*, Australia, 1997.

afford to own more than two properties because their salaries were not high enough to soak up any further cashflow losses.

Does this ring true for you, or someone you know?

3. Using a Mix of Cash and Debt

The third, and most sustainable, way to finance a property portfolio is to combine some of your own money with cash derived from other sources. Of course, the critical issue becomes, 'What percentage mix do you use?' Strangely enough, I believe the answer can be found with porridge!

Do you know the story of Goldilocks and the three bears? This is where Goldilocks gatecrashes the house of Mr and Mrs Bear, helps herself to a serving of yummy porridge, and then curls up for a nap afterwards. In sampling the porridge before eating, Goldilocks comments that Mr Bear's porridge is too hot, Mrs Bear's is too cold, but Baby Bear's is just right.

We need to adopt the same approach with our property investing. No, I'm not suggesting breaking and entering! I'm advocating that we should search for a mix of cash and debt that's just right for our experience and skill as investors, and also for the prevailing real estate market conditions.

What's The Right Mix of Cash and Debt?

Opposite is a matrix I've created to summarise my suggested guide to sustainable debt levels given your skill and experience, and also the current state of the property market. The key figure to look for is the percentage of your property portfolio (at current market value) that should be held as debt.

For example, if you were a novice in terms of skill and experience, and the property market was down, then I'd suggest that your debt be kept within a range of 50% to 70% of the current market value of your portfolio. In this case, if your property portfolio was worth (at current market prices) $600,000, then an ideal amount of debt would be between $300,000 (which is 50%) and $420,000 (which is 70%).

Guide to Sustainable Debt Levels					
Investing Skill and Experience	Trend of the Property Market				
	Crash	Down	Flat	Up	Boom
Novice	<50%	50% to 70%	60% to 75%	70% to 85%	75% to 90%
Average	<50%	50% to 75%	65% to 80%	75% to 90%	80% to 95%
Expert	<60%	60% to 80%	70% to 85%	80% to 95%	85% to 100%+

I've included more details about my definitions for skill and experience, and also the various stages of the property market, in Appendix A. This should help you to use this matrix and to understand how to define both your own position and the markets in which you operate.

MEET VANESSA

There's been a fair bit of theory in this chapter, so let's look at a practical example to illustrate how debt levels ought to vary as market conditions change. Vanessa is a property investor from Sydney and one of the people whom I've worked with as part of my R.E.S.U.L.T.S. mentoring program.

In the past, Vanessa has used the equity in her home to buy investment properties, and then as prices rose further, borrowed against the equity in her investment properties to buy even more real estate. This strategy worked well for her in an uptrending market since she was been able to expose her portfolio to rising prices given she owned more properties.

You'll see a full summary of Vanessa's current portfolio on page 95, but here are the key figures.

Key Figures in Vanessa's Portfolio	
Current market value	$3,150,000
– Property debt	$1,489,500
= Current equity	$1,660,500
Annual cashflow	–$53,237

My initial observations about Vanessa's portfolio were that:

➲ she had a strong growth focus

➲ her properties were concentrated in the one region (in and around the Sydney area), and

➲ her portfolio was very negatively geared.

While Vanessa had achieved good results, my fear was that her portfolio was too focused for growth given the declining market. Specifically, I thought she had the following potential problems:

➲ It might be hard for Vanessa to borrow any more money as lenders would be nervous about her ability to make the loan repayments with her existing negative cashflow.

➲ Her negative cashflow would deteriorate further if interest rates continued to rise.

➲ She seemed to have all her properties in the one Sydney basket. If there were a sudden downturn in that area she would be highly exposed.

➲ She was under huge pressure to keep working in order to continually earn enough money to finance her negative cashflow.

Vanessa's complete portfolio is shown in the table opposite. Applying the debt levels matrix from the previous page, I'd class Vanessa as an average investor and therefore her ideal debt levels would be between 50% and 75% of the value of her property portfolio, given the gloomy market.

Address and Description	Purchase Price and Closing Costs	Estimated Current Value	Current Loan Outstanding	Net Equity	Annual Cash Received	Annual Cash Paid	Annual Cashflow
Vanessa's Property Portfolio As Submitted							
Investment Property							
Property 1 3-bdr townhouse, 7km from Syd. CBD	$625,300	$600,000	$600,000	$0	$20,800	$44,168	–$23,368
Property 2 2-bdr unit, 15km from Syd. CBD	$274,500	$300,000	$155,000	$145,000	$12,480	$14,169	–$1,689
Property 3 4-bdr house, 7km from Syd. CBD (on beach)	$529,500	$950,000	$384,500	$565,500	$31,200	$33,085	–$1,885
Subtotal	$1,429,300	$1,850,000	$1,139,500	$710,500	$64,480	$91,422	–$26942
Home: 5-bdr house, 12km from Syd. CBD	$1,275,500	$1,300,000	$350,000	$950,000	$0	$26,295	–$26,295
Grand Total	$2,704,800	$3,150,000	$1,489,500	$1,660,500	$64,480	$117,717	–$53,237

At the time of writing her debt was sitting at 62% of current market value ($1,850,000 ÷ $1,139,500), so this would seem to be okay.

Her biggest problem is her high negative cashflow and the potential for that to escalate out of control with higher interest rates. In the worst case scenario, Vanessa could become a desperate seller if she were to lose her job and/or experience a sudden drop in equity as a result of a downturn in the Sydney property market.

I came up with the following plan to help mitigate the risks that Vanessa faced.

Action #1: Set Growth Benchmarks

My first suggestion was to set some goals that identified a desired growth target for each property. Vanessa had been just accepting whatever the market served up and, as such, had no firm idea whether each of her properties was helping or hindering her long-term wealth aspirations. Establishing a growth plan isn't rocket science, it could be as simple as the numbers in the following table.

A Simple Growth Plan			
	Current Value	Budgeted Growth %	Budgeted Growth
Property 1	$600,000	8%	$48,000
Property 2	$300,000	8%	$24,000
Property 3	$950,000	5%	$47,500
Next review date: 15th March 2007			

Action #2: Sell Property 1

I'd strongly consider selling Property 1 as this deal represents 53% of her total investment debt and 87% of her total negative cashflow. Vanessa had told me that the property was not currently growing, so it would probably be worthwhile selling it, as this would enable her to repay debt and to improve her overall cashflow situation.

Action #3: Consider Selling Her Home

This may sound a little radical, but if Vanessa and her family could get over their emotional ties to their home, then selling would release a tax-free gain and result in the pooling of a significant amount of cash with which she could invest. The plan would be to rent in the short term and then to buy back another (better) home at a later date using the profits made in the course of investing.

Selling their home would also significantly reduce the amount of her negative cashflow, which would take a lot of pressure to earn money off Vanessa. This, in turn, might allow her to work less, thereby freeing up her time to look for deals rather than having to slave away in her job.

Note: I'm *not* saying that everyone should sell their homes! I'm just pointing out that selling a home is an emotional decision. From an investing perspective, owning a home eats up valuable capital that could be used as money for deposits, at the same time as reducing your ability to borrow since you already have home-related personal debt.

While the ideal portfolio that I mapped out for Vanessa will show you the full picture (Portfolio B overleaf), the summary table below indicates that Vanessa could sell her home and wipe off her investment debt, which would turn her cashflow loss into a cashflow surplus.

A Summary of Vanessa's Position			
	Vanessa Now	Steve's Ideal	Difference
Current market value	$3,150,000	$1,250,000	–$1,900,000
– Property debt	$1,489,500	$0	$1,489,500
= Net equity	$1,660,500	$1,250,000	–$410,500
Annual cashflow	–$53,237	$35,680	$88,917

In addition to the above Vanessa would have about $380,000 to use as deposits to purchase other investment property.

Portfolio B — Steve's Suggested Ideal Property Portfolio							
Address and Description	Purchase Price and Closing Costs	Estimated Current Value	Current Loan Outstanding	Net Equity	Annual Cash Received	Annual Cash Paid	Annual Cash flow
Investment Property							
Property 2: 2-bdr unit, 15km from Syd. CBD	$274,500	$300,000	$—*	$300,000	$12,480	$3,000*	$9,480
Property 3: 4-bdr house, 7km from Syd. CBD (on beach)	$529,500	$950,000	$—*	$950,000	$31,200	$5,000**	$26,200
Grand total (now)	$804,000	$1,250,000	$—*	$1,250,000	$43,680	$8,000	$35,680
Was (comparison)	$2,704,800	$3,150,000	$—	$1,660,500	$64,480	$117,717	–$53,237
Difference	–$1,900,800	–$1,900,000	–$1,489,500	–$410,500	–$20,800	–$109,717	–$88,917

* I have assumed that the money from the sale of the house has been applied against the property debt. There would still be approximately $380,000 in surplus cash remaining.

** Rates, repairs, etc.

Action #4: If Vanessa Wanted to Keep Her Home...

Should the family not be willing to sell their home, then another possibility that may be worth investigating is selling Property 1 and Property 2, then taking some of the cashed-in equity from the sales and paying down the loan on Property 3.

This would result in Portfolio C, as described in the table overleaf. In summary, this would see the following outcome (from an investment property perspective):

➲ no change to the net equity position of Vanessa's investment portfolio

➲ positive cashflow from her investment portfolio (but an overall negative position when we include her home too)

➲ $900,000 less in investment debt.

Portfolio C Summarised			
	Vanessa Now	Steve's Changes + Keep House	Difference
Current market value	$3,150,000	$2,250,000	–$900,000
– Property debt	$1,489,500	$589,500	$900,000
= Net equity	$1,660,500	$1,660,500	—
Annual cashflow	–$53,237	–$18,030	$35,207

CHANGING TIMES

As the graph on page 101 shows, provided Vanessa is proactive in taking action as the market changes, her situation can be made much less risky by reducing the amount of debt she's carrying. For example, under the Portfolio B scenario, Vanessa owns less property but has a far superior cashflow. She will also have a significant bank balance behind her, which she can use to purchase great opportunities as they come onto the market in a downturn.

Portfolio C — If Vanessa Chose to Keep Her Home

Address and Description	Purchase Price and Closing Costs	Estimated Current Value	Current Loan Outstanding	Net Equity	Annual Cash Received	Annual Cash Paid	Annual Cash flow
Investment Property							
Property 3: 4-bdr house, 7km from Syd. CBD (on beach)	$529,500	$950,000	$239,500	$710,500	$31,200	$22,935*	$8,265
Home							
5-bdr house, 12km from Syd. CBD	$1,275,500	$1,300,000	$350,000	$950,000	$0	$26,295	–$26,295
New grand total	$1,805,000	$2,250,000	$589,500	$1,660,500	$31,200	$49,230	–$18,030
Was (originally)	$2,704,800	$3,150,000	$1,489,500	$1,660,500	$64,480	$117,717	–$53,237
Difference	–$899,800	–$900,000	–$900,000	$—	–$33,280	–$68,487	–$35,207

* Lowered by $145,000 × 7% on the basis that the loan is paid down with the equity from the sale of Property 2.

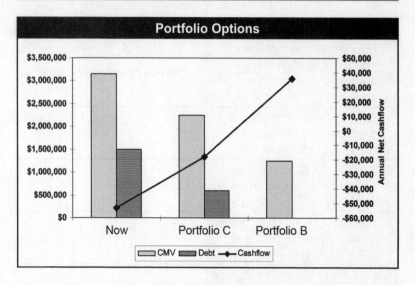

Portfolio Options

Are you in a similar position to Vanessa in that you're carrying debt that could financially cripple you as the property market softens? Don't make excuses — become proactive in managing your debt or you may find that it starts to manage you.

WRAP UP

In winding up this chapter I invite you to complete the table overleaf and then compare your answer with the debt matrix on page 93. Can you conclude that your current property debt levels are appropriate to both your skill and experience and also the current state of the property market in which you invest?

Don't wait for disaster. Take action before you're forced into an outcome in which you lose control. In the next chapter I'll show you how to read the Steve McKnight 'Property Clock' so you can minimise the impact of a potential property melt down, while also positioning yourself to take advantage of the next real estate boom.

Are Your Debt Levels Appropriate?	
1. How would you rate your skill and experience as an investor? (Circle your answer)	Novice / Average / Expert
2. What is the total amount of property debt that you're carrying at the moment?	$
3. What is the current market value of your entire property portfolio?	$
4. What is your debt to current market value percentage? (#2 ÷ #3) × 100	%
5. Looking at the debt matrix table on page 93, what is the suggested debt to current market value percentage for your level of skill and experience?	%
6. What action, if any, do you need to take?	

SOLUTION TO INVESTMENT PROFITABILITY

(See page 90.)

Investment Profitability	
Annual rent	$26,000
– Rental management	$2,340
– Annual costs	$3,050
– Interest	$31,200
= Cashflow	–$10,590
+ Expected annual growth	$30,000
= Net profit	$19,410

Chapter 6 Insights

Insight #1:

Remember, it's your responsibility to repay the money you borrow.

Insight #2:

If you have a plan for getting into debt then have a plan for how you'll get out of debt too.

Insight #3:

As the property market changes, the amount of debt you carry needs to change too. When the market is rising, borrow more. When the market is falling, start reducing your loan balances.

Insight #4:

If property prices fall and your debt remains the same then you may end up in financial hot water. Do whatever you can to avoid becoming a distressed seller!

Insight #5:

Sometimes repaying debt is the best investment option. This softens the impact of rising interest rates at the same time as giving you an equity buffer that will protect you against falling home values.

Insight #6:

It's important to know and to understand the numbers behind your property portfolio as this will allow you to make an accurate investment decision about which assets are under-performing and need to be sold.

Insight #7:

Don't wait for the big bad 'property downturn' wolf to blow your house down. Always be proactive when managing your debt.

The Steve McKnight Property Clock

I had to laugh. The other night my little three-year-old daughter, who's infatuated with Disney Princesses, wanted to show me a Cinderella lunch box in a junk-mail catalogue that had been left in our letterbox. As she flicked though the pages I had to hide my smile because she was holding it upside down. As I helped her turn the brochure around the right way, she laughed and said, 'That's better.'

My daughter is not yet able to read, so her sophistication is limited to her ability to see and to interpret pictures. Many property investors find themselves in the same boat. That is, they're unable to read the property market for themselves and so they rely on others to help them find what they're looking for. The property market is a complicated beast, so a one-size-fits-all generic investing system (such as long-term buy and hold) is, at best, likely to result in a mediocre long-term outcome. If you want to outperform the market then you need to tailor your approach so that you can capture the momentum of each market trend.

Steve's Investing Tip

Always invest in a way that makes the trend your friend.

Many investors make the mistake of trying to create the equivalent of an ocean liner out of their portfolio. They do this in the belief that something big and heavy will be robust enough to ride out any potential price storms. This is flawed thinking though, because a ship that's big and bulky is difficult to manoeuvre and can only operate in deep water. The Titanic was considered unsinkable, but it now rests on the ocean floor.

Just as a yacht is better able to quickly manoeuvre out of trouble, a flexible investing approach can help you to thrive in any market conditions. A flexible investor is able to quickly change direction in response to market movements, and is agile enough to manoeuvre through the shallow waters of lean times.

Looking at the properties you own, are you like the Titanic with a huge equity hull that's needed to support massive debt? Are you a yacht that can sail after quick profits in tough times? Or are you more akin to a tin dinghy that's leaking water and about to go under in rough seas? The aim of this chapter is to increase your sophistication as a real estate investor by enhancing your understanding of the property market.

THE THEORETICAL PROPERTY MARKET

There are only three possible directions in which property prices can move: up, down and sideways. Over the long term, because of inflation, prices will always trend upwards. For example, homes sell for a whole lot more today than they did in 1978, and part of this will be due to a dollar today buying far fewer goods and services than it did a few decades ago.

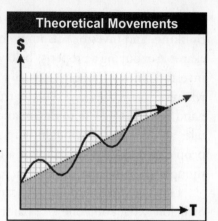

The graph opposite shows the theoretical movement of property prices over time. Take a second or two to locate:

➲ the three uptrends (growth)

➲ the two downtrends (decline)

➲ the sideways trend, and

➲ the long-term uptrend.

If you try marking the ideal selling and buying points at the top and bottom of each market cycle, you'll discover it's not hard in theory. How great would it be if we all had crystal balls that allowed us to buy at the bottom and sell at the top? I'm yet to find such a device though, so instead I have to rely on my understanding and reading of the market in order to form a considered opinion. Unsophisticated investors skip this step and invest on gut feeling based on what they hope will happen, rather than what they reasonably expect will occur.

Steve's Investing Tip

Property speculators act on hope. Property investors use reason to form an opinion and then act accordingly.

Digressing for just a second, the difference between speculator thinking, and investor reasoning, can be demonstrated using the example of buying a property 'below market value'. Knowledgeable investors know they can't actually do this because, as the buyer, whatever price they pay sets the true market value! On the other hand, speculators like to dream and to feel good, so they concoct tales about how they bought bargains based on what a few other people (whom they mistake for a representation of 'the market') thought the property was worth.

Don't get me wrong, you can buy below appraised value, or below what someone else paid, or below what you think the property is worth. Just avoid the hype about buying below market value, as this is often marketing jargon used to entice you to purchase in the first place.

Returning to the theoretical property market, investors have two strategies that they can use to try to make a growth profit from real estate.

1. Buy and Sell Higher

This is where the real estate investor buys a property and then looks to sell down the track at a higher price, ideally before the market turns and values fall.

2. Buy and Hold

These property buyers plan to hold forever as they intend to ride the long-term uptrend and wait out any short-term glitches should prices fall. I deliberately haven't used the word 'investor' in my description of those who follow this practice because, in my opinion, most would fail to qualify. Remember, investors are always seeking to maximise their returns, so the idea of owning property that was falling in value would simply not be acceptable. Only those who don't know when to sell end up holding property in a downturn.

Steve's Investing Tip

A property investment that loses money is a liability, not an asset. Holding too many liabilities will send you broke!

I'm a firm believer that 'timing the market' is much more important than 'time in the market'. Yes, I know this flies in the face of most so-called expert opinions on how to invest in real estate, but I make it a rule to think differently and let my results back up my claims.

WHEN IS THE TIME RIGHT TO BUY?

Trying to buy at the bottom of the market involves pure guesswork. While you might get lucky, if you're wrong then you'll lose money as prices fall further. For example, some investors may decide to buy at point A in the first graph below on the basis that prices had fallen a long way from their peak. Sadly, they'd be wrong and losses would follow because, as shown in the second graph, the values continued to tumble to Point B.

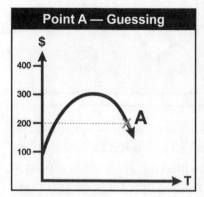

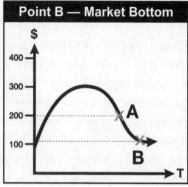

In practice, since you only can only identify the bottom of the market in hindsight, the best time to buy is once prices have bounced off their lows and a new uptrend is established. The theoretical best time to buy is shown on the graph opposite. This allows you to benefit from the full growth cycle.

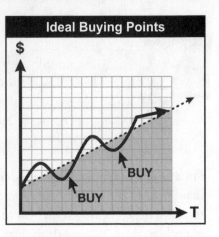

WHEN IS THE TIME RIGHT TO SELL?

Just as buying at the absolute bottom of the market is purely guesswork, so too is attempting to sell at the very top. As shown in the graph provided, the best you can hope for is to identify the change in market sentiment and sell before prices fall too far. If you second-guess the market and exit prematurely then you run the risk of leaving a substantial amount of money in the deal.

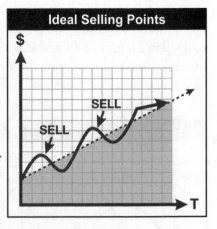

Brian, a friend of mine, is the perfect example of this principle. He bought a property in suburban Melbourne during a sideways trend and, five years later, found his investment was worth about what he paid for it. He finally decided to sell and to do something else with his money, only to just miss out on a price explosion when his ex-property doubled in value over the next two years. His poor timing ended up costing him a fortune.

It's true that owning property for the long term is a sure-fire way of making some money. However, making a little profit is not the same as maximising your wealth. As outlined in my second book, *$1,000,000 in Property in One Year*, between 1980 and 2004, the Australian property market trended upwards for one third of the time, and down or sideways for two thirds of the period. I don't know about you, but I wouldn't want to invest using a strategy that was ineffective for 66% of the time. The message I'm trying to convey is that you should buy when the price trend is up, and sell when the price trend has peaked and is falling. In a sideways market I'd buy, create value, and then sell for a quick profit.

What's your investment strategy? How has it evolved over the past few years to reflect the changing trends of the property market?

THE PROPERTY CLOCK

Have you heard of the 'Economic Clock' before? This is where the varying stages of an economic cycle are shown as time intervals on a clock. For example, you have rising interest rates at 1 o'clock, falling shares prices at 2 o'clock, falling commodity prices at 3 o'clock, and so on. Well, I've taken this concept and applied it to a theoretical real estate cycle.

Phase 1: Post-Upturn Flat Patch (12 to 3 O'Clock)

Unlike shares where price movements of 5% in a day are not unusual, property values take longer for a trend to be established and then, once set, that trend tends to last for many years. Following the up and down phases are periods in which the market catches its breath and prices move sideways.

In the first phase of my property clock you should expect to see growth in real estate values start to taper off as buyers run out of steam. For example, buyers may become spooked by a slight deterioration in the economic fundamentals (such as an interest rate rise or a tax hike).

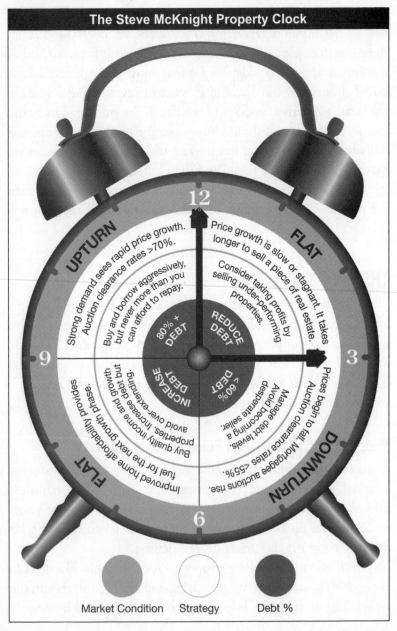

The Steve McKnight Property Clock

UPTURN — Strong demand sees rapid price growth. Auction clearance rates >70%.

Buy and borrow aggressively, but never more than you can afford to repay.

80%+ DEBT

FLAT — Price growth is slow or stagnant. It takes longer to sell a piece of real estate.

Consider taking profits by selling under-performing properties.

REDUCE DEBT

<60% DEBT

Prices begin to fall. Mortgagee auctions rise. Auction clearance rates <55%.

DOWNTURN

Manage debt levels. Avoid becoming a desperate seller.

INCREASE DEBT

Buy quality income and growth properties. Increase debt but avoid over-extending.

FLAT — Improved home affordability provides fuel for the next growth phase.

Market Condition   Strategy   Debt %

Alternatively they may become less inclined to believe that the money-making fairytale can last forever if the demise of high-profile investors and celebrities are featured in the paper.

In the Australian market both happened at the end of the last boom — interest rates bounced off their lows in May 2002, and we had futures traders nearly sink the NAB. At the same time, high-profile company directors were publicly shamed and sent to jail. One indicator in isolation wouldn't have caused more than a glitch, but added together, the psychological mindset of the average investor changed from being optimistic to slightly cautious.

Should investors not shrug off their doldrums and return to happier profit-orientated thoughts, then a flat trend that holds for longer than six months may indicate the changing of the property season. When prices start to fall, that's my signal to take profits on marginal deals.

Phase 2: Downturn (3 to 6 O'Clock)

A downturn is more than prices falling slightly on a few houses in a few suburbs. There will usually be headlines and stories of hardship like the article that appeared in *The Sydney Morning Herald* on August 21, 2006 titled 'Housing Crash Puts Sellers In Debt Crisis'. This article featured a property in Sydney's west that reportedly sold for $260,000 at a mortgagee auction. The distressed vendor purchased the same house three years earlier for $450,000. Ouch!

Survival is the name of the game in a downturn. Specifically, you want to avoid becoming a desperate seller since you may be forced to accept a low sale price, perhaps even less than the debt you still owe your lender, in which case you'll lose the asset and still owe money!

The one benefit of a downturn is that home affordability increases as prices fall. Eventually, home buyers will return to the market on the basis that the financial gap between owning and renting is diminishing. Otherwise, investors start to compete in order to snap up perceived bargains. Alternatively, the economic fundamentals will improve (through falling interest rates or tax incentives) to make property ownership more attractive.

Phase 3: Post-Downturn Flat Patch (6 to 9 O'Clock)

Prices won't rise overnight since buyers will need to regroup in order for demand to be high enough to stimulate growth in home values. There will be some degree of pessimism in the minds of investors since many will have suffered some pain during the downturn.

The market is like a pressure cooker in that the right conditions need time to simmer away, and it can take several years for the hurt to be forgotten. I'd be happy to tentatively buy good value deals that had sound growth or income prospects. I wouldn't bet the lot on a deal though, or go into crazy amounts of debt, as the risks would be too great should the market slip back into a downturn.

Steve's Investing Tip

If a property failed to perform during the boom times, then how likely is it to produce profits in a flat market?

Phase 4: Boom (9 to 12 O'Clock)

Bring out the streamers and pointy hats — there's a property party going on! Any fool can make money in a boom, and enough do so as to entice their buddies to join in on the action. Naturally, when you have enough silly people, doing enough silly things, then you're certain to have silly outcomes.

During the last boom there were commentators — the Reserve Bank of Australia was one of them — suggesting that the boom couldn't, and wouldn't, last forever. That was like telling a child that the ferris wheel would come to an end halfway through the ride. 'Don't be silly', they think, 'the ride's still going around and around'.

Yes, all booms do eventually end, but there are fortunes to be made while the good times last. It's the speculators who force prices higher because they don't pay any attention to economic sensibilities or sustainability — just the ease with which the money can seemingly be made. If you add tax incentives like the First Home Owner's Grant, a falling interest rate climate and deregulation of the lending market, then there's enough fuel for a price explosion.

'All aboard!' is the message you'll hear in a property boom. Buy as much property as you can possibly afford, and then sit back and enjoy the ride as the growth escalator takes you to the top. Be careful that you don't fall asleep though. There's a saying in the stock market that applies equally to property too: the bulls climb up the stairs while the bears jump out the windows. Bad news travels fast, so don't be left overcommitted once the momentum turns sour.

USING THE PROPERTY CLOCK

The first step in improving your investing ability is to shut out the noise of what others think, and to form your own opinion on what's happening in the property market.

Once you've done that then you need to tailor your investing approach to the prevailing conditions. For example, it's appropriate to be aggressive during a boom and conservative during a downturn. The property clock can help you to align your investing to the current state of the market.

Have a go for yourself by trying to complete the table overleaf.

Ask Yourself the Following Questions	
What time is it in your investing area?	
What is the appropriate debt management the clock suggests for the current market?	
How does that compare with your debt management?	
What comes next in the property cycle?	
How can you be better prepared should this eventuate?	

THE REAL WORLD

While extremely useful as a teaching aid, the property clock presented in this chapter is too simple in its design to be relied upon completely. For example, the stages of the real estate cycle are divided evenly whereas in reality the periods are more likely to be:

- **booming:** 30% of the time

- **flat:** 60% of the time

- **downtrending:** 10% of the time.

Furthermore, property cycles tend to exist on a micro level, which means that one area or state could be in a boom and another area or state in a downturn. This is certainly happening at the time of writing with Western Australia experiencing price growth while Sydney is experiencing a general decline in home values. The property clock should therefore be used as one of many tools at your disposal. Ask yourself how you can use this resource to help improve your investing.

Okay, it's time to get controversial so in the next chapter I'm going to debunk one of the biggest myths of property investing! I'm going to show you how holding equity can dramatically restrict your ability to create massive wealth.

Chapter 7 Insights

Insight #1:

The real estate market moves between cycles of price growth and price decline. Time is needed for a new trend to emerge, and prices generally move sideways during these periods of uncertainty.

Insight #2:

Sophisticated investors adapt to changing market conditions by varying their approaches so that they capture the benefit of an uptrend while also mitigating the prospects of being wiped out in a downturn.

Insight #3:

It's impossible to buy at below market value because whatever price you pay as a buyer defines fair market value!

Insight #4:

You can only identify the top or bottom of a market after it's occurred.

Insight #5:

The property clock summarises the four phases of the theoretical property market. It's a guide to help you keep one eye on what's happening right now while your other eye can be assessing what's likely to happen next.

The Secret to Massive Lifetime Wealth

As legend has it, Sir Isaac Newton was sitting under a tree one day when a juicy red apple fell down and donged him on the head. Inspecting the offending fruit, Sir Isaac became inspired to create his Law of Universal Gravitation, upon which the popular saying 'what goes up must come down' is based.

Newton's theory doesn't just apply to apples and hot air balloons. To the chagrin of those who think that home values only ever increase, Sir Isaac's observations are also relevant to the property market. For instance, equity is usually seen as a property investor's good and trusted friend; a safe-house of untapped profit that can be accessed in a tax-advantaged way. However, property prices *can* and *do* fall, and should they tumble to below what's owed then disastrous financial consequences can be just around the corner. This chapter is written to shed light on the dangerous way that many property investors use their equity. Make sure you don't fall for these same traps!

EQUITY EXPLAINED

Equity is what's left over when you deduct a property's debt from the dwelling's current market value.

Equity = Current Market Value – Debt Outstanding

For example, if you owned a property portfolio that was valued at $1,200,000, and you had borrowings against that property of $1,000,000, then your equity would be $200,000 (see below).

Calculating Your Equity	
Property portfolio (at current market value)	$1,200,000
– Property debt	$1,000,000
= Your investment equity	$200,000

Equity, sometimes also called net worth, can be calculated on a per property basis across your entire property portfolio, or across all your assets.

THE SECRET TO BUILDING WEALTH

Right! Grab a highlighter as I'm about to share with you the secret to building massive lifetime wealth. You may be surprised by the straightforwardness of the answer, but don't be fooled by its simplicity.

Okay, the suspense is killing me! Here's the solution:

Grow your equity faster
than you grow your debt!

Having revealed the secret, the rest of this chapter will be devoted to explaining what it means in practice. It's simple but not easy.

ADDING EQUITY

Have you ever seen or played basketball before? It's a game that I know inside-out because, at one stage in my late teens, I was either playing, coaching or umpiring every night of the week. No wonder my knees are creaky now! Conceptually, basketball's a pretty simple game. Two teams try to earn points by throwing a ball through their opponent's hoop. The winner is the team that has the highest score at the end of the game.

Basketball centres around two main strategies — offensive and defensive. If you're playing an offensive game then you're totally focused on rapidly outscoring your opponent. On the other hand, in a defensive game you're channelling all your efforts into stopping the opposition from scoring. While a strong defence can save a game, a team won't win unless it can score goals. That is, a nil-all result is only a draw.

While basketball and wealth creation may not seem to have much in common, on closer inspection the opposite is true. For example, it's next to impossible to build massive wealth by solely using a defensive spending strategy to save money. However, wealth can be quickly accumulated by purchasing clever assets using offensive buying strategies.

With that in mind, imagine that coach McKnight has just stepped on to the court during a time-out to give you some words of wisdom about how to win the property investing game. After commending you on your efforts thus far, I'd whip out my trusty clipboard and sketch out something along the following lines.

1. Offensive Buying Strategy

It's true that you can tell the quality of the investor by the assets that he or she owns. A poor investor owns assets that depreciate

— things like cars, electronic gadgets, clothing or expensive furniture. It follows that the foolishness of the investor can be determined by the amount that his or her assets have fallen in value against what was paid to acquire them. On the other hand, a skilled investor owns assets that appreciate — items like property, shares, businesses and collectables. In this case, skill can be determined by the amount of net equity achieved.

Steve's Investing Tip

Buy assets that appreciate. Limit or avoid assets that depreciate.

Of course, assets purchased for growth could end up as depreciating duds. For example, a property that falls in value would usually be classified as a poor investment notwithstanding that it was purchased for growth and might one day be worth more.

The aim of your offensive investing game should be to acquire assets that will build equity by increasing in value. For example, how much equity would you have 'created' if you bought an investment property for $200,000 that was valued at $250,000 two years later?

It's not a trick question, the answer is $50,000. The graph opposite shows the 'equity zone' that's created when a property appreciates in value. As you would expect, the greater the equity zone, the better the wealth-creation outcome.

2. Defensive Strategy: Debt Reduction

Increasing your equity by decreasing your debt is a powerful and much overlooked defensive wealth-creation strategy. For example, working with the same numbers as those in our previous example, let's imagine that you'd managed to pay down your property loan so that the amount owing at the end of year two was $150,000.

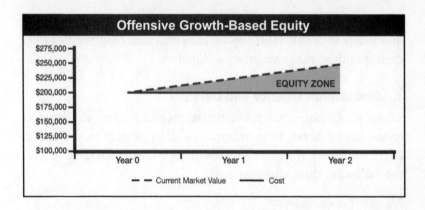

Assuming zero growth, your equity would again be $50,000 (that is, the amount of money that you had repaid). The graph below shows how an equity zone can be increased even when property prices are flat.

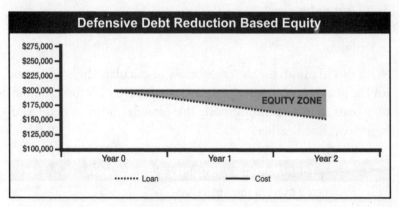

The two ways to eliminate property debt are:

1. making periodic repayments, or

2. selling the property and repaying all the debt.

As drastic as it sounds, selling a property can be a quick way to repay debt and to dramatically solidify your equity (since the capital appreciation is converted into cash).

Positive cashflow investors looking to fast-track their equity may prefer to channel their cash profits into debt repayments rather than spending them on lifestyle expenses.

3. Combination Offence and Defence

As you might expect, the basketball teams that tend to win the most games have a penetrating offence as well as a disciplined defence. In the same way, the most effective wealth-creation strategies have the following three components:

1. *Asset accumulation*
   Where the investor purchases quality assets.

2. *Asset maximisation*
   Where those assets are used in the best possible way so as to unlock maximum profit for minimum risk.

3. *Debt reduction*
   Where the investor also has a plan for controlled repayment of debt.

With this in mind, use the table below to calculate the equity zone for the imaginary property you purchased (page 122) for $200,000 two years ago, combining both the growth and debt reduction figures outlined earlier.

Your Imaginary Property's Equity Zone	
Property's current market value	$
– Property debt	$
= Total equity	$

A solution can be found at the end of the chapter.

Having calculated the total equity, take a moment to split it into its 'appreciation' and 'debt reduction' components.

How much of your own property equity is due to growth, and how much is due to debt reduction? Does your answer reveal a weakness in your offensive or defensive game?

Appreciation and Debt Reduction Components	
Equity from appreciation	$
+ Equity from debt reduction	$
= Total equity	$

A solution can be found at the end of the chapter.

Steve's Investing Tip

The most powerful equity-building strategies incorporate buying assets using other people's money, and then repaying those borrowings in a controlled manner.

The graph below reveals that the quickest way to grow your equity zone is to combine an offensive buying strategy with defensive debt minimisation.

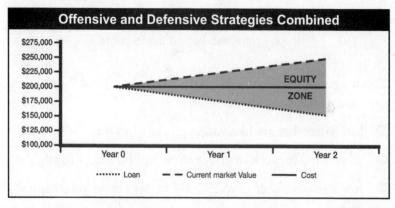

It would be remiss of me not to take this opportunity to remind you of the essential message from the last chapter — that your choice of offensive and defensive equity building strategy needs to be tailored to the current state of the property market. For instance, if you're overly aggressive in a down market then you run the risk of using up all your precious working capital in a period of declining values. That is, if a great opportunity were to present itself then you might be too financially exhausted to grab it!

It would be better to conserve your energy by focusing on repaying debt, as this would preserve your working capital while also improving your borrowing ability. I'm not saying that you shouldn't buy anything in a down market, just that you need to be more selective about the deals you acquire!

In summary, I'm worried that a scary number of investors disregard the importance of defence and instead solely focus on building equity by purchasing more and more property. Can you see the danger of this approach in a down market?

THE WORST WEALTH-CREATION STRATEGY EVER!

Having outlined the best wealth-creation strategy — building equity — let me also share the worst wealth-creation strategy in existence. It's this:

Borrowing against equity
to pay for lifestyle and living costs.

This is a popular topic at wealth-creation seminars and the standard spiel goes something like this:

➲ buy assets that are likely to appreciate in value

➲ allow time to work in your favour and for prices to rise

➲ never sell the asset as you'll have to pay tax on your capital gains

➲ borrow against the equity (which doesn't attract capital gains tax) and use it to pay for lifestyle and living costs.

Let's take a closer look at two prominent examples of this dangerous concept and how it works in practice.

1. *A large bank's 'Equity Mate' campaign*
   I have a mental picture of a TV ad where a guy has a new
   boat parked in his driveway. His jealous neighbour, peering
   over the fence, says, 'Where did you get the money for
   that?' The proud boat owner points to his home and says
   'Equity, mate!'

2. *Reverse mortgages[1]*
   Another TV ad sees a grandmother tuck a brick into
   her handbag on her way to visit her grandson. Over the
   dinner table she proudly produces the brick and places it
   on the table announcing that it will be used to pay for her
   grandson's future education.

What's being proposed in both cases is that home equity be used as
collateral for a loan that will pay for lifestyle expenses. Let me reveal
the danger of this approach by building an example around Mr Boat
— the guy who's using his home equity to buy a boat. To do this I'm
going to need to make the following assumptions. Prior to redrawing
his equity, Mr Boat's financial position was as follows:

- ⊃ He earned $70,000 per annum.

- ⊃ He bought his home eight years ago for $200,000. It's now
  worth $400,000.

- ⊃ He originally borrowed 80% of the value of his home
  ($160,000). He has not paid any money off the loan as it
  was lent on an interest-only basis at 7% per annum.

- ⊃ He paid $40,000 to purchase his fully equipped boat
  (including trailer).

---

[1] A reverse mortgage involves accessing the equity in a house by way of a loan. Interest
is capitalised so there are no repayments. Upon death or sale, the loan is repaid. It
can be very dangerous because the borrower wouldn't normally be able to afford the
loan repayments on his or her current income, which is why the interest is capitalised
in the first place.

Now, the nice employees at the Australian Taxation Office will only allow tax deductions on expenditure that's made in the pursuit of earning income that will be taxed.

Steve's Investing Tip

It is the way money's used, rather than where it comes from, that determines whether tax deductions apply.

Even if Mr Boat was borrowing against an investment property, because those funds will be used for private or personal purposes (to buy a boat), his new pride and joy won't qualify for a tax deduction. This little piece of information can have very serious financial consequences. Let's have a look at a few.

Serious Interest Issues

The interest payable on the $40,000 equity redraw would not be tax deductible. The best way to illustrate this concept is by walking you through the interest consequences of his redraw:

The Interest Consequences of a Redraw	
Equity redrawn for boat	$40,000
× Interest paid	7%
= Annual interest	$2,800

Logically, for Mr Boat to pay this $2,800 from after-tax money, he'd need to earn $2,800 plus tax. So, if we assumed that his average income tax rate was 25%, then Mr Boat would need to earn $3,733[2] before tax, to end up with $2,800 after tax.

---

[2] $2,800 ÷ (1 − average tax rate [i.e. 0.25])

The essential principle to learn is that interest on non-deductible borrowings will need to be repaid using after-tax dollars.

Loan Repayments After Tax

Not only will Mr Boat's interest need to be repaid using after-tax dollars, his loan will need to be too. Have a go at trying to work out how much Mr Boat would have to earn in before-tax dollars to repay his $40,000 equity redraw.

The After-Tax Earnings Required	
Equity redrawn for boat	$
÷ (1 − average tax rate)	
= Pre-tax earnings	$

Can you see how much harder Mr Boat would have to work in order to repay his debt? It's not dollar-for-dollar, in his case he'll need to earn $1.33 to end up with one after-tax dollar.

Falling for the trap of using equity to pay for lifestyle costs is very easy to do. However, doing so means you'll be purchasing a depreciating asset using borrowed money. This is the ultimate wealth-creation whammy!

Steve's Investing Tip

The ultimate wealth-creation whammy is using borrowed money to buy depreciating assets!

By the way, the answer to the question above is that Mr Boat would have to earn $53,333 to repay his $40,000 redraw.[3]

---

[3] $40,000 ÷ (1 − 0.25)

THE PERILS OF USING EQUITY TO FUND RETIREMENT

While Mr Boat's decision is unwise, he can at least cover the interest and loan repayments from his future salary. This option is not usually available for those who have retired from the workforce and thus are not earning an income.

The Marketing Pitch

A few years back I was invited to a special meeting with marketing staff at a high-profile company. They wanted me to endorse their company's housing product. Their pitch was to encourage investors to buy several investment properties, and then to use their equity gains to pay for their future retirement.

Whereas they saw opportunity, I saw danger because I believed the strategy would result in ever increasing non-deductible interest payments at a time of life when incomes were falling. Thinking ahead, it was likely that a debt spiral would be created since retirees would need to continue redrawing equity in order to pay their interest charges. This, in turn, would only lead to higher interest. That is, interest on the interest, on the interest!

Eventually, their only option would be to sell their properties in order to ease the interest burden. Tragically, although the loan may be covered by the sale, the sale would trigger a capital gain and should most or all of the equity have already been accessed, the retiree would then have the issue of finding the cash needed to pay the capital gains tax.

As I pointed this out to the marketing staff, all they could say to me was, 'That's not our problem.' With this attitude it was no surprise that, five years on, their company went bankrupt owing creditors many millions.

Do you know people who are planning to use equity to fund their retirements? If so then you can email them this chapter for free by visiting <www.PropertyInvesting.com/book3> and then selecting the 'Free Chapter' option.

THE MARGIN OF TERROR

To have negative equity is to be in a situation in which you owe more than your property is worth. For example, in the last chapter I included the case of the western Sydney property that was reportedly purchased for $450,000 in 2003, and was then sold under distressed circumstances for $260,000 in 2006. At the time of sale the loan outstanding was allegedly $405,000 which means there was negative equity of $145,000.

Do you think that the vendor gets to say, 'Sorry', to the lender and walk away from the $145,000 shortfall? I don't think so. The bank will sue him personally for the difference and seek to sell other personal or investment assets. If the debt cannot be fully recovered then it may even bankrupt the vendor.

A few years back I bought a property in unusual circumstances. It was an ex-motel site that had been converted into a block of 27 bedsitter units. The vendor tried to save a dollar by self-managing the property, but sadly suffered both health and family breakdowns before deciding to sell. I could see why when I saw the property because it was inhabited by druggies and squatters.

Nevertheless, I paid a fair price and expected to settle on time as per the contract. The day before settlement I received a phone call from the vendor saying that the only way that he could afford to settle was if I left some money in the deal. Even though the sales price was higher than his loan outstanding, the vendor had failed to pay the service fees on the property. In response the council had slapped a caveat on title preventing the property from being sold until the seller paid the $50,000 or so he owed in back-rates and penalties.

The crux of the problem was that the vendor didn't have the money and therefore couldn't provide clear title. Without clear title I wouldn't settle, and without settlement his property loan kept accumulating interest resulting in the vendor continuing to receive letters from his lender threatening impending foreclosure.

In the wash up ...

- ⊃ *The vendor agreed to:*
  Push out the settlement date by a few months as this helped me to move out the current tenants and to begin renovation works. Since there was no settlement, and therefore no loan, I didn't have to pay any interest during this period.

- ⊃ *While I agreed to:*
  Accept a shortfall on settlement so that the mortgage and caveat could be removed. I then carried back this shortfall as a personal loan to be repaid on an agreed basis.

I often call negative equity the 'margin for terror'. Those in this situation usually can't afford to keep owning, because they're sinking under the weight of the debt repayments, but at the same time they can't afford to sell because they owe more than the property is worth. With no obvious way to escape their troubles, negative equity holders try to hang in there in the hope that things will turn around. If times don't improve then they eventually suffer financial breakdowns that can also carry over into their personal lives.

Using the example of the $200,000 property we discussed earlier, I have extended the timeframe to Year 3 and Year 4 as shown in the table below.

A Four-Year Timeframe					
	Year 0	Year 1	Year 2	Year 3	Year 4
Cost	$200,000	$200,000	$200,000	$200,000	$200,000
+ Growth	$—	$25,000	$25,000	–$50,000	–$50,000
= CMV	$200,000	$225,000	$250,000	$200,000	$150,000
– Loan	$200,000	$175,000	$150,000	$200,000	$200,000
= Equity	$—	$50,000	$100,000	$—	–$50,000

I have assumed that the property was refinanced at the end of Year 2 so that 80% of the current market value (CMV) was borrowed (that is, 80% of $250,000). Unfortunately, in Year 3 and Year 4 there was a downturn in the property market and the value of the property fell. Here's a graph plotting the movement over the four years:

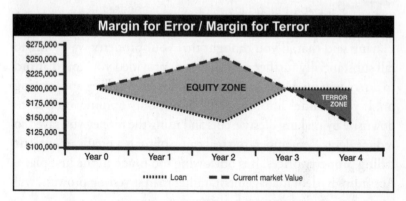

Margin for Error / Margin for Terror

You can now see that there are two shaded areas. The first one is the 'Margin of Error', which is another name for the equity safety zone. Clearly, the greater the margin of error, the more fat you have in the deal, which you can draw upon when you need to. The second area is where the darker shaded 'Margin of Terror' exists, when the loan is higher than the current market value of the asset.

Considering your entire property portfolio, which margin area would you say you're in at the moment — the margin for error or the margin for terror? It can be a valuable exercise to track your progress over time.

Escaping the Terror Zone

There's no quick escape from the Terror Zone. The best you can do is to avoid becoming a desperate seller who is forced to accept a fire-sale price. Instead, try to either ride out the storm or else exit the deal on your terms.

Falling home values are a problem, but such markets will correct themselves over time. Meanwhile, the more immediate issue is making sure that you can cover your loan repayments.

Steve's Investing Tip

Experienced investors cut losses fast!

Having said that, if you thought that your property was going to fall substantially further in value then, provided you could afford to do so, you might decide to cut your losses by selling and moving on. If you couldn't afford to sell then the only option would be to downsize by making lifestyle cuts and using the money you saved to reduce debt. Remember, the real cause of such a predicament isn't falling property prices, it is borrowing too much in the first place. Accordingly, debt management, rather than investing prowess, will be the key to escaping such a situation.

If you ever find yourself in such a predicament, it would be unwise to try to trade your way through the difficult times without changing your approach. Become more active and work hard to improve your investment and debt management. Don't go it alone. Swallow your pride and seek help from your financial adviser.

LAZY MONEY AND IDLE EQUITY

So far I've outlined the characteristics of equity, and the dangers of being caught in a situation where you owe more than your property is worth. There's another nasty side to equity that tends to affect more affluent investors who are benefiting from a bulging net worth. It's called lazy money.

Lazy money loafs around doing next to nothing. In its most common form, it's a spare $500 here and a $1,000 there, sitting in bank accounts earning little or no interest. Property investors often have lazy money too that exists in the form of idle equity. Like most things, the best way to explain the concept is using a financial illustration. Take a moment to look at the table opposite.

An Illustration of Lazy Money					
	Year 0	Year 1	Year 2	Year 3	Year 4
Annual rent	$10,400	$10,400	$10,400	$10,400	$10,400
Cost	$100,000	$100,000	$100,000	$100,000	$100,000
Growth	$—	$20,000	$20,000	$20,000	$20,000
CMV	$100,000	$120,000	$140,000	$160,000	$180,000
Gross rental return (on cost)		10.4%	10.4%	10.4%	10.4%
Gross rental return (on CMV[1])		10.4%	8.67%	7.43%	6.50%
% Growth (on cost)		20.0%	20.0%	20.0%	20.0%
% Growth (on CMV[1])		20.0%	16.7%	14.29%	12.50%

[1] Current market value at the beginning of the year.

Can you see in the table above how the percentage gross return falls as the current market value increases? If we used cost as the basis for our evaluation then the gross rental return stays at 10.4% ($10,400 ÷ $100,000). However, if we use current market value then the gross rental return in Year 2 falls to 8.67% ($10,400 ÷ $120,000). Why is this so? The answer is lazy money.

In effect, the increase in equity is earning no extra cashflow return, so the property's value is growing faster than its income. The result is a falling rental return percentage!

The same is also true for the growth percentage too. Using cost, it remains at 20% per annum. However, looking at Year 3, it falls from 16.67% to 14.29% because the same growth is being achieved ($20,000), but the property is increasing in value.

I have prepared two graphs, overleaf, that show how the Idle Equity zone is increasing. The table that follows reveals how much rent and growth would be needed in order to achieve a constant 10.4% gross rental return, and a 20% growth return each year.

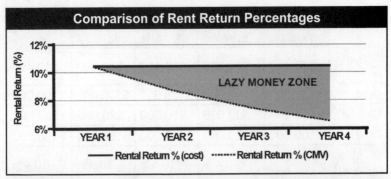

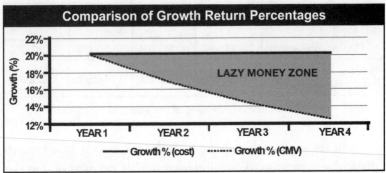

Rent and Growth					
	Year 0	Year 1	Year 2	Year 3	Year 4
Annual rent	$10,400	$10,400	$12,480	$14,976	$17,888
Cost	$100,000	$100,000	$100,000	$100,000	$100,000
Growth		$20,000	$24,000	$28,800	$34,560
CMV	$100,000	$120,000	$144,000	$172,000	$207,360
Gross rental return (on cost)		10.4%	12.48%	14.98%	17.89%
Gross rental return (on CMV[1])		10.4%	10.4%	10.4%	10.4%
% Growth (on cost)		20.00%	24.00%	28.80%	34.56%
% Growth (on CMV[1])		20.00%	20.00%	20.00%	20.00%

[1] Current market value at the beginning of the year.

Steve's Investing Tip

Smart investors base their decisions on current market value rather than cost.

Are you sitting on an equity goldmine? Perhaps you've owned a property that has gone up substantially in value without an equivalent increase in rent. If this is the case then I'd encourage you to calculate your rental return based on current market value rather than historical cost. You may find that the real return on your money is far less than what the banks are currently offering on term deposits.

Perhaps give it a go now by selecting a property you've owned for a while and that's appreciated in value. Crunch the numbers using the format suggested in the table below.

Crunch the Numbers Yourself	
Current weekly rent	
	× 52
= Annual rent	
÷ Current market value	$
= Gross rental return (on CMV)	
Annual rent	
÷ Purchase price	
= Gross rental return (on cost)	

EQUITY THAT'S TRIM, TAUT AND TERRIFIC

In chapter 11 I'll show you how I successfully used equity to acquire multiple properties in a sustainable manner. For the meantime, though, it's enough to say that tapping into equity will only build wealth if the return on your investment is higher than your additional interest cost. For example, if you used equity to borrow $100,000 at 7% interest, then you'd need to purchase an investment property that made more than $7,000 in growth and/or income earnings in order to be building wealth.

MR BOAT'S BEST BET

My final comment in this chapter is to reveal how Mr Boat could have had his pleasure craft without the personal debt consequences. Mr Boat could have simply bought an investment property that generated a net cash return high enough to cover the cost of leasing (rather than owning) the vessel. By doing this he'd be no worse off cashflow wise, because his lease payments would have been covered from the profit derived from his investment property. On the plus side:

➲ he would benefit from any capital appreciation his dwelling gained, and

➲ he wouldn't have the risk associated with the falling value of a depreciating asset. When the lease was over he'd hand back the boat and walk away.

DON'T MISUSE YOUR EQUITY

The wealthy pay for their trinkets using ongoing cash profits derived from their investments. The alternative is to use personal debt, which, for the average person, must be repaid from future wages (which effectively ties them to ongoing employment). In summary, to redraw equity to use for lifestyle expenses is the worst wealth-creation strategy ever and the secret to building massive wealth is to simply grow equity faster than debt.

What practical tips and insights have you gleaned from this chapter that you can apply in your personal and investment life?

In the next chapter I'll continue my safety lesson and show you how to avoid the biggest mistake anyone can make when buying an investment property.

EQUITY SOLUTION

(See pages 124 and 125.)

Your Imaginary Property's Equity Zone	
Property's current market value	$250,000
– Property debt	$150,000
= Total equity	$100,000

Appreciation and Debt Reduction Components	
Equity from appreciation	$50,000
+ Equity from debt reduction	$50,000
= Total equity	$100,000

Chapter 8 Insights

Insight #1:

Equity can be built by purchasing appreciating assets and/or repaying debt.

Insight #2:

The best property investment strategies have offensive and defensive components that work together to maximise the equity zone.

Insight #3:

Avoid borrowing money to purchase depreciating assets. That's a formula for wealth-creation woe!

Insight #4:

Borrowing against equity to fund retirement is a flawed and dangerous approach. A much better option is to acquire assets that generate income that can be used to pay for lifestyle costs.

Insight #5:

Negative equity often results in a distressed sale. You can avoid this through prudent asset management and sensible debt reduction.

Insight #6:

Watch out for lazy money and idle equity as these can drag down your investment returns.

Insight #7:

Smart investors use current market value rather than historical cost when evaluating their investment performances.

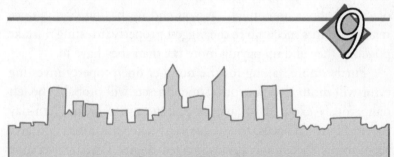

Avoiding the Biggest Mistake in Property

Your ability to become wealthy hinges on two key variables. Not only do you need to make enough money, you also need to retain as much of it as possible. After all, how much prosperity will be preserved if you make $1 million and then spend it all on a glitzy, glamorous lifestyle?

Steve's Investing Tip

How much money you *keep* is more important than how much money you *make*.

While you can limit your spending on avoidable non-essentials, if you want to stay out of jail then you'll need to calculate and pay the correct amount of income tax. You may be surprised to learn that, as a property investor, you have a considerable degree of choice about how much tax you end up paying. Sadly, since many investors succumb to the biggest property investing mistake possible, they end up paying more tax than they have to.

Furthermore, falling for the number one property investing error will mean that your investment assets will probably be left dangerously exposed to lawyers pretending to be modern-day Robin Hoods. That is, they'll sue you, take your assets and give them to their seemingly disadvantaged clients. I'm sure everyone would agree that we live in an increasingly litigious environment. No-one wants to be sued, but accidents can and do happen.

Consider the real life story of poor Mr Shanahan.[1] On the 28 August 1994, on a clear and sunny day, he decided to have a round of golf at the Magnetic Island Country Club. He was a relatively inexperienced golfer having only played a few previous rounds on the course. That day he was one in a group of four. On one particularly fateful hole, two of Mr Shanahan's group teed off without incident. It was Mr Shanahan's turn and he hit the ball further than he expected. It landed on a hard patch of ground (apparently some sort of rock), before bouncing and striking another golfer in the head. Sadly, the injured golfer ended up with permanent brain damage.

In his defence, Mr Shanahan said that he didn't see the golfer ahead of him as his vision was obstructed by nearby trees. Although not malicious, Mr Shanahan was found to be negligent in that he teed off when he ought to have waited, given that there were other players further up the fairway that were at risk of being hit by a stray golf ball. He was ordered to pay compensation in the amount of $2.6 million. This was on top of legal fees!

I'm told that he tried to claim on the golf club's public liability insurance policy, but that he was unsuccessful due to certain clauses in the fine print. Without any insurance to rely upon, Mr Shanahan was left to pay the full amount from his own pocket.

---

[1] *Ollier v. Magnetic Island Country Club Inc. and Shanahan (2003) QSC 263.*

As I said, accidents can and do occur. They happen to people like you and me every day, of every week, of every year. While we can insure ourselves against the obvious risks, we can also do a lot to protect our investment assets from unforeseen attacks. In writing this chapter, my aim is to introduce you to ideas about how you can protect your investment assets at the same time as minimising your income tax. If this is of interest then read on!

CHANGING YOUR MINDSET

Accountants often use the word 'structuring' to describe the way you own, control and secure your wealth. Just remember this as you read the rest of the chapter.

Would it surprise you to learn that I've never owned a single piece of real estate? It's true! No, I haven't made up the story of what I've achieved — I really did purchase over 260 properties in seven years — it's just that I'm structured in such a way as to enable me to control assets without actually owning them. It may seem like semantics, but there's a world of difference between what you own and what you control.

Steve's Investing Tip

The ultimate aim of all investors is to control lots, but own little.

For instance, what you *own* can be taken away, but if you can *control* and benefit from an asset without possessing it, then you'll achieve the outcome you desire (a share in the profits) without carrying the same risk (that someone could potentially snatch your asset away).

Not only do I avoid having investments in my name, I also limit the amount of personal assets I hold. For example, my wife owns the family home. I have deliberately done this for the following two reasons.

1. I Have a Higher than Average Risk of Being Sued

Given I'm a landlord with many tenants, and given that I'm trained and work in the accounting, finance and investment sector, I have a higher than normal chance of being sued. While I carry public liability and professional indemnity insurance, I take the view that you can never be too careful, so I also avoid holding private assets in my own name that could be up for grabs if I were sued.

2. I Am a Personal Guarantor on Many Loans

When purchasing real estate, I use a series of personal and investment trusts. Most lenders are happy with this arrangement, however, they request that I provide a personal guarantee. This means that I'll have to repay the loans should the trusts default on the debts. While I have no plans to default, I pay my accountant big bucks to limit my exposure should I be sued in unforeseen circumstances. For example, even if I lost all my wealth, because of the way I'm structured, with personal assets in my wife's name, our family home and private possessions would all be safe.

This talk of splitting personal and investment assets raises an important concept, that I call 'the fall guy'. No, I'm not talking about the popular 1980s TV show staring Lee Majors. I'm talking about identifying a person who can 'take the fall' by accepting the risk of being sued. The idea is to then heap as much risk as possible on the fall guy, thereby freeing up others to own personal assets in a way that limits the damage in the event of a law suit.

Who is the fall guy in your household?

THE BIGGEST MISTAKE REVEALED

Since the name of the wealth-creation game is to control rather than to own assets, one of the biggest mistakes you can make in real estate is to buy an investment property in your own name.

Steve's Investing Tip

Avoid buying property in your own name.

Individuals and Asset Protection

While buying in the name of an individual is cheap and it's easy to understand, purchasing an investment property in your own name immediately mixes your personal and investment assets. As such, if you're sued by (say) a tenant, then all your personal assets will be up for grabs, and if you're sued personally then all your investment assets will be at risk too. The end result is that you could work very hard over a number of years to build up substantial net worth, only to suffer an unfortunate Mr-Shanahan-type experience and potentially lose the lot.

Individuals and Income Tax

Although the federal government has increased the thresholds, individuals remain the highest taxed of any entity, with a top marginal income tax rate of 46.5% (including the Medicare levy). Even if you don't earn a huge salary, should you sell one or more profitable property investments then your taxable income may spike for that particular year and push you into the 46.5% tax bracket. In fact, the biggest reason why people buy property in their own name is to access the losses arising from negative gearing property (where expenses are greater than income), since these losses can be used to offset their salary income, thereby lowering the overall amount of income tax paid.

However, what seems to make sense in the short term may end up biting them later on if they sell and become potentially pushed into the top marginal tax rate for individuals!

Individuals and Leverage

When you buy property in your own name, the mortgage will also be registered in your name too. As explained earlier, the two critical variables that determine how much a lender will allow you to borrow are:

1. your income, and

2. your personal net asset position.

Once you've reached your borrowing limit then it doesn't matter how many other lenders you approach, they'll all consider you to be maxed out because they all apply the same lending rules. For example, let's say that you reach your limit with the Commonwealth Bank and you then decide to try your luck with Westpac. You tell the staff your income and they calculate how much they'd be willing to lend you. The next step in the process will be for them to look at how much debt you're already carrying, and it won't take them long to conclude that you're already at your limit. 'Sorry', they'll say, 'no loan for you!'

Is there anything else you can do to overcome being maxed out? Yes, but the pill may be bitter to swallow as you'll either have to:

➲ earn more income

➲ find a more flexible lender, or

➲ sell some property to reduce debt.

The truth of the matter is that, had you been correctly structured to begin with, you could have avoided the problem altogether. For example, the way I'm structured has allowed me to borrow against my income and asset statement many times rather than just once. While a detailed explanation is beyond the scope of this book, the secret is to carry the investment debt as a guarantor rather than in your own name. That way, when you max out with one lender you head up the road to the next and start the process all over again. If you're interested in finding out more about this concept then you'll find *Wealth Guardian* to be a great resource. You can find out more by visiting <www.PropertyInvesting.com/wealthguardian>.

In summary, buying investment property in your own name:

1. provides very low asset protection since there's no distinction between your personal and investment assets

2. means you may pay up to 46.5% income tax on your property profits, and

3. will place a glass ceiling on how much money you can borrow because the debt is in your own name, and once you max out, the only way to borrow more is to earn more income or reduce debt.

GETTING STARTED

As you can tell, I'm not much of a fan of purchasing real estate as an individual. I do make an exception though if you're just testing the investing waters before jumping in. For example, you're unlikely to get into too much hot water by purchasing one investment property in your own name. Ideally though, if you have grand plans for building a sizeable real estate empire, then invest a few thousand dollars to visit your financial advisers and have them set up a structure that's appropriate to your investing needs.

A Warning on Partnerships

As my friend Martin Ayles says, 'The only ship certain to sink is a partnership!' Legally, a partnership is a very, very dangerous arrangement because each partner is joint and severally liable for all the partnership debts. Yes, I know that's a mouthful, but the consequences can be diabolical, because it means that a partner with a 1% share is still liable for 100% of the partnership's debts.

I know too many real-life stories about partnership deals going sour to make a joke about this important issue. Unless you have a compelling reason to set up a partnership, I would work hard to find another structuring option. If you and a friend are combining forces to start up an investing empire, it would be wise to sit down with an adviser to discuss the merits of a unit trust as opposed to a partnership. It usually results in the same outcome with much less risk.

Borrowing Against Your Home

In chapter 8 I wrote about the dangers of using home equity to fund lifestyle costs. You may be wondering, 'Is there the same risk when you use home equity to purchase investment properties?' This is a relevant question for many people given that Australians typically have a lot of money tied up in their homes. That is, a well-trodden path to achieving the great Australian dream is to buy a home as soon as possible, work hard to pay it off, and then to later tap into the equity to purchase investments.

Steve's Investing Tip

Your home is a lifestyle asset rather than a financial investment.

I always grimace when asked the question, 'Should I borrow against my home to buy investment property?' because I honestly don't know any better answer than, 'it depends'.

My typical response is to try to point out the difference between a lifestyle asset (which is something you buy to enjoy) and an investment asset (which is something you buy with a view to making a profit). Can you plan to combine both? Not really because the mindset and motive underpinning each class of asset is substantially different.

My home is a good example of a lifestyle asset. My wife bought it a few years back for around $390,000, and then proceeded to spend another $100,000 or so on renovating it. In the meantime the real estate market has taken a dive and if we tried to sell it now we'd be lucky to break even. As a property investment it's a shocker.

I'm not losing any sleep, though, because this is our home, and I'm not too concerned about the financial implications. Yes, it would be nice if it skyrocketed in value, but that would be incidental to my enjoyment of the property as a home. Furthermore, we paid for the dwelling out of investment profits and there is no personal debt owing on it.

My house is a perfect example of the fact that some dwellings make better homes than investments!

Steve's Investing Tip

Use after-tax investment profits to buy lifestyle assets.

As a guideline, it's more sensible to use after-tax investment profits to buy lifestyle assets (such as homes) than it is to use borrowed money. This raises a problem though. Many people don't like to wait until they can afford to pay for lifestyle assets — once they know what they want, they want it immediately.

The following thoughts may seem quite drastic, but here are my suggestions for those weighing up the buy versus rent versus equity redraw debate:

Start By Renting, Not Owning

I started by renting rather than owning a home as it allowed me to buy investment property with the money that would otherwise have been used up as a home deposit.

Furthermore, I didn't have the same obligation to hold down a job to cover the mortgage payments (which would have been about twice the cost of the rent). This provided a less stressed and more flexible situation because I could take the time during the day to look for investment properties rather than working in a job and then coming home to squeeze in my investing when I was mentally fatigued.

I'm not saying that you have to rent forever. A model that I've seen used effectively is to use after-tax investment profits to pay for your home deposit, and then fund the ongoing mortgage payments out of the positive cashflow your property portfolio generates.

If You Own Your Home, Seriously Consider Selling It

I can almost hear you saying, 'Surely you're not serious Steve? Sell my house? I don't think so!' While it may seem risky, I think selling your home and investing the proceeds can be a very smart option because:

- ⊃ it gives you a pool of working capital to use for investing

- ⊃ you'll eliminate the personal debt of your home mortgage

- ⊃ the burden of having to work to pay your mortgage will disappear — yes, you'll still have to pay the rent, but you won't have to pay the rates, repairs and so on

- ⊃ provided you invest in more property, you'll still be in the real estate market so you'll continue to benefit from any growth.

While it may make financial sense, the biggest drawbacks when selling your home will be the emotional hurdles you have to come to grips with. Things like fond memories or the idea of selling a house that you've just finished getting exactly as you wanted and returning to the hassles of renting again.

Of course, like any investing proposition, there is a potential financial downside too. For example, there is a risk that you'll sell the home, invest and then lose money. In the end there is always pain and risk, it's just a question of whether there's more to gain than to lose. Remember, you're only planning to rent temporarily — perhaps for a few years. The eventual plan would be to pay for another even better home out of investing profits rather than personal debt.

Refinance Some of Your Home Equity

I sometimes ride my hybrid push bike to work. A hybrid bicycle is a cross between a mountain bike and a racer. While there are some benefits, you rarely see serious cyclists on this type of bicycle because what you lose with such a compromise is the best of either extreme. That is, I couldn't use my bike on serious mountain trails, and I wouldn't be competitive in a road race either.

The same compromised principle exists for those who use large slabs of home equity for investment purposes. That is, they aren't able to use the full value of their equity since mainstream lenders will only allow borrowings of up to 80% of the value of the property. They will also be placing their homes at potential risk should their investments fail.

If you do decide to keep your home and use your equity to invest with then I suggest you:

- ➲ Limit your borrowings to less than 60% of the value of your home. This gives you a safety buffer should values drop. Even if you are forced to sell, you'll still have a pool of money from which to start again.

- ➲ Have an action plan for repaying the home equity redraw as soon as possible.

- ➲ Consult with an insurance broker to consider the merits of income protection, both personally and over your property portfolio too. I would also get advice on life insurance. For example, in my case, I thought it wise to take out life insurance so that all my investment debt would be repaid in the event of an untimely death.

In summary, what I'm advocating is that if you decide to use your home equity then make sure you mitigate the risks of potentially losing your principal place of residence. Hopefully you can see that there isn't a black or white answer to the question of whether or not you should use home equity. In the end it's a matter for all investors to weigh up according to their risk tolerance and emotional situations.

A QUICK INSIGHT INTO MY STRUCTURE

I'm often asked about the way I structure my affairs. I believe the following points provide a good summary of this entire chapter, so I'm happy to share them but please understand that what's right for me may not be right for you as our financial and life situations will be different. Make sure you seek tailored financial advice!

As you read these points see if you can tell how I've applied the theory as outlined in this chapter.

I Separate My Personal and Investment Assets

There is no reason why I need to hold personal assets in my own name, so I actively avoid doing so. My wife and I have a happy arrangement — I own the investment assets and she owns the lifestyle assets. We work hard to keep the two separate and independent so that if there is a crisis with one then the other can carry on regardless.

I Have Insurance

By its very nature insurance is something you take out when you feel there is a risk of potential loss worth mitigating. For example, I have life insurance because people die unexpectedly. I have fire insurance because I see on the news from time to time that houses burn down. I have home and contents insurance because I've been burgled before. I don't want any of these things to happen to me, but if they do, then I know that I am protected.

I Control Multiple Entities

If you hold all your investments in the one entity then you run the risk that every asset could be potentially up for grabs should there be a lawsuit. For example, if you own 100 properties in the one structure, and the tenant in property number 62 falls down the steps and injures herself, then any uninsured compensation will potentially have to be met from selling one or more of the 100 properties.

The safer option is to progressively set up more structures as your empire expands. There is no hard and fast rule about when to set up a new structure except to say that it's worthwhile when the benefit outweighs the cost.

As an illustration, if you had five independent structures that each contained 20 properties, then the most you could lose to the suing tenant mentioned above is that parcel of 20 properties in the affected structure.

I'm the Fall Guy for My Empire

I'm the company director and the guy who signs all the loan documents. If something goes wrong then I'm the one who suffers the financial consequences. Since I've taken on this role, my wife avoids any involvement with our investments so we run no risk of mixing our personal and investing assets.

I Legally Lower My Income Tax Through Income Splitting

My wife enjoys being a full-time mum, and because it is a full-on time commitment, she earns very little income. However, because I use a trust structure, I'm able to distribute investment income to her so as to take advantage of her low marginal tax threshold. Even my children receive small, tax-effective trust distributions each year. Furthermore, sensible structuring for asset protection purposes has the by-product of legally capping the maximum amount of income tax I pay on my investments at 30%. If this revelation is news to you then see your accountant or get a copy of *Wealth Guardian*. See <PropertyInvesting.com/WealthGuardian>.

I Increase My Borrowing Ability by Leveraging My Income

My trust structure is the entity that buys the property. However, because my trust has just been set up, it won't have any income in its own right. Accordingly, financiers will be reluctant to lend any money unless I sign on as a guarantor and lend my debt repayment ability to the deal. When done correctly, I can use my income-earning ability as a guarantor to secure multiple loans, thereby allowing me to control far more property than if I were borrowing in my own name.

I Pay My Accountant a Lot of Money

Good accountants aren't cheap, but they're inexpensive when compared with the cost of ignorance. Don't think of accountants as avoidable expenses — treat them as you would a physician who sees you for regular checkups to ensure you don't get sick in the first place. If you're not meeting with your accountant at least quarterly then there's something wrong.

HOW MUCH RISK DO YOU FACE?

I've been trying hard to keep the accounting jargon out of this chapter, which is difficult because I have skirted around some very complicated issues without being able to go into a lot of depth. My desire was to give you a helicopter view of some very important matters and to give you some items to discuss with your accountant when you hook up next quarter.

As we wrap up our discussion, have a go at completing the financial questionnaire below to gain an understanding of your current investment risk. This is pretty simple to complete. All you need to do is circle YES or NO in answer to each question.

How Much Risk Do You Face?		
Question	Answer	
Do you own your home and investment assets within the one entity?	Yes	No
Are you and your spouse both 'fall guys' in that both your names are on the property title(s) and the loan document(s)?	Yes	No
Do you know of a serious risk to your investments that you haven't insured against?	Yes	No
Have you thought about making a will but as yet have not got around to getting it done?	Yes	No
Has it been more than three months since you saw your accountant?	Yes	No
Are you either at, or near, your lending limit?	Yes	No
Are you involved in a partnership?	Yes	No
Do you own investment property in your own name?	Yes	No
Have you earned a lot of money in the past few years but have very little to show for it?	Yes	No
Have you borrowed more than 50% of the value of your home and used those funds for investment purposes?	Yes	No

Count up the number of times you circled YES and then check your score in the table that follows.

Scoring	
8 or more	Heck! If you haven't yet imploded then disaster is probably just around the corner! Seek urgent help from an experienced adviser before you lose the lot.

Scoring *(cont'd)*	
5 to 7	It looks like you have quite a few loose ends that need tidying up. I wouldn't invest in any property until you've seen an adviser and sorted out the bigger risk areas.
3 to 4	You have some weak areas that need to be tightened up. Be proactive in taking care of these issues rather than allowing them to drag out.
Less than 3	Well done. You seem to have most of the bases covered. Just make sure you keep on top of changes as they occur.

Chapter 9 Insights

Insight #1:

The amount of money you keep is more important than how much money you earn.

Insight #2:

An effective structure is one that allows you to control and profit from assets without owning them.

Insight #3:

Insurance is a key component to minimising risk. If you can't afford insurance then don't invest to begin with.

Insight #4:

Buying property in your own name is the biggest real estate mistake you can make. Not only is there poor asset protection, but you are subject to the highest income tax rates and you also place a glass ceiling over your future borrowing ability.

Insight #5:

I hold my assets in multiple trust structures to gain maximum asset protection. This also allows me to legally lower my income tax to the lowest level possible for my situation.

Insight #6:

Be very careful when using home equity to buy investment property.

Insight #7:

If you assessed yourself as being in a risky situation then take steps to correct your problems.

10

How to Survive and Thrive in a Property Downturn

Have you heard the Walter Swan story? Walter is an American who came up with a clever marketing campaign for a book he wrote called *Me 'n' Henry*. I haven't read it but I believe it's an innocent story about Walter's life growing up with his brother (Henry) in Arizona. Try as he might, Walter couldn't find anyone who was even remotely interested in publishing this book. Unperturbed, he decided to self-publish and then sell the book through his own tiny shopfront, which he rented in Bisbee — a small town in Arizona just down the road from the more famous Tombstone (yes, that's Wyatt Earp country).

Now, Walter didn't come from a Harvard business background, he was an ex-plasterer who retired as a result of ill health and pursued writing as a way of filling his time in retirement. What's particularly interesting about this story is that Walter called his shop 'The One Book Bookstore' because, as you can probably guess, it only sold his book! Even more strange was that it was right next door to a mainstream bookstore that sold thousands of titles! I'm told that Walter would often sit in the store window, dressed in his overalls and a cowboy hat, and wave to tourists as they walked past, inviting them to come inside for a chat. Anyway, Walter became famous once the TV channels heard his story and ran bulletins about his novel idea (excuse the pun). Soon he was a regular on TV talk shows and the rest, as they say, is history.

With his new-found success Walter was inspired to write a second book called *Me 'n' Momma*. I'm sure you can guess what it's about. If you want a copy then it's only for sale at 'The Other Book Bookstore'.

Now you're probably wondering what this has to do with property investing, right? Well, this chapter contains my ideas on how to thrive and survive in a property downturn. The first point I'd like to make is the importance of having and exploiting a niche, just like Walter did with his book.

1. HAVE A SALES AND MARKETING NICHE

I doubt any of Walter Swan's books have won literary awards, but that doesn't mean they're not bestsellers. His success hasn't been due to his writing ability, or the thrilling subject matter of his books, it's been based on his ability to market and sell in a competitive environment. This should be an encouragement to all aspiring investors because it shows that you don't need to have the best product in the marketplace to be a success. You just need a sales and marketing edge that places you at the forefront of your target audience's minds.

For example, if you're into renovations then you don't need to win any Housing Industry Association awards for your work to make a lot of money. However, you do need a way of completing your renovations so that you're price competitive and market attractive. Price competitive means avoiding overcapitalising, and this can be done by making sure you have the right housing product that's pitched at the right price to the right end buyer. Market attractive means that you sell your property in a way that makes it appealing to potential buyers.

Nigel is a R.E.S.U.L.T.S. mentoring participant who decided to use the renovation strategy to make money. He did well to complete his project on time and within budget. He felt it was the right product at the right price, so he was a little confused when it didn't sell as quickly as he thought it would. My advice to Nigel was to spend a Saturday morning looking at all the other renovated houses in his area that were also for sale at around the same price, and to ask himself, 'What makes my dwelling stand head and shoulders above the rest?'

I told Nigel that throwing extra commission incentives at real estate agents to sell it faster was far less effective than spending a few extra thousand to make the house a little more appealing for his target audience (who, after all, were the people he thought would buy it).

Featured in my second book, *$1,000,000 in Property in One Year*, Brett and Tiffany from New South Wales followed this same advice and it led to them incorporating a home theatre system into their renovations. The basis for this move was that the $5,000 in extra cost would be partially recovered in the sales price, and partially recovered by interest saved by a quick sale.

This theory doesn't just apply to renovations. It has equal relevance to the problem of finding tenants. For example, it doesn't take much skill to sign up a tenant at 50% below appraised market rent. It's a different proposition though to get someone to happily pay $20 a week above appraised market rent.

You can achieve this with some pretty basic marketing by agreeing on the rent and then offering various upsell options. For instance, you could say, 'With summer coming the house can become a little hot. I tell you what, how much extra rent would you be willing to pay if I installed ceiling fans in the main bedroom?'

If the answer is 'Zero', then wait until the middle of summer and make the offer again. If ceiling fans don't win your tenant over then there are thousands of other options — a new heater, a new stove, a new clothesline or new curtains. All you need to do is find the right solution for the tenant's needs.

I'll expand more on the equity building power of this technique in chapter 12. Again, you don't need to be the best at what you do to make money in a downturn, you just need to be the best at *selling* it! I doubt McDonald's make the healthiest hamburgers in the world, but the company sure sells a lot of them! What could you do to improve the price competitiveness and market attraction of your investing?

2. NEVER STOP LEARNING

Education provides knowledge and, as renaissance author Sir Francis Bacon famously said, 'Knowledge is power'. With this in mind, I take the view that education is a life-long pursuit rather than a once-off experience. To me, enhanced knowledge adds a depth to thinking and understanding, which is extremely valuable in investing as it helps you to identify and profit from opportunities.

Steve's Investing Tip

Rarely is a great property deal purchased. Instead it needs to be assembled by bringing together various components.

I quite like the saying 'Change is the only constant'. Surely it makes sense that, as the property market changes, so too will our thinking need to change as we need to re-educate ourselves to ensure our strategies remain relevant and profitable. Perhaps look at it this way — how many people do you see wearing shorts in the middle of winter? There is a good reason why they don't, and similarly, we need to vary our investing approaches for the different investing seasons.

There's no shortage of people who sell information designed to improve your investing ability — just spend 10 minutes on the internet and you'll uncover a few dozen or so experts who claim to have the secrets to lifetime wealth. Perhaps they do and perhaps they don't — it's up to you to sort the wheat from the chaff and to find out. What I would say, though, is make sure you don't just buy investing theory — enquire as to whether the writer or presenter is actually practising what is preached. Before taking action it would be sensible to bounce the main ideas off your financial adviser too to ensure that what you're considering is legal and safe.

While you could spend big bucks going to an investment seminar, the first place I'd go for help is the forum boards at <www. PropertyInvesting.com>. Over the past few years I've spent countless hours and several hundred thousand dollars making this Australia's biggest and best online forum for serious property investors. There are over 160,000 posts that cover every possible real estate investing topic — from the basics right up to more advanced concepts. Best of all, it's free and available 24 hours a day.

Those on a shoestring budget may like to attend the multitude of free investment seminars you see advertised in newspapers. Just be mindful that you'll probably be asked to buy something since someone has to pay for the room hire and coffee. Should you have a little more money behind you then it might be wise to consider attending a more expensive structured investment seminar. The better ones charge an upfront fee and provide education rather than a big sales spiel.

The rules I apply before buying information are as follows.

Is There a Genuine 100% Money-Back Guarantee?

If you're paying more than $100 for something then I'd be immediately sceptical about any presenter or product that did not back up any claims with an unconditional, money-back guarantee. Watch out for fine print clauses such as having limited time periods to exercise your decision, having to pay for resources provided, or being stung with hefty 'processing' fees. I like to pay by credit card because I can then make a claim against the provider if I make a refund request that's not honoured.

Research

As an ex-auditor, I have been trained to always seek evidence to support every fact I'm told. Before I part with one dollar I want to make sure that the person providing information to me is really an expert and has successfully done what will be advocated.

Length of Successful Track Record

The wealth-creation industry is littered with fly-by-nighters who start up companies and then collapse them in mysterious circumstances. The anonymous environment of the internet allows people to operate sham enterprises that appear credible but are actually run from someone's garage.

Make sure that any promoters or people you deal with have genuine businesses, which means that they have staff, phone lines and offices. Clearly, you also want to make sure that the person giving the information has some sort of qualification and/or relevant practical experience.

What After-Care Service is Provided?

Paying a fortune to attend a seminar is one thing, but who will be there to help afterwards if you encounter a problem when you try to apply the information in the real world? The better information providers also offer after-care services so you can ask questions about how to apply the new ideas you've paid to acquire.

Genuine Success Stories from Ordinary People

A good way to test the integrity of the information is whether or not ordinary people can apply the teachings. Make sure that the person behind the promoter's testimonial is not a friend, relative or someone paid to give a favourable comment.

Search the ASIC Database

The Australian Securities & Investments Commission (ASIC) maintains a database of dodgy investment experts and exposed scams. You'd be wise to spend five minutes searching it to see if the expert you're considering paying has been blacklisted. Be sure to keep your wits about you — there are plenty of sharks about in the wealth-creation industry.

Paying for education is an established principle — I spent four years of my life and thousands of dollars to gain an accounting degree. I've spent even more time and money finetuning my investing ability. Markets change so make sure you keep up to date with the latest teaching and techniques.

What percentage of the value of your investment portfolio do you spend on education each year? Is this reflected in the results you are achieving?

3. MANAGE PROACTIVELY

Just yesterday Katrina, another of the R.E.S.U.L.T.S. mentoring participants, mentioned to me how the tenant in one of her investment properties did a mysterious runner. That is, he packed up and left without telling anyone. Katrina didn't have cause to be suspicious because his rent was paid up to date, however a tell tale sign that something was not right was when she received a call from the local police to say the place had been burgled and trashed.

Some people would fly into a rage and blame the tenant, the vandals, the rental manager — anyone but themselves. Katrina is more sophisticated than that, though. While unhappy about what happened, Katrina quietly went about the business of taking charge of the situation and controlling proceedings to get the outcome she desired. She liaised with the insurance company, rang and co-ordinated various tradespeople to fix the damage, and filed a report with the police.

Katrina's story provides a good example of how unexpected events happen, and how good management can quickly rectify problems, thereby returning the asset to income-earning status. Proactive management is essential during down times because market conditions can quickly change. It follows that your ability to make a quality investing decision will depend on the quality of the information at your disposal. Therefore, if you don't have your finger on the pulse then you run the risk of making a poor investment decision.

Do you have an ongoing investing problem that you've been wrestling with for some time? What's needed to fix the issue once and for all? Don't make the mistake of trying to do all the day-to-day property management yourself. Smart investors value time more than money because they know that thinking can lead to unlocking profits.

Steve's Investing Tip

Your job is to manage the manager.

Your job is to set up some kind of system so that you can manage the property managers rather than become bogged down doing the necessary, but time-consuming, administration tasks.

4. FINETUNE YOUR STRUCTURE

The previous chapter contained plenty of ideas about how to structure your affairs so that you could gain asset protection while also legally minimising income tax. As the property market softens, though, I would work hard to take care of the following issues.

➲ *Untangle Your Home from Investment Borrowings*
If you have used your home as security over investment borrowings, then perhaps try to restructure your affairs so that your house is left out of the collateral mix. This may involve selling or refinancing. The time to do this is well before a crisis eventuates.

➲ *Avoid Cross-Collateralising Assets and Personal Guarantees*
Cross-collateralising occurs when a lender secures one property loan against other properties in a portfolio. For example, let's say that you borrow 80% of Property 1 resulting in a first mortgage being registered against title as security. Six months later you decide to use the same lender to purchase Property 2. Again you borrow 80% and again the lender takes a first mortgage, but this time the loan documentation also mentions that the borrowings are secured (that is, cross-collateralised) against Property 1 as well. Lenders like to do this because it reduces their risk. I'm vehemently against the idea though because I think it's total overkill. In a worst-case scenario all you need is one asset to go bad in a cross-collateralised portfolio for a domino effect to occur which puts every asset at risk.

➲ *Tidy Up Your Structure While You Can*
You may have survived without any problems during the boom times, but the quality of your structure will be tested when difficulties arise, such as when losses rather than profits eventuate. The time to see your accountant is as you feel the market changing. It will be too late to take action after disaster has occurred.

Which of these three areas do you need to finetune?

5. TAKE CASH PROFITS

A common mistake made by real estate investors is that they think owning property is like creating a time capsule — once acquired the titles are buried in a dark place for long periods of time. I take a different view. I tell my real estate agents that every property I own is for sale should a buyer come along at the right price. When the agents enquire as to what that 'right price' may be, I politely tell them that I'll consider any reasonable offer. I do this for two reasons:

1. it's very hard to sell a property that's not for sale, and

2. the best way to keep track of the market is to listen to what it's trying to tell you.

I know that selling property is often thought of as taboo. However, I approach the issue by using the principles I've gleaned from auditing successful businesses rather than from urban investing myths. For instance, in all my years as an accountant I didn't come across a single profitable business that only bought and never sold. In fact, those that couldn't sell their stock ended up broke. For the life of me I can't see why real estate is any different! While it's always wise to recycle profits, it's even more important to do so in a down market. Choosing to sell will:

➲ decrease your debt as you repay the mortgage. Provided your income-earning circumstances are the same then you can always borrow the money back again at a later date.

➲ convert your unrealised capital gains into cash, thereby locking in your profits.

➲ increase your borrowing ability because the profit will flow through to your income-tax return (ITR). Of course, it's your ITR that lenders will use to determine how much you can theoretically afford to borrow.

If you're maxed out and unable to borrow more money then you're probably like a business with a warehouse that's full of stock and bursting at the seams. It'll take much longer to build a bigger warehouse, so the best option to make room is to sell some stock!

Are your cash reserves running a bit thin? If you are still holding on to a property that underperformed during the boom, how much worse may it fare in a downturn?

6. BE VIGILANT COMPLETING YOUR DUE DILIGENCE

Investors buy on fact whereas speculators buy on opinion. The difference can be summed up by comparing what you know with what you think you know. Due diligence is a word accountants use to describe the fact-finding mission associated with discovering information that's not obvious at first glance.

While not recommended, investors can get away with doing minimal due diligence in prosperous financial times because mistakes are masked by booming prices. The same can't be said for softer economic periods where values are flat and expensive oversights lead to significant losses.

BuyerBeware (see <PropertyInvesting.com/BuyerBeware>) is a resource I've written that contains checklists and templates that I use when I do my due diligence. It's a resource in which I talk about the importance of completing the following actions.

Accurately Crunching the Numbers on Potential Deals

This helps to identify the key variables that you can then research to test the validity of the potential profit.

For example, the common variables in a buy and hold property are:

- ➲ *Rent:* I would want to make sure that the rent being quoted was backed up by a signed and current lease, and that the tenant was also paying the right amount on time.

⊃ *Finance:* A small change to interest rates can have a dramatic impact on cashflow. In testing the numbers I consider what the consequences would be if interest rates rose up to 3% higher.

⊃ *Ownership costs:* It doesn't take much to find out the likely ownership costs rather than guessing at the numbers. The more accurate the information you have, the better the quality of the investment decision you'll make.

Evaluating a Property's Structural Integrity

This will help you to identify areas that may be costly to fix. In property, it's the problems you can't see that end up costing you the most money. If you can't afford a building inspection then don't invest to begin with.

Making Sure Tenancy Agreements Are Documented

Make sure that any existing tenancy you inherit comes with all the appropriate documentation including a current lease, bond receipt, condition report and full rental history. I suggest you make this a condition of your purchase and pass the responsibility back onto the vendor to supply this information.

Sloppy due diligence is a sure sign of a weak investment mindset. I'll never understand why property investors try to save a few dollars by cutting due diligence corners, only to have to pay thousands later as a result of their laziness.

Hopefully you wouldn't buy a $250,000 used car without a mechanical inspection or without taking it for a test drive. It would be just as ridiculous to buy an investment property without some investigative research.

7. NEGOTIATE A FAIR PRICE

It's difficult to negotiate favourable terms when prices are booming; however, vendors are a lot more accommodating when properties are taking a lot longer to sell. While it's bad form to take blatant advantage of a distressed seller, I'm always keen to negotiate a win–win outcome by varying the price or the settlement terms to make the deal more attractive.

A buyer in a down market has a lot more bargaining power, and I suggest you use it to your advantage (without seeming opportunistic). There are many possible options including:

⊃ Offering a reduced price. This can work but many vendors will have a minimum amount they need to clear in order to repay their mortgages.

⊃ Asking the vendor to fix up the issues identified on the building report. Pay particular attention to areas where any money you spend won't add extra value to the property. For example, your property is unlikely to be worth much more as a result of repairing fences, fixing roof leaks, replacing spouting, changing faulty hot water services or fixing broken windows. Yet these repairs often need to be done. A good example that comes to mind is a property we bought where we included as a purchase condition that:

- every broken window be repaired

- all the absconding tenant's junk be removed, and

- all the bric-a-brac, and the considerable refuse around the outside of the house be taken to the tip.

This saved us several thousand dollars but was of little cost to the vendor since she rang her friends and organised a working bee to get the job done.

⊃ Extend the settlement period if it's in your interests to do so. This may be appropriate if you're considering subdividing the property since it can take several months to get council planning approval. If you're thinking about subdividing then make sure the purchase contract includes words to the effect that the vendor will sign forms and allow access to the property so that everything that needs to be done can be promptly completed.

➲ Consider asking for early access to the property (before settlement) to start doing minor renovation works so that you can get the project underway as soon as possible. Of course, you won't pay any loan interest until you settle.

As you can see, there's a lot you can negotiate aside from a cheaper price. When times are tough, every dollar you save is a dollar added to your bottom line.

8. CHANGE YOUR INVESTING STRATEGY

Earlier in this chapter (Point 2) I mentioned that your chosen investing strategy needs to be tailored to the current conditions of the property market. Expanding on that theme, here are some ideas for a flat or downtrending market.

Invest with an Income, Not Growth, Focus

If you take the view that property prices are going to trend sideways or down, then alternative investment options will probably provide higher growth returns. If you're going to invest in property, do so with an income focus rather than a bias for long-term growth.

Look to Make Fast Profits with Quick Cash Deals

Renovating and developing can still unlock good profits provided you add more in perceived value than actual cost. Just be sure to remember the importance of price competitiveness and market attractiveness.

One change I'd be inclined to make in softer economic times would be to sell and to cash in some profits, reducing debt, and to then borrow against my equity to fund the expansion of my property portfolio. Both of these topics are discussed in a lot more detail in Part III.

How have you changed your approach to better reflect the current state of the property market?

9. THERE'S NO 'I' IN TEAM ... BUT THERE IS A 'ME'!

Scientists have studied the power of migrating birds that fly in a 'V' formation. Apparently researchers have discovered that a flock of 25 birds can fly up to 70% further than a single bird using the same amount of energy. Property investors can certainly apply the benefits of working as a team rather than flying solo. There's more to it than simply pooling knowledge and benefiting from strength in numbers. Even elite sportspeople need coaches and support teams around them to help maintain peak performance. Sometimes you'll be too close to your problems to see the obvious solutions, which is why in tough times it's more important than ever to seek counsel with fellow investors and trained experts.

Property investing is not a unique science. You can learn a lot from studying the success of others in seemingly unrelated fields and then applying the same principles in an investing context. Just as the squeaky wheel tends to get oiled, most people will only offer help if you ask for it.

WE MAKE OUR OWN CIRCUMSTANCES

Hopefully the ideas expressed in this chapter will help you to realise that investors should be able to make money in any market. When property prices are slumping, strategies that worked in times of booming prices will need to be changed. By committing to learn different investing skills and to being proactive, investors can stay on top of these changes. Particular care needs to be taken with managing debt levels and protective structures when the market softens and belts tighten.

Nevertheless, skilled investors can make the most of any market conditions and a market downturn should be an opportunity to thrive and flourish, not just to survive.

Chapter 10 Insights

Insight #1:

In a down market it will be more important than ever to work on improving your sales and marketing. You don't need to have the best product, just a compelling offer that reaches your target market.

Insight #2:

The day you stop learning is the day you die. If you aren't willing to invest in your own education then perhaps you shouldn't invest at all.

Insight #3:

Passive investors who let life happen around them tend to experience higher losses in a down market. Be proactive in managing your property managers by setting performance targets and clarifying your expectations.

Insight #4:

Have your accountant review your structure before disaster strikes.

Insight #5:

Selling property recycles debt, locks in profits and improves borrowing ability.

Insight #6:

You ought not to complain about unexpected costs, expensive repairs or large profits unless you do a thorough due diligence.

Chapter 10 Insights (cont'd...)

Insight #7:

Buyers in a down market are better able to negotiate more favourable terms. Remember that every dollar saved is an extra dollar of profit.

Insight #8:

Make sure you tailor your investing strategy to the prevailing market conditions.

Insight #9:

Sometimes you are too close to the problem to see the solution. Seek regular support from fellow investors and expert counsel from paid advisers.

PART II SUMMARY

A lot of ground has been covered in Part II and much of it dealt with the importance of protecting yourself. With the market softening many investors who exposed themselves to property in the boom times will need to learn new skills to adapt to the changing seasons.

The cornerstone of all successful investing has to be money management. Personal debt has never been more available or acceptable, but to delay gratification and to avoid the temptation is a key to investing success.

Of course, investment debt is a different animal, as some borrowings are essential in order to maximise your wealth through property. Investment debt is like fire — it's a good servant but a terrible master. In summing up successful wealth-creation strategies, you must grow your equity faster than your debt in order to grow your wealth. Conversely, the worst wealth-creation strategy ever, is to borrow against equity for lifestyle expenses.

Once you have mastered the basics it is prudent to consider your structure before you go too far down the property investing road. Buying property in your own name might allow you some tax savings in the short term but cause you to pay more tax when you sell and expose you to unnecessary risk.

To buy as a person or as a partnership is one of the biggest mistakes you can make. Successful investors use structures that allow them to control their assets without owning them.

In conclusion, changing seasons call for changing strategies and flexible investment approaches.

PART II SUMMARY (CONT'D)

While much has been made of the gloomy market, successful investors should be able to thrive and prosper in any conditions by tailoring their activities to the prevailing situation.

In the next section we're going to throw caution to the wind and look at some positive, offensive options to help equip you with the tools you need to continue investing successfully, Steve McKnight style.

PART III:

Real Estate 'Steve Style'

11

Building a Massive Property Portfolio from the Ground Up

In sales and marketing circles there's a famous story that goes something like this: three top-selling New York hot dog vendors were gathered together and asked, 'What would you choose if you could have just one competitive advantage that only you could apply?' The first vendor replied, 'The freshest and tastiest buns. If I could get my hands on those buns then I'd have the best hot dogs in the land'. The second vendor said, 'The juiciest and most succulent frankfurts. If I could get my hands on those then I'd have the highest quality hot dogs on earth!' The third vendor thought for a moment and then said, 'All I want is a hungry crowd. If I could find hungry people then I'd sell out in seconds'.

Do you see the difference in mindset that the third vendor had over his competitors? The first two had been focused on their products while the third vendor concentrated on his market. The same principle applies to real estate. The prevailing mindset of inexperienced investors is overwhelmingly focused on the product — which in real estate is the style of the house, the number of bedrooms, the location and so on. Upon creating their housing product, investors then try to convince the market that it needs such a product.

The Uncertain Path to Profit

Buy

Renovate

Convince purchasers

Make sale

Bank profit

For example, a commonly used strategy is to buy a property and then to spend time and money renovating it. Upon completion the home is then put back on the market with an expensive sales campaign designed to convince potential buyers to purchase.

Steve's Investing Tip

If you want to take profits from the market, then give the market what it wants.

My success has come from thinking differently. I don't care what I buy, so long as there's a hungry market for what I'm selling. If I were to use the renovation strategy, my preferred option would be to spend a lot of time interviewing agents to find out what type of property, and what style of renovation, was selling the fastest and then I'd simply give the market what it wanted.

Notice that the difference between the two profit making paths illustrated is that I've replaced 'convince the market' with 'listen to the market'. I've done this because the harder it is to convince the market that it needs what you're selling, the longer it will take to sell your property, and the less profitable it will be.

To think differently is the first and most important step for those looking to acquire a mammoth property portfolio. Instead of telling the market what it needs, investors need to focus their energies on listening to the market and supplying it with what it wants.

The Proven Path to Profit
Listen to the market
⇩
Buy
⇩
Renovate
⇩
Make sale
⇩
Bank profit

AUTOMATIC VERSUS AUTOMATED PROFITS

It is also vital to know the difference between an automatic and automated property profit. A booming property market is the best example of how an automatic real estate profit is made. That is, with little effort on your part, buyers will compete to secure deals at a frenetic pace and automatically increase house prices. You don't need to be very clever to make a nice profit in an automatic real estate market. All you need to do is to buy something, and then wait for market forces to lift your wealth higher and higher.

An automated property profit is different. Instead of being market based, it's dependent on a four-tiered system that stems from the following mantra:

Steve's Investing Tip

Automated property profits occur when you buy the right property, at the right price, using the right strategy, targeted at the right person.

Let's look at each of the components in more detail.

THE RIGHT PROPERTY

While real estate agents might tell you otherwise, not every property that's for sale will make a good investment. At the risk of stereotyping, I categorise potential purchases into the following two categories:

1. Solutions

Solution properties make poor investments because the opportunity to add value by solving potential problems has already been claimed by someone else. Serviced apartments are a good illustration of solution properties since there is a long line of people who all make a profit before the investor, such as:

➲ *The Developer*
   The developer takes the first bite of profit by having the vision and system to convert a problem block of land into finished apartments.

➲ *The Builder*
   The builder also takes a margin for solving the problem of constructing the dwellings.

➲ *The Bank*
   The bank takes a profit for providing the finance.

➲ *The Real Estate Agent*
   Any commission paid to the real estate agent is likely to be factored into the off-the-plan sales price.

➲ *The Management Company*
   Even after buying, the management company takes a profit for handling the books, managing cleaning and so on.

Last of all comes the poor old investor who is convinced by the clever real estate agent to buy a low-maintenance investment that is sure to increase in value over time. A phrase to remember is,

'The further down the profit chain you are, the less profit you stand to make'.

In the absence of a problem to solve, investors who purchase solution properties must rely on automatic profits (that is, those provided by general market forces).

Steve's Investing Tip

If you buy a solution property then you will only make money in an automatic property market, where prices are rapidly increasing.

It stands to reason that in soft market times, solution properties tend to underperform since the after-inflation price growth is negligible. Other examples of solution properties include renovated dwellings, off-the-plan purchases and any houses with little opportunity to add value, where the landscaping has been done and there is no room to extend.

2. Problems

When you think about it, every employed person is paid a wage or salary to solve someone else's problems. Now, I can let you in on the unwritten pay structure secret that most bosses use: the more problems you can solve, the more we're prepared to pay!

Real estate investing is no different in that the deals that offer the highest profits also come with the most problems. Therefore, if you want to increase your profitability, start looking for more problems! For example, when I visit real estate agents' offices, I'm not all that interested in the glossy brochures that advertise all their high-priced homes. I want to know about the property that's been for sale the longest, or the ugliest house, or the one that the vendor is keenest to negotiate a quick sale for. Be careful though. Buying a property problem that you don't know how to solve (or that you don't even know who to turn to for advice on how to solve) is a sure-fire way of losing lots of money.

Part IV of this book contains six case studies of people who made tidy profits by turning problems into solutions. As I mentioned, not every property that's for sale will make a good investment. If you want to maximise your money-making potential then turn problems into solutions in an uptrending market.

THE RIGHT PRICE

Many real estate agents advise their clients to auction their properties rather than sell them privately. This is because there's a general feeling in the industry that auctions create an emotional environment that causes buyers to pay more than they otherwise would. For instance, I'm sure that most readers would have seen or heard about an auction where multiple anxious bidders forced the price much higher than the seller's reserve. It often happens. It's for this very reason that I rarely buy properties at auction. In fact, the only auctioned property that I've ever bought was acquired several days after the auction on the basis that it was still for sale because no bidders turned up!

Before buying anything, astute investors identify their maximum purchase price on the basis of their minimum acceptable profit. Speculators, on the other hand, tend to buy property with little regards to price, and this leads to a very uncertain outcome.

Even if you find the right property, if you can't buy it at the right price then it's unlikely that the deal will eventuate in your planned profit. If you can't otherwise make the deal work then walk away as there's no shortage of property available for sale. When determining what might be the right price, I suggest you come up with three possibilities:

1. A price you'd be happy to pay. This is your best-case-scenario price.

2. A price you might be forced to pay. This is the maximum that you're willing to pay, given your expected profit outcome.

3. A price that you won't pay under any circumstances. This is anything above your maximum price.

To finish up, here's a little negotiating tip: Before walking away from a deal tell the agent, 'Sorry, I can't make the deal work at *that* asking price'. Often the agent will reply, 'Well, what price can you pay?' This is your invitation to submit a lower offer in a way that doesn't seem like a dreadful low-ball negotiating technique.

THE RIGHT STRATEGY

Just as a hammer isn't much use when you need a power drill, the only way to convert a problem into a solution is by using the right strategy. For example, you can quickly overcapitalise on a renovation if you spend more money on completing it than you make through the extra value added to the property.

Your choice of strategy will depend on whether you're trying to solve a property problem or a people problem.

➲ Property problems relate to making better use of the land and/or housing structure.

➲ People problems relate to helping people occupy a home that they couldn't otherwise afford on their own.

Steve's Investing Tip

You'll make the most money on deals where you solve both property and people problems.

An example of how you might solve both a property and people problem is to convert vacant land into three townhouses, and then sell them off the plan to investors on a no-deposit basis, where you finance some, or all, of the buyer's purchase price (charging interest, of course). This solves the property problem by converting the vacant land into liveable dwellings, and also solves the need of investors who want to buy but have limited capital and/or borrowing ability.

Even if you have the right property that's purchased at the right price, you won't be able to maximise your profit unless you apply the right strategy, and market it to the right person.

THE RIGHT PERSON

Bank accounts are held in the name of people, not houses, so if you're planning to make money from real estate then you *must* tailor your strategy to meet the needs of a living, breathing, chequebook-owning person. Naturally, not all people are the same, which is why the property market can be broken down into the following three broad categories:

1. *The Top Tier*
    These are the most expensive homes, priced in the top 15% of dwellings in their area.

2. *The Middle Tier*
    These are average-priced dwellings and make up the bulk of the property market.

3. *The Bottom Tier*
    These are the cheap properties that comprise the bottom 15% of prices in their area.

There has been plenty of conjecture about which is the best 'market' to invest in. High profits can certainly be made in the top tier, since expensive homes facilitate high margins. However, profits can also be made in the middle and bottom tiers as well. Ultimately your decision about which market to invest in will be determined by your available time and money. Clearly, if you don't have much money behind you, then the top tier of the property market is going to be a difficult place to start. Personally, my target market can be summarised in the diagram below.

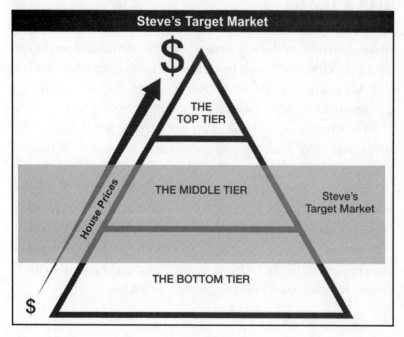

Irrespective of whether I'm buying to rent or to resell, I try to aim for where the majority of the market competes. In my mind this is the top third of the bottom tier, and the bottom two-thirds of the middle tier.

In case you're wondering, I don't invest in the top of the market because of what I call the 'Foible Factor'. Buyers at the top of the market tend to be very particular about their tastes, so any slight deviation from exactly what they're looking for can leave a property sitting for sale for quite some time.

At the other extreme, the bottom of the market is where it's most price competitive, since home occupiers have the lowest incomes and are the most affected by higher costs of living. Therefore, factors like interest rate rises and petrol price increases can conspire to keep prices down.

SEEK A SYSTEM

In summary, my target market aims to capture lower and middle income earners on the way up, and top income earners on the way down. I deliberately look to compete in a market where there is a steady volume of activity as that limits my chances of having a property sit vacant or for sale over a long period of time.

How much thought have you given to the target market that you invest in? What strategies do you have in place for attracting the right person?

There are two ways that real estate prices increase. The first is when general market forces automatically lift all property values higher. This is largely beyond the control of any single investor. The second, automated profits, is more strategic. Like Henry Ford who pioneered the factory line by automating the manufacture of motor vehicles, your job is to create systems for:

➲ finding the right property

➲ paying the right price

➲ using the right strategy, and

➲ attracting the right person.

If you can do this then success will be just around the corner.

THE PROPERTY TREE

Instead of looking to buy just any type of property that might make just any kind of profit, another secret to building a mammoth property portfolio is to match your desired profit to your chosen strategy, and your chosen strategy to your desired investing objective.

By doing this you have a choice of either using a top-down approach (where your profit dictates your investing objective) or else a bottom-up approach (where your investing objectives dictate your desired profit). As you'll soon see, my preference is to use the latter option.

Let's explore this concept further using a diagram I've created called 'The Property Tree' (see below).

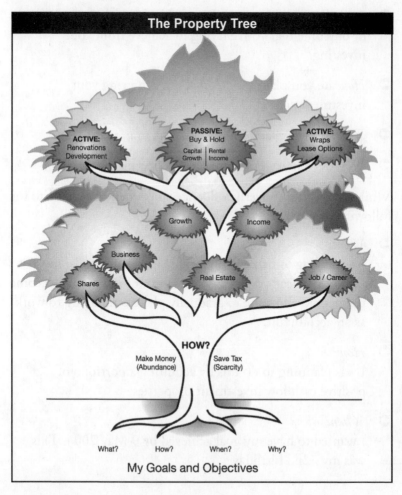

The Property Tree

ACTIVE: Renovations Development

PASSIVE: Buy & Hold
Capital Growth | Rental Income

ACTIVE: Wraps Lease Options

Growth   Income

Business

Shares   Real Estate   Job / Career

HOW?
Make Money (Abundance)   Save Tax (Scarcity)

What?   How?   When?   Why?

My Goals and Objectives

The Base (Strong Roots)

While I don't profess to be an arborist, I understand that a tree's root structure acts as an anchor to hold it firmly in place. This is particularly important in helping a tree withstand damaging winds. In the same way, your property empire needs a strong root system to prevent it from being upturned when the winds of change sweep the property markets. At the root of your investing activities will be your answers to some important questions.

- Aside from making a profit, *what* is the underlying purpose or outcome that you're trying to achieve from your investing?

- *How* are you planning to go about achieving your investment goals?

- *When* do you plan to have achieved your goals?

- *Why* are you even investing in the first place?

While I hope I don't overly influence you, when I began I had the following answers mapped out:

- *What?*
  I was trying to become financially independent. In my mind this meant establishing a source of investment income that would allow me to gradually phase out having to work as an accountant.

- *How?*
  I was planning to do this by acquiring a portfolio of positive cashflow investment properties.

- *When?*
  I wanted to have my goal achieved by 9 May 2004. This was my 32nd birthday.

➲ *Why?*

I was investing in the first place because I really didn't like my job as an accountant, and because I wanted to spend more time with my kids as they were growing up rather than having to work long hours in a job.

Hopefully you can see that by answering these questions I started to come up with a context for my investing. For example, there was no point in me pursuing a negatively geared portfolio as this would have meant that I'd have needed to work longer in a job to fund the negative cashflow.

If you've never thought through these issues before then it would be easy to gloss over them. However, to do so would be a mistake because almost all investing problems I'm asked about stem from a lack of clarity about why the person is investing in the first place. Perhaps look at it this way, at any one point in time there are probably tens of thousands of houses for sale in Australia. How will you ever know which one to buy if you don't know what you're looking for in the first place?

The Main Trunk

Once you've thought through the preliminary planning questions behind your investing, the next issue to consider is your preferred avenue for creating wealth. At a very basic level you will need to choose between saving tax (scarcity thinking) and making money (abundant thinking).

Saving tax is often chosen, but the truth of the matter is that the tax office only allows a deduction for the loss made, and I can't think of one business I know where making a loss is seen as a good idea. As outlined in earlier chapters, if you select 'saving tax' then you immediately place a limit on how high your real estate tree can grow because you'll only be able to afford a couple of loss-making investment properties.

The other option is to make money. If you select this broad option then you'll need to choose from a range of vehicles:

➲ *Shares*
Making money from share-based capital appreciation and dividends, or else trading shares and derivatives thereof.

➲ *Businesses*
Making money buying, selling and operating businesses.

➲ *Real Estate*
Making money from rent and/or capital appreciation.

➲ *Career (Selling Your Time)*
Building a career and being paid for solving problems.

My suggestion would be to specialise in one option, but to also have an interest in the other three. In my case I:

➲ control a significant share portfolio

➲ control multiple businesses across many industries

➲ control multiple investment properties that deliver both growth and income returns, and

➲ earn money from speaking engagements and other events.

Take a minute now to try to work out how much money you earn per annum from each of the four possible sources. Use the table opposite to record your answers. Also calculate how much each contributes as a percentage of your overall income.

What have you gleaned as a result of completing this table? From what source is the majority of your income derived, and how would you like that to change in the near future?

Contributions from Each Source		
Area	$ Per Annum	% of Total[1]
Shares	$	%
Businesses	$	%
Property	$	%
Career	$	%
Total income	$	100%

[1] As an example, the percentage contributed by shares would be calculated: (Value of shares ÷ $ Total income) × 100.

YOUR REAL ESTATE OPTIONS

While I could write quite a lot on each category, since this is a real estate book, let's stick to analysing our options in that area. Having decided to use real estate as your way of making money, you then need to choose what type of profit you want — either growth (capital appreciation), income (cashflow), or a mixture of the two. A choice is needed to help narrow down the number of potential properties that you might be interested in.

Steve's Investing Tip

Let your desired profit outcome dictate the property you buy, rather than the other way around!

The next chapter contains more information on the difference between growth and income profits in property.

Cash Versus Cashflow Property Deals

Instead of talking about property profits as being either growth or income orientated, another approach we can adopt is to reclassify each deal as being either a 'cash deal' or a 'cashflow deal'. A cash deal is one in which you can expect to make a lump-sum gain, whereas a cashflow deal provides ongoing surplus income above costs.

Varying the terms helps to ensure that we remain focused on the end goal. For example, capital appreciation may be the catch cry, but growth only becomes realised when the price gains are converted into cash through a sale.

Until a short time ago I'd been completely sold on the virtues of cashflow deals to the extent that I was blind to other money-making opportunities that involved cash deals. A changing market has necessitated a changing mindset though, and today my thinking has evolved into an understanding that I need to have a property portfolio with an appropriate mix of both cash and cashflow deals.

A Mix of Ingredients	
Cash Strategies	Cashflow Strategies
Buy and hold (growth) Renovation Development	Buy and hold (income) Lease options Wraps Flips

Which is Better, Cash or Cashflow?

I'm often dragged into a debate about which I think is better — cash deals or cashflow deals. The answer is that neither and both are better, since the value of any outcome depends solely on how well it helps an investor meet his or her objectives. That is, for growth-orientated investors, a lump-sum cash outcome is great. On the other hand, income-orientated investors will see an investment that delivers a positive cashflow return as superior.

Rather than arguing about superiority, I'd simply urge all investors to make sure that they use the right strategy on the right property to ensure that they have the best chance possible of securing their desired investing outcome.

Active Versus Passive Investors

Before you rush out and buy something, though, it's wise to consider whether you want to be an active or passive investor. Active investors seek to drive their profits higher by energetically participating in their deals. On the other hand, passive investors prefer 'set and forget' type investments. Another way of looking at the difference is that passive investors usually buy their profits, whereas active investors are more likely to make them.

Rather than buying a property and applying a strategy, I'd encourage you to select a strategy and to then find a suitable property on which to apply it. That is, have a strategy focus rather than a property focus.

I've prepared two tables below that summarise how active and passive growth and income investors may like to apply each investing strategy.

Growth Focus Strategies		
	Growth Focus: Passive	Growth Focus: Active
Buy and hold	Buy a solution property that's in a good growth area and wait for market forces to drive prices higher.	Buy a problem property and create equity through price competitiveness and market attractiveness.
Renovation	Complete small scale projects — usually 'do it yourself' jobs that don't require a lot of effort or significant skill.	Take on larger projects such as extensions and more complicated works. Adopt an active role in managing the subcontractors.
Developments	Usually avoided.	Completed according to a detailed plan and a budget. Mainly outsourced to contractors.

Income Focus Strategies		
	Income Focus: Passive	Income Focus: Active
Buy and hold	Buy a property that has a net positive cashflow outcome.	Look for ways to create positive cashflow, either through increased rent and/or by adding more streams of income.
Wraps	Usually avoided.	Create a deal to meet the specific needs of the buyer.
Lease options	Usually avoided.	Create a deal to meet the specific needs of the buyer.

Note: Should you desire more information about the various strategies outlined above then please visit <www.PropertyInvesting.com>.

If you follow my suggested approach by starting at the bottom of the tree and then working your way upwards, you'll gain greater clarity about your investing and also more certainty about what type of property deals are most likely to help you to achieve your wealth-creation goals.

A PROVEN RECIPE

The recipe for building a mammoth property portfolio is 65% thinking and planning, and 35% follow-through action. The alternative approach is to rush out and to buy a property. To do so without appropriate planning and forethought will result in a disjointed and haphazard investing outcome that may be profitable, but which will also place severe restrictions on your ability to reach your full potential.

Typically investors who fail to plan soon hit a severe motivational crisis. Also common are serious restrictions on borrowings, use of an inappropriate accounting structure, and investments that compete with, rather than complement, each other. Make sure that your Property Tree is the right way up because a tree that has its roots in the air is certain to die.

Let's take a pause here and finish up the chapter. When you're ready to continue, turn to the next chapter and we'll look at one of the most effective strategies for profiting in gloomy conditions — taking small chunks of quick profit from multiple deals.

Chapter 11 Insights

Insight #1:

The easiest way to make money is to discover what the market wants, and then to simply supply it.

Insight #2:

Give yourself the best chance of real estate success by selecting the right property at the right price, and adopting the right strategy that's targeted to the right person.

Insight #3:

My target market ranges from the top third of the bottom tier, to the bottom two thirds of the middle tier. This is where there is always likely to be a steady demand.

Insight #4:

The Property Tree model highlights how effective planning can drastically narrow down the number of potential properties you may be interested in buying. This is essential for good time management and for allocating your available capital to the most profitable opportunities.

Insight #5:

I believe many real estate investors have their Property Tree upside down. That is, they rush out to buy a property with everything else left as an afterthought. This invariably leads to stunted growth. Avoid making this mistake by heeding the approaches outlined in this chapter.

Cashing in on Fast Growth

The presence of sharks around some of our beaches is a fact of life that Australians have had to come to grips with. I'm told that there are around 166 species of shark that inhabit Australian waters, from the small lantern shark (which is about 15cm long) right the way up to the massive whale shark (which can be 12 metres in length — about as long as a bus!) While you've probably heard about Great Whites, Hammerheads and Grey Nurses, I doubt you've ever seen many TV documentaries that feature *Isistius Brasiliensis* — the Cookie-Cutter Shark. These ocean lurkers grow to about 50cm in length and have a unique way of feeding. Instead of trying to kill their victims outright, they prefer a 'grab and run' approach. They use their sucker-style lips to latch on to their larger prey and then, once attached, spin around so that their small upright teeth carve out a chunk of flesh. A Cookie-Cutter shark bite certainly inflicts a serious injury, but it's rarely fatal. Quite often larger fish in deep oceans have scars and bite marks indicating many attacks by various nasties such as the Cookie-Cutter.

As the property market changes, I suggest you vary your approach to that of the Cookie-Cutter Shark. That is, instead of trying to make a killing out of one or two investments, it's a lot smarter to take regular small profit chunks across multiple deals. The aim of this chapter is to reveal how you can profit from quick cash transactions.

$76,385 PROFIT IN 4.5 MONTHS

A Commercial Deal

Let's start by examining a real-life deal that made a very tidy quick cash profit. In the previous chapter I outlined my philosophy for making profits by buying problems and selling solutions. In this case, the vendor had a tenant problem which made it difficult for him to sell. Specifically, the tenant had been there for three years and knew that he was paying well under market rent. Wanting the good times to last forever, he would baulk at allowing prospective buyers to see inside the building. It seems he was worried that if the property was sold then his rent would be jacked up substantially.

The agent selling the property mentioned that it had been on the market for around a month, however no offers had been made because no-one wanted to buy the property without having a builder do an internal appraisal. The shop contained 500 square metres of retail space and was rented on a month-to-month lease for $500 per week. Ringing around various real estate agents, we were told that commercial space was currently renting for between $65 to $75 per square metre. Have a go at working out the potential market rent using the tables opposite, assuming a conservative $65 per square metre.

Potential Market Rent	
Total square metres	
× per square metre rate	$
= Conservative market rent	$

My answer is $32,500 (that is, 500 × $65). Okay, having established that the property was under-rented, our simple strategy was to buy, increase the rent, and then sell for a higher price. On the basis that we could increase the rent to $32,500, have a go at trying to work what the potential sale price might be assuming an 8% rental return.

Potential Sale Price	
Conservative market rent	$
÷ Rental return %	
= Potential sales price	$

My answer is $406,250 (that is, $32,500 ÷ 0.08). Given the asking price was $250,000, what was the potential gross profit before purchase and sales costs?

Potential Gross Profit	
Potential sales price	$
– Purchase price	$
= Gross profit	$

My answer is $156,250 (that is, $406,250 – $250,000). There seemed to be enough profit in the deal, the next issue to address was how could the risk of not inspecting the property be mitigated? In this case a builder was engaged to walk around the building, examine the roof, and look at the adjoining walls in the properties next door. He also walked into the shop as a browsing customer. The feedback we received was that the building seemed structurally sound.

Due to the vendor's financial circumstances, a full price offer was submitted to allow him to clear his mortgage. In return though, he agreed to a six-month settlement and a low deposit on signing — just $2,500.

Our Strategy

Even though the property may have been worth up to $406,250, the strategy was to sell quickly at an attractive rental return. For example, if the market was willing to buy property at an 8% return, then offering this deal at 9%, plus also solving the access problem, should have meant that it would sell very quickly.

Have a go at trying to work out what our asking price would be, and our potential profit, on the basis of selling on a 9% yield.

Our Asking Price	
Conservative market rent	$
÷ Attractive rental return	
= Potential sales price	$

My answer is $361,111 (that is, $32,500 ÷ 0.09).

Our Potential Profit	
Potential sales price	$
– Purchase price	$
= Gross profit	$

My answer is $111,111 (that is, $361,111 – $250,000). Soon after our offer was accepted the tenant decided to move out since he knew that a rental increase was imminent. Rather than have the shop sit empty for five months, the vendor put a 'For Lease' sign in the front window.

Call it luck or good fortune, but a short while later a person drove by who was interested in buying rather than leasing the shop. Somehow or other he ended up with our phone number, and a few weeks later a deal had been agreed in which he would buy the property from us for $340,000. Here's a summary of our actual numbers.

A Summary of the Numbers	
Purchase price	$250,000
+ Closing costs	$16,037
= Total purchase price	$266,037
Sales price	$340,000
− Sales costs	$800
+ Settlement adjustments	$3,222
= Net sale proceeds	$342,422
Net sale proceeds	$342,422
− Total purchase price	$266,037
= Pre-tax profit	$76,385

Even though we might have been able to hold out for a higher sales price, the prospect of making a quick cash profit was more enticing than the possibility of making another $10,000 or $20,000.

In summary, you could say that our profit was made on the basis of buying on a rental return of 10.4% ($26,000 ÷ $250,000), and then selling on the lower rental return of 9.6% ($32,500 ÷ $340,000). Even at 9.6%, the purchaser picked up a good deal, which highlights an important principle that a property will sell a lot quicker if you leave some profit on the table for the next buyer.

TIME AND MONEY

The deal above introduces an important point about the connection between the state of the property market and the timing and potential profit in a cash deal. When the real estate market is running hot then you can sit pretty while the buyer frenzy pushes prices higher and higher.

On the other hand, in a down or sideways market, you'd be well advised to consider clipping your profit for the sake of making a speedy exit.

Steve's Investing Tip

The aim in less prosperous property times is to make less profit per deal, but more often so you end up with more overall.

Even though your profit may be lower, you can compensate for this shortfall by increasing the volume of deals that you have on the go. For example, even though our profit of $76,385 is less than it might have otherwise been if we'd held out for top dollar, being able to access and then reinvest this money allows us to pay for portfolio growth using realised cash profits. This is a safer and more sustainable option than using third party debt, particularly in a flat or down market.

15 TIPS FOR ACHIEVING ACCELERATED GROWTH

Passive investors sit back and wait for growth to happen around them. Active investors take a far greater hands-on role and adopt home-grown strategies to speed up their capital appreciation. As a quick glimpse of what's ahead in this chapter, here are 15 ideas for fast-tracking potential growth:

1. Find a suburb that is experiencing good growth and then look to buy in an adjoining area. That way you'll be well positioned for spill over demand once the booming suburb becomes unaffordable.

2. When renovating or developing, equity is created by adding more in perceived value than actual cost. This being the

case, I suggest spending a good portion of your budget on anything a potential buyer sees and touches within the first 10 seconds of walking into the property.

3. Before buying, investigate potential lifestyle attractions in that area and then link them back to the target market of possible future buyers. For example, trendy restaurants appeal to young professionals whereas parks are more attractive to families.

4. Make a list of the local amenities that are within a 10-minute walk of the property. This includes shopping centres, public transport, schools, bike tracks, medical centres, swimming pools, sporting arenas and major arterial roads. The closer the property is to major amenities, the more convenient it is for the homeowner or tenant and this will result in greater demand over the long term.

5. Housing shortages almost always result in higher home prices, so investing in areas that are experiencing increasing populations will help you to achieve above-average price growth.

6. Quick profits can be made by purchasing properties with a higher than normal rental return percentage. You can find such deals by looking for homes with problems that can be solved in a cost-effective way. Once you've solved the problem then you can put the property back on the market and look to bank a fast profit.

7. There are thousands of strategies you can use to increase the rent. Be creative and remember that the higher the rent, the more your property will be worth to another investor.

8. Gaining planning approval can be a real pain, but if you can put in the groundwork then your property may be worth more. For example, I recently helped out a mate in

an unusual situation. He owned a parcel of land that was separated by a water authority easement. My suggestion was that his land would be worth a whole lot more if he could buy the easement as it would allow him to get planning approval for more dwellings.

My friend was unaware that easements could sometimes be bought, and was even more surprised when the water authority consented. I'm expecting a thank-you card and a box of expensive chocolates in the mail!

9. The more dwellings a property has, the more it will be worth because there's scarcity associated with a deal that can't be rebuilt due to planning code changes. Even if you could build again, the cost of doing so would be prohibitive given that materials and labour become more and more expensive each year.

10. If you're a little short of land then you can always approach your neighbour and try to buy some of his or her block. This is particularly useful if you fall just short of the minimum subdividable block size for your area.

11. Try to identify areas that are benefiting from jobs and/or wages growth. Experience shows that housing values rise sharply when people have more money to spend.

12. For selected buyers, you might want to consider offering vendor's terms to help finance their purchase. In return, you can increase the selling price given the extra risk involved. The same is also true if you were offering a second mortgage.

13. Values of houses in areas experiencing infrastructure improvements tend to rise at a higher than normal rate. For example, the new toll road in Melbourne's east will reduce travel time to the outlying suburbs, thereby making it more attractive for commuters to live there.

Again though, it may be smarter to buy in surrounding suburbs that experience spill-over growth, rather than the more obvious areas where the benefit of the new infrastructure has already been priced into home values.

14. Time is money, so make sure that all your deals are very carefully planned so that you're not held up by delays — particularly when renovating or developing.

    For example, be diligent in planning the timing of tradespeople as there is nothing more frustrating than a clash of schedules, or a project coming to a standstill when you can't get the right tradesperson at the right time.

15. Change your attitude and become more proactive! Bite the bullet and invest some time and money into maximising your growth rather than waiting for the market to do it all for you.

VALUE IS IN THE EYE OF THE BEHOLDER

Now I'd like to share some more detailed observations about value and how you can add it to a property. A commonly held misconception is that houses appreciate in value. When you think about it though, the truth of the matter is that dwellings actually depreciate, so that each physical property becomes worth less, not more, over time.

For example, a 100-year-old house that was in 'original condition' would have been severely damaged by exposure to sun, wind and rain. No doubt the weatherboards would be rotten, the roof would leak, and the plumbing and electrics would be obsolete. It's hard to see then how such a weather-beaten house would be worth more than property that had been built in the last few years.

Steve's Investing Tip

Houses don't appreciate, they depreciate!

Given that houses actually depreciate, what causes rising property prices? I believe the answer is that:

> Values increase according to buyers'
> perception of potential scarcity.

I shared this observation recently with Grant, a R.E.S.U.L.T.S. mentoring participant from Queensland. Grant was looking to buy vacant land in a new estate, and he was particularly interested in two blocks that had been earmarked as the only sites that had planning approval for the construction of duplexes rather than stand alone homes. (Duplexes are two houses side-by-side that are joined by a common wall down the middle.) I told Grant that I generally wasn't a fan of vacant land for two reasons.

1. there was generally no income, and

2. in the case of new estates, there was usually little scarcity.

However, in his case, the notion of buying the only two blocks in the estate that could be turned into medium-density housing was appealing on the basis that Grant had a monopoly in that particular market. That is, there was scarcity in those duplex blocks given he would have four streams of income at the same time as benefiting from the economies of scale driving his construction costs down since he would be building two properties side-by side rather than stand alone dwellings.

At the other less sensible extreme, some friends I know purchased a block of what they were told was prime land in regional New South Wales. They were wrong, though, because soon after their purchase a glut of new estates were released. In the end they were committed to building in a softening market and were lucky that they only lost $20,000.

Scarcity only needs to be perceived in order for it to be effective. For example, real estate agents often try to build an urgency in buyers' minds by using comments like, 'We don't have another one like it' or 'This is a one-of-a-kind property.' Of course, this is just marketing hype designed to get you to pay more.

THE SIX TYPES OF SCARCITY

Having shared with you that scarcity is the secret ingredient to increasing property prices, it stands to reason that you'll be well positioned to earn above-market growth if your property can tap into one or more of the following six types of scarcity.

1. Lifestyle or Convenience

The mantra of 'location, location, location' does not fully explain the connection between the position of a house and its potential to achieve price growth. That is, if 'location, location, location' were the answer, why would traditionally poorer suburbs go up in value, sometimes far more in percentage terms than the more expensive areas?' Places like Redfern in Sydney, Yarraville in Melbourne, Elizabeth in South Australia, Armadale in Perth and Darra in Brisbane.

If you want to turbo-charge your capital appreciation and maximise your growth return then you need to do much more than buy a property in a blue-ribbon postcode. What's required is that you draw a link between the location and the potential buyer's lifestyle tastes and/or convenience needs.

As busy people, we live in an era in which we're used to paying a premium price for lifestyle appeal and convenience. For example, just the other day I was in the supermarket and noticed that pre-sliced, prepackaged mushrooms were nearly double the cost of loose and whole mushrooms that you had to pick and pack yourself.

Steve's Investing Tip

You can generate your own growth if you can link your property back to lifestyle and/or convenience factors that will benefit the next owner.

Lifestyle tastes are factors that increase the enjoyment or appeal of the property. For example, ocean views, proximity to popular restaurants or positioning in trendy areas. Convenience relates back to access to public transport, distance to local schools and ability to access major roads and freeways.

Don't get me wrong, properties perceived to be more exclusive certainly sell for more than those in lower socioeconomic areas. However, the issue ought not to be which is the nicer suburb. As investors, we only need to worry about which suburb provides the best growth opportunities for outperforming the market.

2. Potential Return (Yield) or Value

As mentioned, blue-ribbon houses aren't the only ones that increase in value. Home prices in poorer areas will also appreciate, not because of their location, but because of their price attractiveness.

That is, as other areas increase in value, those wanting to own but who are squeezed out of the higher priced areas will often decide to buy in an inferior location in order to gain a foothold in the market. Another name for this phenomena is 'The Ripple Effect'.

Not only do homebuyers compete with each other to buy affordable housing, they must also try to outbid investors looking to snap up properties that offer high returns. For example, investors will be happy to buy in less respected areas provided they can earn a higher rental return. That is, which of the following two properties would you be interested in buying if you were looking for an income return — a house in a well-respected suburb that was offering 2% return, or a house in a blue-collar suburb that was offering a 6% return?

Even though home owners and investors have different objectives, quite often they'll compete for the same properties and force prices higher.

3. Planning or Zoning Restrictions

The planning and building codes of yesteryear were much more flexible as to what could be built than those that exist today. For example, private open space considerations are now a lot more stringent, as are shadowing issues and permit requirements.

As a general rule, councils that make it difficult to improve or to build property run the risk of scaring developers away, and when you remove that buying segment from the market then you risk the following two unpleasant consequences:

1. You impinge on the demand for properties and this will put pressure on prices to stagnate or fall.

2. You prevent the modernising and upgrading of the area since developers are required to also contribute to infrastructure costs such as better roads, parks and other amenities.

The reverse is also true in that councils that provide a hospitable renovating and developing environment encourage favourable price competition, while also making the area more desirable to live in.

4. Density

Following on from the previous comment, the evolution of stricter building codes has meant that you are no longer able to build the same density of housing that was allowed even five or 10 years ago. For example, before you ever buy a property it is wise to become an area expert. This means that you invest time and effort to get to know the place like a local. This allows you to gain insider information that can help you to avoid making an expensive mistake. For example, the average out-of-town investor wouldn't know that anywhere in Ballarat that has been backfilled runs the risk of soil contamination, since the backfill often came from mining sites where the tailings were treated with arsenic. A soil test is an absolute necessity in these locations.

One way that you can become an area expert is to walk around the streets paying attention to the changing style of housing. As you do this you will quickly notice that unit developments built in the 1970s or early 1980s have far more properties on the blocks than what is allowed today for developments built on the same sized parcels of land.

A good illustration of this principle is the block of 27 bedsitter units plus a communal laundry (see chapter 8) that I bought from a vendor who couldn't afford to settle. There's no way that you'd get a planning permit to build that kind of dwelling on planet Earth again today because the planning code now requires that each unit have its own laundry.

It stands to reason that the more dwellings you can get on a block, the higher the potential overall return. For example, if you wanted to bulldoze the site and rebuild, then you could probably gain planning approval for 14 one-bedroom units. However, doing this would be expensive and in the end you would receive far less rent than what you would presently collect from the existing 27 units.

5. Style or Appeal

Some architectural housing styles tend to be more popular than others. For example, Ballarat contains several beautiful federation-style homes that look absolutely breathtaking, particularly if they've been tastefully renovated. Local real estate agents will tell you that these properties are always in high demand

and fetch superior prices because the market perceives that they're more valuable due to their scarcity and street appeal.

6. Land Size

A general rule of real estate is that the larger the block size, the more likely it is that the property will grow at a greater rate than similar style houses on smaller blocks. This is because cashed up home-owners and developers will see the value in larger backyards, and both of these segments tend to pay higher prices for better quality sites. Look at it this way, if there are 20 blocks of land in an estate that are the one size, and one block that is 20% bigger, which do you think will be in the highest demand and therefore attract the highest price over time? All half sensible real estate agents will be able to quickly tell you how the size of the block compares against others in the area, as they have access to databases that record that information.

CASHING IN ON SCARCITY

Having revealed the six types of scarcity, here's an outline of how you can use each to up-size your growth potential.

1. Lifestyle or Convenience

Before you buy, spend some time walking and driving around your chosen area and write down all the lifestyle and convenience factors that you feel make the suburb an attractive place to live. This will help later when you sit down to work out what kind of improvements you want to make, as the most value will be added to the property when any improvements are tailored to the needs of the next buyer.

For example, if you thought that there was a lack of family restaurants then you may like to make an outdoor barbecue area one of the features of the property. Similarly, if there was a lack of nearby parks and you wanted to make the property more appealing for children, then placing some swings and a cubby house in the backyard might do the trick.

Remember that any improvement that costs more than the value it adds will eat into your profit margin, so the more accurate you are with identifying potential buyers, the smarter you can be with your investment dollars.

2. Potential Return (Yield) or Value

Rather than buying in a suburb that's already boomed in value, consider buying in a neighbouring or adjoining area. Perhaps consider paying slightly more for a property that has future development appeal (because it features a large block of land), as these properties will out-perform the market when the suburb becomes more popular.

You can also drive your growth higher by increasing the rent. I will explain this concept in more detail shortly.

3. Planning or Zoning Restrictions

Be sure to do your due diligence homework to see how lenient a council is towards development applications. Look out for heritage overlays and nasty fees and charges on mandatory permits. For example, I read the other day that some Sydney councils are charging as much as 5% of the renovation cost to issue a permit. This can be a substantial chunk of your profit.

In other cases councils require an infrastructure contribution. Once again, this can quickly swallow up potential profits. Since every council is different, there's no quick way to solve the problem. The only option is to spend the time and money to become familiar with the planning ground rules in your chosen location.

4. Density

There's not much you can do to improve the density of existing dwellings. The point to note is that the more units you can fit on a block, the higher the growth will be over time. For example, if you have a block of 12 units built in the 1970s with small backyards situated next to a block of 9 units built in the 1980s with larger backyards, the block of 12 will always be worth more since rent is attached to dwellings rather than yard sizes.

5. Style or Appeal

Interview several real estate agents and ask them about the kind of properties and renovations that buyers tend to pay premium prices to acquire. For example, in some areas polished floorboards will be seen as more appealing than carpet. If you can find out what's popular then you can target your improvements to build maximum equity.

6. Land Size

Go to the effort to compare your block size to others nearby. Also be sensitive to gardens that make a yard look crowded rather than spacious. Be sure to check council regulations on minimum subdividable block sizes — if yours can be subdivided later on then your property will command a premium price.

THE RENTAL MULTIPLIER EFFECT

Hopefully you can now appreciate that there's lots you can do to position yourself to achieve above-market growth returns by being savvy about how you assess scarcity. Let's now look at another way to profit. Smart investors know that a great way to build extra value is to find ways to encourage a tenant to pay more rent. For example, consider two theoretical properties — Home A and Home B. They're identical three-bedroom brick houses, situated next door to each other and positioned on similar-sized blocks. They were even built by the same builder 10 years ago. In fact, the only difference is that the tenant in Home B pays $10 a week more in rent.

Given this situation, which home do you think would be worth more? The answer has to be the one that has the higher rent — Home B.

Steve's Investing Tip

The higher the rent, the more a property will be worth.

The rental multiplier effect explains the relationship between a property's value and its associated rent. Through the use of a formula (see below) we can estimate how much extra value will be added to a property after a rental increase.

$$\text{Extra home value} = \frac{\text{Additional annual rent}}{\text{Rental return percentage}} \times 100$$

For example, imagine that you own an investment property valued at \$200,000 that rents for \$300 per week. Furthermore, you've just negotiated with the tenant to increase the rent by \$10 per week. Applying the formula above, all you need to do is plug in the variables and you'll be able to calculate an approximate figure for the extra value you've added to the property.

Let's do it together using the three steps outlined in the following table.

Calculating the Extra Value You've Added	
Step 1: What is the Extra Rent Collected Per Annum?	
Extra weekly rent	\$10
	× 52
= Total extra annual rent	\$520

Calculating the Extra Value You've Added *(cont'd)*	
Step 2: What is the Rental Return?	
Annual rent (before increase) *(calculated $300 × 52)*	$15,600
÷ Current value	$200,000
= Rental return	0.078
	×100
= Rent return %	7.8%
Step 3: Extra Home Value Formula	
Total extra annual rent	$520
÷ Rent return percentage	7.8%
= Total extra value	$6,666

As shown above, the extra rent brings in an additional $520 of income at the same time as increasing the value of the property by $6,666. Instead of looking at the overall increase in value, we can also calculate how much equity is created per dollar of extra rent collected. The formula below reveals that the answer for our example property is $12.82 (1 ÷ 0.078).

$$\text{Rental multiplier effect} = \frac{1}{\text{Rental return}}$$

This is a powerful number to know since you can use it to determine whether the cost of an incentive to increase the rent is worth the extra value added. For example, let's imagine that you have a property with a Rental Multiplier Effect of $8.50. You are considering whether or not to spend $2,000 on a non-essential improvement to the property that you believe will allow you to increase the rent by $200 per annum.

Overall $200 × $8.50 = $1,700, and as this is less than the $2,000 cost, the improvement would perhaps be uncommercial.

Have a go at trying to work out how much extra value will be created in the following three scenarios.

Scenario 1: Basic Rent Increase

Your rental manager tells you that she has negotiated with the tenant of your investment property to pay an extra $20 per week in rent. Your property currently earns a rent return percentage of 3.5%. How much extra value would be created?

Extra Value Created	
Additional annual rent	$
÷ Rental return %	
= Extra value created	$

The answer is $29,714, which means that every dollar of extra rent contributes $28.57 in additional value (that is, 1 ÷ 3.5%).

Scenario 2: Assessing Extra Value

You're interested in purchasing an investment property that is currently rented for $140 per week. The agent tells you that the current owner likes the tenants and hasn't increased the rent for 5 years. You are told that a more realistic market rent would be $200 per week. Similar properties are selling on a 5% rental return. How much equity would be created if you bought the property and increased the rent up to the market level?

Extra Value Created	
Additional annual rent	$
÷ Rental return %	
= Extra value created	$

The answer is $62,400. In this case, you could buy the property, do a partial renovation, and then put it straight back on the market and expect to make a quick pre-tax profit of around $40,000 after closing costs.

Scenario 3: Improvements

You're approached by one of your tenants to purchase and install a ceiling fan in the main bedroom. In return the tenant will pay $10 per week in extra rent. Speedy Sparky, a local electrician, has quoted you $550 to do the required works. The property is currently returning a 4% rental return. Is it cost-effective to proceed?

Extra Value Created	
Additional annual rent	$
÷ Rental return %	
= Extra value created	$

At first glance the proposal seems borderline since the cost of installing the ceiling fan is not recouped in the extra first year's rent. However, if you take a wider view and look at the $13,000 of extra value that's created, who in their right mind wouldn't invest $550 to receive back $13,000 (that is, a 2,363% return)?

Astute readers will pick up that the rental return percentage underpins the multiplier effect. Perhaps strangely, the lower the rental return percentage, the higher the multiplier effect (since you are dividing by a smaller number).

The percentage rental return is set by the market and, as such, it's largely outside your influence or control. The best you can do is gain an understanding of an indicative rate based on other rents and asking prices of similar properties in the area.

SUMMARY

My aim in writing this chapter was to open your eyes to the many ways that you can increase your property's value without having to wait for general market gains. Which of the 15 tips outlined could you immediately implement? Did you learn anything from examining the six types of scarcity? Have your investments included properties with any of these features, and can you use them now to position yourself for maximum profit?

Finally, rental returns are often a key tool used in assessing the value of any property. As such, if you can find a strategy to quickly increase the rent then you'll be well positioned to add value to your property and make a quick-fire profit.

Having addressed the topic of growth, in the next chapter let's tackle the issue that I'm asked more often than any other — where do you find positive cashflow properties?

Chapter 12 Insights

Insight #1:

In a flat or down market it's better to take small but regular bites of profit rather than trying to make a killing out of every deal.

Insight #2:

Remember that a prime rule of wealth creation is to buy assets that appreciate. Given that over time houses depreciate, you're really investing in future perceived scarcity. If you want a property that earns above-market growth then before buying make sure you research how the property stacks up against the six types of scarcity.

Insight #3:

Since investors pay more for properties that offer higher returns, upping the rent is a great way to also increase the value of your investment.

Insight #4:

If you want to sell quickly then make sure you leave some profit in the deal for the next person.

Insight #5:

Proactive investors know there are lots of ways to increase a property's value without having to wait for the market to do it for them. Will you adopt this mindset too?

13

Proven Ways to Find Positive Cashflow Properties

Everyone knows that gold can be found in the ground, but did you also know that it's in sea water? Apparently it's true, there's US$10 trillion plus worth of it floating in the ocean. However, before you rush off to your local beach, the concentration is extremely diluted — just 10 parts of gold per trillion litres of water. So, if you're planning to create your fortune that way then you're going to need a very big pot!

Let's talk more about gold. What mental picture comes to mind when I mention gold mining? Is it a romantic notion of the old days with shaggy-bearded prospectors crouched by a river panning specks? Or is it perhaps a more modern vision of massive open cut and underground mines with huge machinery carrying out enormous piles of dirt that are then processed to extract tiny amounts of metal? I think it's fair to say that times have changed for the gold mining industry, and it's now almost unheard of to stumble across chunks of surface gold worth hundreds of thousands of dollars. That's not to say that smaller but very profitable nuggets aren't still out there. No doubt each weekend a small army of fossickers comb the countryside with metal detectors, hoping to hear a hum or beep indicating that they've struck it rich.

Trying to find a positive cashflow property has a lot in common with the above description of gold mining. That is, the recent boom in prices has made it a lot more difficult to rush out and to buy a positive cashflow deal by just skimming the surface of the market. While it's still possible for you to get lucky and to stumble across a fantastic opportunity, nowadays you can expect to work a lot harder to create positive cashflow deals by bringing various components of the deal together.

12 APPROACHES

In this chapter I'll reveal 12 approaches to finding and creating positive cashflow outcomes. In doing so I'll share with you the details of a billboard deal I've just bought that proves that great opportunities remain available.

Approach 1: No-Brainer Residentials

The no-brainer way to make positive cashflow profits is to try to buy the outcome. As mentioned, this is going to be a tough ask in the current residential market, unless you target outlying or regional areas where prices are low. For example, I know that quite a few people in the R.E.S.U.L.T.S. mentoring program have been snapping up positive cashflow properties in Western Australia and Queensland, in towns that are near major mines. Even though the asking prices may seem high, the rents being paid are even higher because there's an extreme shortage of decent rental accommodation for mine workers.

Cam and Lisa

Take the experience of Cam and Lisa. They bought a smallish three-bedroom property in regional Queensland for what may seem a very expensive $232,000. However, price is always relative to the rent collected, and in this case a major mining company was willing to sign up on a long and lucrative lease at $550 per week. Here's an outline of the numbers on their deal:

The Numbers on Cam and Lisa's Deal	
Purchase price	$232,000
+ Closing costs	$9,347
= Total purchase price	$241,347
– Amount borrowed	$241,347
= Cash down	$0
Annual rent	$28,600
– Loan repayments and ownership costs	$17,286
= Cashflow	$11,314

Given that they didn't put any money down, a positive cashflow profit of $11,314 per annum is a wonderful result!

Anna and Friends

At the other extreme, Anna and her team of fellow savvy investors bought a pair of cheapies — two on the one block in outback Western Australia. All up they paid $98,000 and planned to do some minor renovations before leasing them both out for a combined total rent of $350 per week.

These examples are not unique. I hear similar stories all the time, which further convinces me that, with a little extra effort, it's still possible to buy positive cashflow residential properties. However, I think that people become frustrated and instead of going to the market, they expect the market to come to them.

That is, investors with an unrealistic mindset think they'll be able to find positive cashflow properties in conditions or locations that suit them. Again, while you might strike it lucky, having an attitude like that will set you up for a major disappointment.

Anna's budgeted numbers are shown in the table below.

The Numbers on Anna's Deal	
Purchase price	$98,000
+ Closing costs	$3,000
+ Renovation costs	$11,000
= Total purchase price	$112,000
Annual rent	$18,200
– Loan repayments	$6,840
– Ownership costs	$2,700
= Net cashflow	$8,660

Approach 2: Commercial Opportunities

While the residential market may have been heavily scoured, there are still many opportunities in the commercial arena. Again, I wouldn't expect positive cashflow properties to fall from the sky; however, there's no shortage of 10% plus deals for the picking. For example, have you ever considered the merits of advertising billboards? I've just paid $117,500 for a three-in-one monstrosity on 231 square metres of land. It's nicely positioned at the intersection of several roads. A new two-year lease has just been signed, and there are three more two-year options thereafter. The current rent is $11,500 per annum.

At first glance the rental return seems to be 9.78% (that is, $11,500 ÷ 117,500), however, there are a few factors at work that make the deal a lot more attractive.

➲ The purchase price includes GST. If I buy as a GST-registered entity then one-eleventh of the purchase price will be refunded when I lodge my next Business

Activity Statement. Accordingly, the net amount I'm actually paying (before closing costs) is $106,818.

➲ The rent of $11,500 is plus GST and is also annually indexed to inflation.

➲ The 'real' rental return is therefore 10.77% (that is, $11,500 ÷ $106,818).

➲ Unlike residential leases where the landlord has to pay for the rates and insurance, in a commercial lease it's the tenants who (usually) pay for the outgoings and, in my case, the upkeep of the property too. Therefore, the rent of $11,500 is net rather than gross.

➲ Bearing this in mind, so long as my interest rate was less than 10.77%, I could finance up to 100% of the purchase price and still end up with a positive cashflow outcome!

However, rather than take on a 100% loan, let's see how the numbers work out based on 90% financing.

The Numbers with a 90% Loan	
Cash Down	
10% deposit	$11,750
+ Closing costs (say 5%)	$5,875
– GST refund	$10,682
= Cash down	$6,943
Cashflow	
Rent	$11,500
– Interest	$8,460
= Cashflow	$3,040
Cash-on-Cash Return	
Cash back	$3,040
÷ Cash down	$6,943
	× 100
= CoCR	43.79%

I'm not sure about you, but a cash-on-cash return of 43.79% is a deal that I'd be happy to write home about. Just in case you're wondering, I came across this opportunity as a result of an existing relationship I had with a valued real estate agent. He knows what I'm looking for and I was the first person he called when he heard about the deal. I believe the property never actually hit the market, and it certainly wasn't advertised on the internet.

If you're interested in commercial property then bear in mind that the rules are slightly different than what you might have encountered before with residential houses. For example, the interest rate is generally 1% or 2% higher, and the loan establishment fees are higher too. Furthermore, because of the risk, banks usually only lend up to 70% of the purchase price and shorten the loan period to between 10 to 15 years.

One way you can get around the hassles of commercial lending is to redraw equity on residential investment properties and then use that money to pay for your commercial investment. This way you will get access to the cheaper residential housing interest rates in order to save interest and improve cashflow.

Steve's Investing Tip

If you can, try to use equity in residential real estate to avoid paying the higher interest associated with loans for commercial property.

Always remember though — the more you borrow, the higher the risk!

Approach 3: Falling Prices

As a result of the recent price boom, many properties that would have been positive cashflow in the past, would now be negatively geared because of the extra borrowing required to reach their new prices. However, in areas where prices have fallen from their peaks you may be able to again buy a positive cashflow outcome. I'd suggest targeting properties where deals can be negotiated rather than buying top-dollar solutions.

Approach 4: Negotiating Favourable Purchase Terms

While it may sound almost impossible, you can always try to negotiate a situation in which the vendor carries back some (or all) of the purchase price as a 0% loan. Clearly this will reduce the amount of interest you have to pay and will improve the cashflow outcome.

When negotiating, be mindful to meet the vendor with either the price paid or with the sale terms offered. That is, if you get your terms then you may have to give the vendor his or her price. For example, if you can negotiate with the vendor to carry back 30% of the purchase price as an interest-free loan, take a 50% loan from a mainstream lender and kick in the remaining 20% yourself, then this mix of finance will cut your interest cost and may turn a normally negative cashflow property into a positive one.

Approach 5: Borrowing Less Money

While most investors are trying to borrow as much as they can, cutting back on the amount of your loan reduces your interest cost. Since interest is the major expense in a property transaction, this technique will improve your cashflow profitability. Just be wary though, if you contribute too much money then you will lower your cash-on-cash return and this is a sign of 'lazy money' (see page 134). It's certainly only a fine line between borrowing too much, and borrowing too little!

Approach 6: Refinancing Your Loan

Lenders are now literally falling over themselves to attract new business by refinancing existing loans. Quite often you'll be able to save a substantial amount of interest by taking out a new loan at an interest rate that's a little lower. Make sure you do your sums though as costs and penalties for repaying the existing mortgage, as well as fees and charges on setting up a new loan can eat up a lot of your interest savings.

By the way, always ask for a discount off the advertised interest rate. Most lenders have established professional packages and various other affiliations, so the provision for a discount is there — all you need to do is figure out how you qualify to receive it.

Steve's Investing Tip

Always ask for a discount off your interest rate. You never know, you might actually get it!

Approach 7: 11 Ideas to Increase Rents

If you can't lower your expenses then another way to improve your cashflow is to increase the rent! A significant number of landlords are near-sighted with rent adjustments as they think they'll be upsetting their tenants by asking for more money. Personally, I don't believe that it takes much investing skill to charge an under-market rent. However, it takes a lot of nous to have a tenant happily accept to pay above-market rent.

Steve's Investing Tip

When negotiating, expect that you'll have to give something to get something. Don't expect something for nothing!

No-one likes to feel like they gave something for nothing, so the secret to negotiating a rental increase is to offer an incentive in return for the extra rent. You don't necessarily have to provide something expensive (particularly if it breaks easily!), however, offer something that the tenant will value. Here are 11 suggestions that you can use to negotiate a rental increase. Before using any of the tips please ensure that they are legal in your area as state residential tenancy laws can vary.

1. Offer a longer lease in exchange for a higher rent. Tenants may find this appealing as it provides them with more security and peace-of mind that they won't have to leave at a moment's notice.

2. Offer a rent-free period as an introduction to the new higher rent lease. You may only end up slightly ahead in the first year, but you'll make up lost ground in the years that follow.

3. Offer a rental rebate so that part of the rent is credited to a holding account and then refunded back at the end of every quarter, provided that certain conditions have been met (such as paying of rent on time or keeping the property in good repair).

4. If you have quality tenants that are vacating, offer them a bonus (cash, or movie tickets) for recommending friends who may want to move into the property. Experience shows that good tenants have friends who make good tenants too. Before the friends moves in, give them the option of paying a higher rent in exchange for an improvement or luxury (see below). This strategy also works well for finding good tenants for other vacant investment properties you may have.

5. Offer to rent furniture in accordance with the tenant's needs. Rarely does the whole house need furnishing, normally it's only a couch or dining suite or similar item. I suggest the extra rent you charge should recoup the cost of the furniture within 12 to 18 months.

6. Provide for access to technology as needed by the tenant. For example, it's common in student accommodation to provide unlimited broadband internet access. In return you charge a little extra rent per room which adds up to a lot overall.

7. Offer to improve the property in exchange for a rental increase. Ideas include lighting, heating, air conditioning, carpet or painting.

8. Provide quality second-hand items such as whitegoods and computer equipment. These can be bought cheaply on eBay, as can blinds, curtains and light fittings.

9. Charge a premium for allowing pets. Be sure to make it a condition of the lease that a 'pet bond' is paid, and that any pet-related damage is promptly fixed. Make sure there are at least quarterly inspections. Also include a clause that specifies that the house has to be treated for fleas once a year (and on leaving) at the tenant's expense.

10. As silly as it sounds, rent the garage out separately for those looking for some extra storage. Place ads in shop windows and also on bulletin boards. Be sure to check how this impacts on your insurance policy first though.

11. Rent the property by the bedroom rather than by the house. Before doing this make sure that you check council regulations to ensure you're not classified as running a boarding house. Check the wording and fineprint on your insurance policy too.

Approach 8: Buying, Subdividing and Selling to Repay Debt

Another possible strategy that you can use to end up with a positive cashflow outcome is to adopt the four-step approach of buying, subdividing, selling and then allocating some or all of the profit to repaying debt. That is, let's say you buy a rental property on a block that's large enough to subdivide. Next, engage the right advisers to arrange for the subdivision to create the new title(s). When ready, look to sell the subdivided land for a profit, and then use that profit to pay down the loan on the rented house at the front. The interest saving will hopefully result in a positive cashflow outcome for the remaining rental property.

Yet another option is to sell the property with building plans that have been approved by the local council. Be careful to properly research and to understand the planning regulations though since the rules can change dramatically from area to area and council to council.

Approach 9: Working the Ratio

You could also go one step further and actually build. Then, instead of selling everything, you could use the profits from the sale of some of the dwellings to pay down the loan on the remaining properties to the point where they were positive cashflow.

Martin Ayles, an expert property developer friend of mine, has applied this strategy to good effect. He works on the ratio of building five and selling four to keep one that's debt free. The remaining debt-free property is positive cashflow and, if needed, can be used as security for other investment loans. That is, the equity is not redrawn but the title is offered as additional security for debts that Martin carries on his other investment projects.

Approach 10: Using Lease Options

Instead of focusing on the property as a way of increasing the rent, another angle is to look at providing some kind of financing that helps the tenant eventually become the owner. One way you can do this is by offering a 'lease with an option to buy' (that is, a lease option). You can find more information about this strategy on <www.PropertyInvesting.com/leaseoption>, but the essence of the transaction is as follows.

⊃ Tenants agree to rent a property that they might like to own one day.

⊃ The landlord provides the tenant with an option to buy the rented property at an agreed price. This option must be exercised on or before a future agreed date.

⊃ In exchange for the option the tenant pays a once-off option fee (usually a few thousand dollars), plus a higher than normal market rent.

⊃ If the tenant exercises his or her option and goes ahead with the purchase then the option fee and a portion of the accumulated additional rent is treated as a credit against the agreed price.

The aim of a lease option is to provide the investor with a positive cashflow outcome on a property that would otherwise be neutral or negatively geared. The option fee is designed to subsidise the amount of cash the investor needed to buy the investment in the first place. This can be a very effective strategy provided you can find someone interested in taking it up.

Approach 11: Using Vendor Financing

While some see it as a controversial strategy, vendor financing has been successfully used as a means of selling property for well over 100 years. Unfortunately, the technique has been abused by some unscrupulous investors and now it tends to have a bad name.

Nevertheless, provided all parties are aware of the risks and benefits, vendor financing offers a way for those who can't access mainstream lending to own a home rather than renting. Here's how it works:

⊃ When you sell a property you have a choice of either accepting a full cash settlement or otherwise self-financing the purchaser for some or all of the purchase price paid.

➲ Purchasers are not registered as the owners on title until the last payment is made, but they are completely responsible for the property as if they were the owners. That is, they have the right to live in the house at the same time as having the responsibility for paying the rates, insurance and repairs.

➲ In exchange for offering vendor finance the purchase price may be slightly higher to reflect the extra risk in the transaction. This is not dissimilar to what is offered in the retail market where purchases on credit attract a higher price.

➲ Interest is charged on the vendor financed amount at an agreed rate, with the loan being repaid on agreed terms.

Really, vendor finance provides investors with the opportunity to build income streams by making a margin on the difference between their loan repayments and their mortgages, and the vendor finance repayment they receive from their purchasers. The Consumer Credit Code applies to vendor financing, which means that it's very important to obtain accurate legal advice before proceeding with this strategy.

If you'd like more information on vendor financing then visit <www.PropertyInvesting.com/wraps>.

Approach 12: Using Second Mortgage Finance

If vendor financing isn't your cup of tea then another take on the same concept is to carry back part of your sale price as a second mortgage. Under this strategy the title of the property immediately transfers into the name of the purchaser.

Normally the purchaser will use some kind of financing and his or her lender will therefore look to gain the security of a registered first mortgage. Since the first mortgage position is taken, the best you can do is stand next in line (that is, take a second mortgage) to protect the portion of the sale price that you've left behind as a loan. Second mortgage funding usually commands a premium interest rate that is about 5% higher than the standard home loan rate.

Here's an example of a second mortgage: Let's say that you're looking to sell an investment property for $200,000. Bob is an interested buyer but has a problem in that he's only got a $20,000 deposit and approved finance of $150,000.

Untroubled, you offer to sell him the property for $210,000 on the basis that he pays you his $20,000 deposit plus the $150,000 from his financier, and then you'll carry back a $40,000 second mortgage at 12% interest. You also specify the repayment terms, which in this case will be (say) loan repayments of $1,000 per month over four years with the remaining balance due at the end as a balloon payment.

Converting your equity into an interest-bearing loan is a creative way of establishing a positive cashflow outcome. Again, if you want to go down this road then seek expert legal advice.

HOW TO CONVERT A NEGATIVELY GEARED DISASTER INTO A POSITIVELY GEARED GOLDMINE

The final area I want to touch on in this chapter is a quick re-application of the options outlined above since they can also provide solutions for investors looking to convert properties from negative to positive cashflow. As I see it there are four broad possibilities:

1. Increase Rents

The aim is to increase the income to not only cover the higher costs, but to also provide a positive cashflow surplus.

2. Decrease Costs

You can tinker with cost savings such as self-managing the property, but the flipside is that you'll lose time and suffer increased stress.

You'll have the biggest impact by targeting interest savings, and this can be done by refinancing to a cheaper rate or else looking to repay slabs of debt. One way you can do this is by banking a quick profit by subdividing or developing part of the block and applying the proceeds to paying off the loan on the remaining income-producing dwelling.

3. Convert the Property to a Loan

Really, aside from trying to increase the rent or decrease the costs, another option is to convert the asset into some sort of loan, thereby securing an income stream from the interest charged.

Whether you use a lease option, vendor-financed sale or second mortgage will depend on the circumstances of the interested buyer. Whatever you do, make sure the potential buyer can afford the repayments as the last thing you want is the grief and hassle of a repossession.

4. Sell

The old saying 'before you can get out of a hole you have to stop digging' can also be applied to negatively geared property too. That is, sometimes selling is the quickest and best way to eliminate a loss! I can understand that selling means your pride may take a fall, but it's better than suffering the humiliation of going broke. You can then spend the money that you were putting towards your weekly mortgage payments and save up for a deposit on a positively geared investment.

SUMMARY

There's been quite a lot of practical information covered in this chapter. Before moving on I suggest you take a few moments to think about which new ideas you can implement to improve the profitability of your own investing.

Having now given you plenty of tips about cash (growth) and cashflow (income) property, next we'll turn our attention to deal evaluation, beginning with some magic money-making formulas.

Chapter 13 Insights

Insight #1:

Positive cashflow deals do exist, but just not necessarily in the form you may expect or in bold print on page three of your local paper.

Insight #2:

While you can buy a positive cashflow property outright, such deals are the exception rather than the norm. Usually you'll need to apply skill and creativity by bringing together various components and options.

Insight #3:

One approach to achieving a positive cashflow outcome is to increase income and/or decrease costs. Another alternative is to convert your property into an interest-bearing loan.

Insight #4:

A negative cashflow property can be converted to positive cashflow if you change your thinking away from waiting for growth and instead become more proactive in working the deal.

Working the Five Money-Making Formulas

One of my favourite memories from primary school was our regular 'Battle of the Times Tables'. The teacher would call up two students to the front of the class and then fire off questions to test how well we had mastered our maths. 'What's eight times five?' the teacher would ask. Whoever was first in with the correct answer three out of five times earned the right to challenge another pupil. If you were the daily winner then you received a prize plus the right to be the carry over victor for the next day's contest.

Yes, I know, this sounds a little sad now, but at the time it was enormous fun, and there was a lot of playground 'cred' given to the Grand Champion — the child who won the grade round-robin tournament. Unfortunately, my mathematical glory days at primary school were short lived. By the time I hit year nine I was stuck in remedial maths with the other less able students. Given this revelation, you may be wondering how and why I became an accountant. Well, accounting has more to do with times-tables than it does calculus, so I was really in my element!

Like maths, investing can seem full of jargon and complexities, but if you can break up each concept into bite-sized bits, then you can quickly learn and apply a few handy tricks. If you aren't particularly good at maths then breathe easy — you don't need to be an Australian representative in the Maths Olympiad to be able to understand and to accurately crunch the numbers in a property deal.

In this chapter I'll explain the five key formulas used to measure property investing returns. Relax, it will be quite straightforward, but we're really just warming up. In the next chapter, we'll turn up the heat and address some trickier issues.

THE FIVE KEY PROPERTY RETURN FORMULAS

If you can learn to recognise these figures it will allow you to cut through the jargon and understand what you are truly measuring when you talk about investment returns. The five key property investing formulas are as follows.

1. Gross Rental Return (GRR)

You calculate the gross rental return by dividing the (gross) annual rent by the asset's purchase price.

$$\frac{\text{Annual rent}}{\text{Purchase price}} \times \frac{100}{1}$$

Unless you have a specific reason for doing so, the annual rent doesn't need to be adjusted for vacancies or rental management commission — it's simply the amount that the tenant pays per annum. Also, be sure to use the rent as it is — don't be persuaded to use some potentially inflated figure that a real estate agent tells you is a more accurate reflection of market value. Often, if I'm calculating the gross rental return to help me formulate how much I can afford to pay for a property and still meet my profit objective, agents will try to influence the numbers I use. For example, it's common to hear, 'The property is currently rented for $210 per week, but I think this is a little low — it should be $230 per week'.

My response when I'm told this is, 'Well, I'll pay more if you get the tenant to sign a new lease at that higher amount, otherwise my offer will need to be based on how things are at the moment'.

A technique you can use to test the accuracy of what the agent tells you is to say, 'Okay, if you think that's the case, how about we make the new lease at the higher rent a condition of my purchase'. If the agent starts doing a massive amount of back-peddalling then you know to be wary.

Steve's Investing Tip

When crunching the numbers, use the rent as it is now rather than some potentially achievable higher amount.

As far as the purchase price is concerned, use the price as stated on the contract. Unless there's a compelling reason, don't include closing or other costs.

One exception to this rule would be if I was doing a renovation project. In this case I'd calculate the gross rental return based on the following two sets of figures and compare the results:

1. on the figures that existed at the time of purchase, and

2. figures in which I add any renovation costs to my purchase price and the expected additional income to my annual rent.

If the after-renovation return wasn't substantially higher then the only way the project would make sense would be if you could add more value to the property than the cost of the renovation.

Applying the Gross Rental Return

Right! It's time to stretch those mental muscles! Grab a pen and a calculator and have a go at trying to apply the GRR formula. As an example, let's imagine that you're looking at buying a property that currently rents for $450 per week. The agent tells you that the asking price is $300,000. What do you think the gross rental return is?

Calculating the Gross Rental Return	
Annual rent	$
÷ Purchase price	$
	× 100
= Gross rental return	%

A suggested solution is located at the end of the chapter.

My answer is 7.8% and this means that each investment dollar contributes 7.8 cents of gross rent. One way you can interpret this result is to compare it to the interest rate you would pay on your borrowings if you had 100% finance. For example, if your investment loan attracted interest at (say) 8.5%, and your gross rental return was 7.8% then, before any other cost was considered, you should expect an annual cashflow loss of 0.7% of the purchase price (see the table below).

An Annual Cashflow Loss		
	% Purchase Price	$
Gross rental return	7.8%	$23,400
– Interest	–8.5%	–$25,500
= Expected negative cashflow	–0.7%	–$2,100

In order to be profitable, this investment would need annual capital growth of substantially more than $2,100 in order to cover the other non-interest costs.

As you can see, the gross rental return is a quick but simplistic measure. It has its uses, but I wouldn't rely on it in isolation.

2. Return on Investment (ROI)

Given its profit focus, return on investment is a favourite amongst the accounting profession. Here's the formula.

$$\frac{\text{Annual profit}}{\text{Purchase price}} \times \frac{100}{1}$$

This figure's not an ideal measure for property investors because the underlying formula doesn't properly take into account that properties are generally bought using mostly borrowed money. Specifically, while interest is included in the profit figure, there's an assumption that the entire purchase price is paid in cash. Clearly this calculation is not ideal for investors who use leverage to buy multiple properties. Another shortfall in the formula is that unless the property is sold, capital appreciation will not be included in the profit figure.

Traditionally, accountants use ROI to determine how much income each asset generates. As such, a ROI of 10% means there's a contribution of 10 cents of profit for each dollar of asset owned.

Your Turn

Have a go at calculating the ROI for a property based on the following information.

Numbers for Return on Investment (ROI) Calculation	
Purchase price	$300,000
Annual rent	$23,400
Rental management	9% of rent collected
Loan interest	$19,079
Rates, insurance, etc.	$2,500

Return on Investment (ROI) Calculation	
Step 1: Calculate Profit	
Annual rent[1]	$
– Rental management	$
– Loan interest	$
– Rates, insurance, etc.	$
= Profit / (loss)	$
Step 2: Calculate ROI	
Profit / (loss) *(from step 1)*	$
÷ Purchase price	$
	× 100
= ROI	%

[1] For simplicity reasons, assume no vacancies.

A suggested solution is located at the end of the chapter.

My answer was –0.095%, which means that the property loses nearly one tenth of one cent per dollar of asset invested. Since ROI has a limited use for real estate investors, I don't spend a lot of time tinkering with the formula.

3. Cash-on-Cash Return (CoCR)

Our next formula is my favourite. I have a strong preference for using cash-on-cash returns since the formula calculates the cash return for each cash dollar contributed, taking into account that much of the purchase price will be borrowed.

$$\frac{\text{Cash back}}{\text{Cash down}} \times \frac{100}{1}$$

A CoCR of 20% means that every dollar of cash contributed will return $1.20 as a cash payment — that is, the dollar contributed plus an additional 20 cents.

A huge plus is the fact that the formula includes both the interest cost and the loan repayment in the 'cash back' figure, as well as the amount of cash that you've paid to acquire and improve the asset in the 'cash down' figure.

Here are the steps involved in calculating a cash-on-cash return.

- ⮑ Work out how much cash you need to purchase and complete the investment. This is your 'cash down' figure.

- ⮑ Work out how much cash you're going to receive back from the investment. This is your 'cash back' figure.

- ⮑ Divide your 'cash back' by your 'cash down'.

- ⮑ Finally, multiply the result by 100 to turn your fraction into a percentage.

It's up to you to decide on what time basis you'd calculate the CoCR. It can be done either on the project as a whole or, alternatively, as an annual return. Either and both can be appropriate depending on your needs.

Have a go at trying to calculate the annual CoCR given the following variables.

Numbers for Cash-on-Cash Return (CoCR) Calculation	
Purchase price	$300,000
Deposit	20%
Closing costs	5% of purchase cost
Weekly rent[1]	$450 per week
Loan repayments[2]	$427.12 per week
Rental management	9% of rent collected
Rates, insurance, etc.	$2,500

[1] For simplicity, assume there are no vacancies.

[2] Weekly loan repayments on a $240,000 principal and interest loan at 8% per annum over 25 years.

Cash-on-Cash Return (CoCR) Calculation	
Step 1: Calculate Cash Down	
Deposit	$
+ Closing costs	$
= Total cash down	$
Step 2: Calculate Cash Back	
Annual rent	$
– Loan repayments	$
– Management fees	$
– Rates, insurance, etc.	$
= Total cash back	$
Steps 3 and 4: Calculate the CoCR	
Cash back *(from step 2)*	$
÷ Cash down *(from step 1)*	$
Step 3	× 100
= CoCR *(step 4)*	%

A suggested solution is located at the end of the chapter.

How did you go? My answer was –4.55%, which means you'll only receive back $0.95 for every dollar of cash that you've contributed. Cashflow orientated investors won't need me to tell them that this is a poor outcome.

The Risk-Free Return Comparison

Having calculated your CoCR, you can then compare it back to the percentage interest that you could have earned had you simply left your cash in the bank. For example, using the numbers in this example, from a cashflow perspective you could have left your money in the bank earning annual interest at (say) 5%, instead of investing in this deal and losing 4.55% per annum.

Do you accurately and carefully consider what else you could be doing with your money to make sure you are maximising your returns? If not, make it a habit to do so from now on.

Steve's Investing Tip

Your investments need to do more than just make money, they need to outperform all other options, one of which is the interest you could earn if you left your cash in the bank.

4. Growth-on-Equity Return (GoER)

A large number of property investors aim for medium- to long-term growth under a buy and hold strategy, so capital appreciation is their number one goal. This means that the cash-on-cash return formula is less relevant and perhaps only useful in quantifying the minimum growth needed to cover their cashflow loss.

The formula that investors seeking growth returns should apply is the growth-on-equity return (GoER). Here's how it works:

$$\frac{\text{Expected annual growth}}{\text{Current equity}} \times \frac{100}{1}$$

1. Quantify the amount of the annual capital appreciation that you desire from your property in dollar terms. This is your 'annual growth' figure.

    A word of warning: make sure you're sympathetic to the current market conditions when setting your desired annual growth, since a silly expectation will lead to an unachievable outcome.

2. Calculate your 'current equity' in the property. This is done by subtracting the amount you owe on the mortgage from the property's current market value.

Equity = Current Market Value – Total Debt Owing

> **Notes:**
>
> If you've used a line of credit or other facility instead of cash to help pay for your purchase, then include that additional debt in the amount owing.
>
> I'd suggest ascertaining the 'current market value' figure by asking a local real estate agent to give you an appraised (not sworn) value. This should be free.

3. Now you have the variables, divide your 'annual growth' by your 'equity'.

4. Finally, multiply the result by 100 to turn your fraction into a percentage.

Do you think you've got it figured out? Let's see as you try to calculate the GoER formula using the same theoretical property as before, except let's now assume that we're three years into the future.

Numbers for Growth-on-Equity Return (GoER) Calculation	
Estimated current market value	$350,000
Your expected annual growth	$25,000
Current loan balance owing	$229,801

Growth-on-Equity Return (GoER) Calculation	
Step 1: Annual Growth	
Your expected annual growth	$
Step 2: Equity	
Current market value	$
– Current loan balance	$
= Total current equity	$

Growth-on-Equity Return (GoER) Calculation *(cont'd)*	
Steps 3 and 4: GoER Calculation	
Your desired annual growth *(from step 1)*	$
÷ equity *(from step 2)*	$
Step 3	× 100
= GoER *(step 4)*	%

Once again, you can find the solution to this exercise at the end of the chapter.

My answer was 20.8%, and this means that my current equity is earning a return of 20.8 cents in the dollar. This seems quite good when compared to what I could achieve if I sold and put the money in the bank, but whether or not it is exceptional depends on what return I could obtain from other investment opportunities.

For example, how would your assessment change if you could take that equity and invest it in another property with a growth-on-equity return of 40%? Perhaps 20.8% would no longer seem so attractive.

5. Net Profit Percentage (NPP)

Of course, because most property investments involve a combination of both cashflow and growth, it's potentially near-sighted to concentrate solely on one or the other. Accordingly, a formula measuring both offers a powerful and balanced view of the net profitability of your real estate investment. Here it is.

$$\frac{\text{Annual cashflow} + \text{Annual expected growth}}{\text{Cash down}} \times 100$$

You have already identified or calculated the variables, so all you need to do is:

1. Add your 'net cashflow' and 'expected growth' figures.

2. Divide the result by your 'cash down' figure.

3. Multiply this number by 100 to turn your fraction into a percentage.

Using the table below, have a go at trying to work out the net profit percentage using the same information presented for the previous two examples.

Net Profit Percentage Calculation	
Net cash flow (page 248)	$
+ Expected annual growth	$
= Profit	$
÷ Cash down[1]	$
	× 100
Net profit percentage	%

[1] If you've used the equity in another property as a substitute for cash, include the redrawn equity in your 'cash down' figure.

Once again, at the end of the chapter you can check your answer. My answer was 28.78% which means that I will receive back 28.78 cents in net profit (combined cashflow and growth) for each dollar I contributed to buy the investment.

HOW OFTEN SHOULD YOU CHECK THE RETURNS?

I suggest that you crunch all five returns during your prepurchase analysis. Should you end up buying the property, then I'd also crunch the numbers as often as shown in the table opposite.

For example, at the start of the year I'd set a target gross rental return, and then I'd compare my actual result achieved at the end of the year. I'd monitor the cashflow return monthly since a blow out could cause a financial catastrophe. Unless the market were booming or crashing, checking the growth twice a year should be sufficient.

Naturally, you'd calculate the returns even more frequently where the circumstances warranted closer attention.

Timetable for Checking Returns		
	Set a Benchmark	Monitor Actual Results
Gross rental return (GRR)	Annually	Annually
Return on investment (ROI)	Annually	Annually
Cash-on-cash return (CoCR)	Biannually	Monthly
Growth-on-equity return (GoER)	Biannually	Biannually
Net profit percentage (NPP)	Biannually	Biannually

Will You Apply This Knowledge?

How often will you crunch the numbers? Don't risk having a financial heart attack through ignorance. Be sure to budget and then regularly monitor the returns.

Now I've taken you through the investing theory, I'll raise the bar in the next chapter even higher as I take you through my 3–2–1 approach to working out whether the return you've calculated is high enough to justify the risk of the investment.

Stay tuned as in the next chapter you're about to discover my new 'Three Second Solution'!

SOLUTIONS TO CHAPTER CALCULATIONS

Solution for Return on Investment (ROI) Calculation	
Step 1: Calculate Profit	
Annual rent	$23,400
– Rental management	$2,106
– Loan interest	$19,079
– Rates, insurance, etc.	$2,500
= Profit / (loss)	–$285
Step 2: Calculate ROI	
Profit / (loss) *(from step 1)*	–$285
÷ Purchase price	$300,000
	x 100
= ROI	–0.10%

Solution to Cash-on-Cash Return Calculation	
Step 1: Calculate Cash Down	
Deposit	$60,000
+ Closing costs	$15,000
= Total cash down	$75,000
Step 2: Calculate Cash Back	
Annual rent	$23,400
– Loan repayments	$22,210
– Management fees	$2,106
– Rates, insurance, etc.	$2,500
= Total cash back	–$3,416
Steps 3 and 4: Calculate the CoCR	
Cash back *(from step 2)*	–$3,416
÷ Cash down *(from step 1)*	$75,000
Step 3	x 100
= CoCR *(step 4)*	–4.55%

Solution to Growth-on-Equity Return (GoER) Calculation	
Step 1: Annual Growth	
Your expected annual growth	$25,000
Step 2: Equity	
Current market value	$350,000
– Current loan balance	$229,801
= Total current equity	$120,199
Steps 3 and 4: GoER Calculation	
Your expected annual growth (from step 1)	$25,000
÷ equity (from step 2)	$120,199
Step 3	x 100
= GoER (step 4)	20.8%

Solution to Net Profit Percentage Calculation	
Net cashflow	–$3,416
+ Expected annual growth	$25,000
= Profit	$21,584
÷ Cash down	$75,000
	x 100
Net profit percentage	28.78%

Chapter 14 Insights

Insight #1:

You don't need to be a genius at maths to be able to calculate the five key property investing returns. You just need to be diligent and accurate.

Insight #2:

If you're not already monitoring your investment performance then it's time to pull your finger out! Ignorance leads to losses and missed opportunities.

Insight #3:

My two favourite returns are the cash-on-cash return and the growth-on-equity return, as the combination of the two provides a powerful deal evaluation formula that considers both the cashflow and the growth aspects to your investment.

Insight #4:

Make sure you keep a watchful eye on the five key property returns. A quick proactive correction is usually enough to get an asset back on track when a problem is identified early. However, if you leave it too long then you may end up with an incurable loss.

Revealed: 3–2–1 to Easy Deal Evaluations

Do you know how to confidently assess whether an investment's return is worth the risk of buying it? Not long ago Paul approached me during the break of one of my property seminars to ask me about this very issue. He waited patiently as I outlined how I use the net profit percentage calculation before replying, 'Steve, I know how to calculate the percentage — I just don't know how to tell whether or not it's high enough to make the deal attractive'.

The ability to accurately evaluate a potential deal is an essential skill that every real estate investor must acquire. Otherwise, how will you ever know whether the property you're considering is a goldmine or a goose?

Having evaluated literally thousands of properties over the past seven years, I've devised and implemented many different ways to test whether or not the investment return justifies the risk. Today,

I've finetuned the process to make it as easy as 3–2–1. In other words, I quickly take the following action:

- work out the 'Three Second Solution'

- make sure my profit is at least twice the interest paid, and

- calculate a Danger Money Multiple.

Before I share with you how these three powerful techniques work, I'd like to first address an issue that keeps cropping up. Is the '11 Second Solution' test introduced in my first book, *From 0 to 130 Properties in 3.5 Years*, still valid?

DOES THE '11 SECOND SOLUTION' STILL APPLY?

Just in case you haven't read my first book (or alternatively if you need reminding) the '11 Second Solution' is my simple formula that calculates the maximum purchase price you should pay for a property and still expect it to earn a net positive cashflow return. Here's how you can do it:

- identify the current weekly rent

- divide the weekly rent by two, and

- multiply the result by 1,000.

11 Second Solution

Maximum purchase price =
(Weekly rent ÷ 2) × 1,000

Let's imagine that you're interested in buying a property that currently rents for $300 per week. Applying my '11 Second

Solution', the maximum purchase price you should pay and still expect a positive cashflow return is $150,000 (see below).

➲ weekly rent = $300

➲ weekly rent divided by two ($300 ÷ 2) = $150

➲ result multiplied by 1,000 = $150,000.

A lot has happened since the release of my first book. In particular, home values have boomed and interest rates have substantially increased. Nowadays, not only is it more difficult to find an advertised property that meets the '11 Second Solution' requirements, but even if you could locate one, higher interest rate costs mean that there's no guarantee the result would be positive cashflow anyway.

Nevertheless, I'm not ready to write off the '11 Second Solution'. As outlined in chapter 13, positive cashflow deals do exist, and at the very least the technique provides a yardstick to gauge how far out of the positive cashflow range a property may be.

For example, if you're looking at a property that has a weekly rent of $150 and is on the market for $200,000, you can still quickly do the maths to determine that an indicative positive cashflow purchase price would be $75,000, and that $200,000 is a long way away out of the positive cashflow zone.

Don't worry too much about the seemingly limited application of the '11 Second Solution'. With more experience and wisdom, I've created a revised formula that's much easier to use and even more effective. Tongue in cheek I'm calling it 'The Three Second Solution'.

TEST 1: THE THREE SECOND SOLUTION

In the last chapter I showed you how to calculate and apply the five key property investing returns, including the cash-on-cash return, the growth-on-equity return, and the net profit percentage.

In order to pass the 'Three Second Solution', the net profit percentage must be at least three times the average percentage interest rate you pay on your property debt.

Three Second Solution

Net profit percentage must equal at least three times the average interest rate percentage.

For example, if your property loan attracted an average interest rate[1] of 7%, then your net profit percentage would need to be at least 21% to achieve a pass.

Have a go at working out the 'Three Second Solution' in the following circumstances.

Calculating Three-Second Solutions		
Scenario 1		
You borrow 80% of the purchase price from the ABC bank on an interest-only loan at 6%.	Average interest rate (%)	%
		× 3
	Three second solution	%
Scenario 2		
You borrow 100% of the purchase price from the XYZ bank using a principal and interest loan at 8%, but the interest is capitalised for 12 months.	Average interest rate (%)	%
		× 3
	Three second Solution	%

---

[1] By average interest rate I mean the percentage paid for each loan product that comprises the overall property debt.

Calculating Three-Second Solutions *(cont'd)*		
Scenario 3		
You borrow 100% of the purchase price from a private money lender who charges 18% interest per annum.	Average interest rate (%)	%
		× 3
	Three second solution	%
Scenario 4		
You purchase an investment property for $200,000 and borrow $160,000 from the KLM bank at 8% and use $40,000 against a line of credit on your home. The line of credit attracts interest at 6%.	Average interest rate (%)	%
		× 3
	Three second solution	%

The first three were actually really simple weren't they? The solution for the fourth scenario is a little more complicated because you need to work out the average interest rate paid. Here are the required net profit percentages for each scenario:

1.   18% (calculated as 6% × 3)

2.   24% (calculated as 8% × 3)

3.   54% (calculated as 18% × 3)

4.   22.8% (see below).

The table overleaf shows how I went about calculating the result for scenario four.

Time management is the real benefit of this tool. Professional investors look over so many deals that having a handy way to quickly sort out those that may make money from those that probably won't becomes critical.

Sometimes you may elect to set the 'Three Second Solution' benchmark at more than three times the average interest rate. For example, I'd require a much higher return for a rural or country property than a regional or metropolitan property, since the risk of vacancy would be higher and the prospects for resale are more limited in rural areas with lower populations.

As a minimum though, a net profit percentage of at least three times the average interest rate paid on your property debt is a good start.

The Average Interest Rate in Scenario Four			
Interest on:	Interest (%)	% Total Debt	Average Interest (%)
Investment borrowings	8%	80%	6.4%[1]
Line of credit	6%	20%	1.2%[2]
Average debt			7.6%
			× 3
Three second solution			22.8%

[1] 80% × 8% = 6.4%.
[2] 20% × 6% = 1.2%.

Example: Three Second Solution

Let's look at an example based on 'Project X', a theoretical property deal that's just come across your desk. In weighing up whether or not to buy it, you have the following two financing options:

Option 1: Borrowing 80% of the purchase price

Option 2: Borrowing 95% of the purchase price.

The table opposite contains the financial variables under each option. With this information, have a go at trying to calculate the 'Three Second Solution' for each option in the second and third tables on the page opposite. **Note:** You can check your answer against the solution at the end of the chapter.

The Financial Variables		
	Option 1: **80% Borrowing**	**Option 2:** **95% Borrowing**
Purchase price	$250,000	$250,000
Deposit	$50,000	$12,500
Closing costs	$12,500	$17,000[1]
Cash down	$62,500	$29,500
Cash back	$8,125	$3,450[2]
Interest rate	7%	8.5%
Interest paid	$14,000	$20,200
Desired annual growth	$20,000	$20,000

[1] The closing costs are higher in Option 2 because of mortgage insurance and once-off loan fees for the higher borrowings.

[2] The cash back figure is substantially lower under Option 2 because of the extra interest cost.

Net Profit Percentage		
	Option 1	**Option 2**
Cash back	$	$
+ Desired annual growth	$	$
= Total profit	$	$
÷ Cash down	$	$
Cash back	× 100	× 100
Net profit percentage	%	%

Pass or Fail		
	Option 1	**Option 2**
Average interest rate	%	%
	× 3	× 3
Three second solution	%	%
Net profit percentage	%	%
Pass/Fail		

My answer sees both options pass the 'Three Second Solution' with net profit percentage figures of 45% for Option 1 and 79.5% for Option 2.

TEST 2: PROFIT = TWO × INTEREST PAID

The danger in basing your investment decision solely on the net profit percentage is that there's likely to be a bias towards projects that use little of your own money (since these dramatically increase the NPP). This bias can be dangerous though, since higher borrowings mean greater investment risk.

For example, basing your decision on the net profit percentage, which financing option would you go for? Most investors would choose Option 2 and take out a 95% loan since it provides a net profit percentage of 79.5%. However, on the flip side, the cash back figure under Option 2 is only $4,675 (around 57% less than Option 1). Considering the increased risk of borrowing such a large amount of the purchase price, and also the reduced cash back amount, perhaps Option 2 isn't the most attractive after all.

To guard against the bias of a skewed net profit percentage, I add another level of scrutiny to my deal evaluation. It's called the '2 x Interest Paid' test. It requires that in addition to your net profit percentage being three times your average interest rate (in percentage terms), the amount of your (cashflow + growth) profit in dollar terms be at least twice the interest paid too.[2]

Profit = 2 × Interest Paid Test

Cashflow + growth = At least 2 × Interest paid.

---

[2] If you're capitalising your interest, then treat it as if it was paid in cash in this case.

With this in mind, use the tables below to determine whether Option 1 and Option 2, from our last example, pass the '2 × Interest Paid' test.

Profit in Dollars		
	Option 1	Option 2
Cash back	$	$
+ Desired annual growth	$	$
= Total profit	$	$

Pass or Fail		
	Option 1	Option 2
Interest paid	$	$
	× 2	× 2
2 × Interest paid	$	$
Total profit	$	$
Pass / fail		

A worked solution is included at the end of the chapter.

Option 1 passes while Option 2 fails as the total profit is not twice the expected interest paid. Despite the attractive net profit percentage, my conclusion would be that Option 2 is not worth the risk associated with the investment.

Even though Option 1 has passed both tests thus far, it would also need to get the green light on the third test in my arsenal — the Danger Money Multiple test — before I would seriously consider buying the property.

TEST 3: THE DANGER MONEY MULTIPLE (DMM)

The final piece in the deal evaluation jigsaw puzzle is called the Danger Money Multiple test.

This calculation builds in a risk assessment for:

➲ the percentage of the purchase price borrowed (as mentioned, the more you borrow the higher the risk associated with the investment), and

➲ the skill and experience of the investor (if you're inexperienced or unskilled then there's a higher likelihood that you'll make an expensive mistake).

The first step to implementing the Danger Money Multiple is to gain an appreciation of how to calculate the risk-free return.

Risk-Free Returns

Since every investment carries with it the possibility of making a loss, a 'Danger Money' premium needs to exist to make a property project worthwhile. In deciding how much of a Danger Money premium is appropriate, it's worthwhile to calculate your risk-free return. This is how much interest you'd earn if you left your cash in the bank rather than using it to purchase the investment property.[3]

Let's see if you can calculate the risk-free return for Option 1 and Option 2 from our previous example, assuming that you could earn 5% interest by leaving your cash in the bank.

The Risk-Free Return		
	Option 1: 80% Borrowing	Option 2: 95% Borrowing
Cash down	$	$
× Interest percentage		
= Risk-free return	$	$

You can check your calculations against those in the solution at the end of the chapter. My answer was $3,125 for Option 1 and $1,475 for Option 2.

---

[3] If you're using equity rather than cash to fund the purchase, use the amount of interest payable on that equity redraw.

Danger Money Multiple

Having done the calculation, the next step is to weigh up whether or not our Danger Money premium is high enough above the risk-free return to justify taking on the danger associated with the investment. For example, in Option 1 my profit was $28,125 and my risk-free return was $3,125. Therefore, is a Danger Money premium of $25,000 enough to accept Option 1? It's hard to say since investing skills and risk tolerance will vary from investor to investor.

One way that you can interpret the risk-to-return relationship for an investment is to work out how many risk-free returns are included in the profit amount. I call this figure the Danger Money Multiple.

Danger Money Multiple

Danger Money Multiple = Profit ÷ Risk-free return

Have a go at calculating this figure for Option 1 and Option 2 by completing the following table.

How Many Risk-Free Returns Are in the Profit Amount?		
	Option 1: 80% Borrowing	Option 2: 95% Borrowing
Cash back	$	$
+ Desired annual growth	$	$
= Total profit	$	$
÷ Risk-free return	$	$
= Danger money multiple	$	$

The solution at the end of the chapter reveals that the Danger Money Multiple is 9 for Option 1 and 15.9 for Option 2.

Generally, the higher the Danger Money Multiple, the more attractive the investment becomes. However, before making a final decision, you also need to consider the DMM against two other variables:

1. the percentage of the purchase price that you're borrowing, and

2. your skill and experience as an investor as it relates to the investing strategy you're implementing.

The matrix below contains my suggested minimum Danger Money Multiples.

Suggested Minimum Danger Money Multiples				
		Your Skill and Experience with the Investing Strategy Being Implemented		
Debt risk	% LCMVR¹	Novice	Average	Expert
Low	<70%	5+	9+	8+
Medium	70% to 85%	7+	6+	5+
High	>85%	12+	11+	10+

¹ LCMVR stands for Loan-to-Current Market Value Ratio and represents the percentage of debt to the property's current market value.

I can understand that this may seem a little confusing, but let's look at an example of how to read the matrix. Let's say you're considering a renovation project. You've done a couple before, so you rate yourself as having average skill and experience. You are planning to borrow 80% of the value of the property. Looking up the matrix you find that the minimum DMM required is seven plus (the intersection of medium debt risk and average investing skill and experience). In practice, this means that your profit must be at least seven times your risk-free return in order for the project to be worth the investment risk.

Have a go at trying to work out the minimum DMM to qualify a deal for consideration in the following circumstances.

Minimum Danger Money Multiples	
Circumstance	Min. Req. DMM
Annette, a brand new investor, is looking to purchase a negatively geared buy and hold property. She plans to borrow 65% of the purchase price.	
Brent is a sophisticated investor who has purchased 20 positive cashflow properties. He finds another positive cashflow deal, but it requires he contribute 20% of his own money.	
Lisa has done two previous renovations and is looking to do a four-unit subdivision and development. She has the opportunity to borrow 80% of the purchase price and plans to use the equity in her home for the remaining 20%.	
Damian, a carpenter, has owned an investment property for three years. He now plans to renovate and sell it. He doesn't like risk and has no debt.	

My assessment of each investor's required DMM is as follows.

Steve's Assessment			
	Debt risk	Skill level	Min. DMM
Annette	Low	Novice	5+
Brent	Medium	Expert	5+
Lisa	High	Novice[1]	12+
Damian	Low	Average	9+

[1] I rated Lisa as a novice given that renovations are not the same as subdivisions and developments.

While there is always going to be an element of subjectivity in assessing your skill and the condition of a market, to ensure that there is not a huge gulf between our definitions (which would render the tool useless), I've included some broad guidelines in Appendix B. Refer to these if you're having trouble categorising yourself or the markets in which you invest.

Summary of Each Combination

Another way of summarising the DMM Matrix is to reorganise it to reveal the investment risk rather than a numeric multiple required. I have done this for you below.

Suggested Minimum Danger Money Multiples				
		Your Skill and Experience with the Investing Strategy Being Implemented		
Debt risk	% LCMVR	Novice	Average	Expert
Low	<70%	Medium risk	Low risk	Low risk
Medium	70% to 85%	Medium risk	Medium risk	Medium risk
High	>85%	High risk	High risk	Medium risk

As you can see, the riskiest investments are those in which you borrow more than 85% of the purchase price at the same time as having little or average skill. At the other extreme, the lowest risk investments are those in which you have high or average skill and where your debt is only a small percentage of the property's current value.

Danger Money Multiple Example

Let's go back and analyse the Danger Money Multiple for Option 1 and Option 2 from the example examined earlier. As you can see in the table opposite, both options pass the Danger Money Multiple test, although investors with substantial skill may view Option 1 as borderline.

The Danger Money Multiples in Example Scenarios				
	Option 1: 80% Borrowing		Option 2: 95% Borrowing	
Danger money multiple	9		15.9	
Assessed debt risk	Medium		High	
Skill Level Required	DMM Needed	Pass?	DMM Needed	Pass?
Novice	7+	✓	12+	✓
Average	6+	✓	11+	✓
Expert	5+	✓	10+	✓

Let's summarise by looking back over the three tests we discussed. The table below shows how each option rated.

The Three Test Results Collated		
	Option 1: 80% Borrowing	Option 2: 95% Borrowing
Three second solution	✓ Pass	✓ Pass
2 × interest paid	✓ Pass	✗ Fail
Danger Money Multiple		
Novice	✓ Pass	✓ Pass
Average	✓ Pass	✓ Pass
Expert	✓ Pass	✓ Pass
Overall	✓ Pass	✗ Fail

In interpreting the test results in the table above, even though Option 2 passes the majority of tests, it fails to produce the minimum return needed as the profit is not at least twice the interest cost.

So far we've looked at a theoretical example, let's now use a real life deal to see how the numbers come out.

BALLARAT DEVELOPMENT PROJECT

This property in Ballarat South is situated on a block of 1,092 square metres. It has a three-bedroom house in good condition at the front, and boasts a large backyard. The plan is to subdivide the block and then build two new units (a two-bedroom and a three-bedroom) at the rear. We then planned to sell all three. Here's a snapshot of the budgeted numbers for this project.

A Ballarat Project

Ballarat Project — Budgeted Numbers			
	Cash Down	Borrowed	Total
Purchase price[1]	$33,600	$134,400	$168,000
Closing costs[2]	$8,400	—	$8,400
Land subdivision	$5,000	—	$5,000
Building costs[3]	$56,000	$168,000	$224,000
Development costs[4]	$30,000	—	$30,000
Holding costs[5]	$5,000	—	$5,000
	$138,000	$302,400	$440,400
Interest costs[6]	$15,876	—	$15,876
Totals	$153,876	$302,400	$456,276
	Received	Fees	Total
Sales price			
Existing house	$140,000	$3,500	$136,500
Dwelling 1	$170,000	$4,250	$165,750
Dwelling 2	$195,000	$4,875	$190,125
Totals	$505,000	$12,625	$492,375

Ballarat Project — Budgeted Numbers *(cont'd)*		
Cash-on-cash Return (CoCR)		
Cash down	$153,876	
Cash back[7]	$36,099	
Project CoCR	23.5%	

1. Borrowed 80% of the purchase price.
2. Assuming 5% of the purchase price.
3. Borrowed 75% of the building costs.
4. We were not expecting to borrow against the development costs.
5. Insurance, rates, etc.
6. $302,400 × 7% interest for nine months.
7. $492,375 – $302,400 – $153,876.

Before we crunch the numbers, I should let you know that since we plan to buy and sell the property within nine months, our anticipated growth will be converted into cash. This means that our profit will equal our cash back. It's also appropriate in this example to calculate our percentages on a project rather than annual basis. Let's see how you go with crunching the numbers:

Ballarat Deal — Three Second Solution Test	
Net Profit Percentage	
Profit / cash back	$
÷ Cash down	$
	× 100
Net profit percentage	%
Pass or Fail	
Average interest rate	%
	× 3
Three second solution	
Net profit percentage	
Pass / fail	

Ballarat Deal — Two x Interest Paid Test	
Interest paid	$
	× 2
2 x Interest paid	$
Profit / cash back	$
Pass / fail	

Ballarat Deal — Danger Money Multiple Test		
Risk-Free Return		
Cash down	$	
Assume	× 5%	
Risk-free return	$	
Calculate Multiple		
Cash back		
÷ Risk-free return		
= Danger money multiple		
Assessed debt risk	80% LVR, so medium	
Skill and Experience	**DMM Needed**	**Pass/Fail**
Novice	>7+	
Average	>6+	
Expert	>5+	

Note: You can check your answer against the solution at the end of the chapter.

Interpreting the above results, this project would not be accepted since the Danger Money Multiple is too low. The possible exception is for an expert or very experienced investor, for whom the deal would be very marginal. So, before we shut the door on this project, don't forget that an investor always tries to work the deal to see if a variable can be changed to unlock a greater profit. Let's consider three other financing possibilities to see if things change.

⊃ *Option 2:*

The ABC Bank has a loan product where the interest can be capitalised and added to the balance rather than paid periodically during the project.

⊃ *Option 3:*

As per Option 2, plus the bank is willing to provide an end value loan so that 85% of the purchase price, building costs and development costs can be borrowed. The interest rate on this product is 7.25%.

⊃ *Option 4:*

As per Option 3, except that you will use a line of credit against your home to pay for the remaining 15% of the purchase price, building costs and development costs. Your home loan is charged interest at 6.5%.

Here's a summary of how the numbers look under each option:

Four Options Examined				
	Option 1	Option 2	Option 3	Option 4
Cash down	$153,876	$138,000	$81,700	$48,400
Cash back	$36,099	$35,532	$32,471	$29,029
Interest	$15,876	$16,443	$19,504	$22,946
Average interest rate	7.00%	7.25%	7.25%	7.14%
Risk-free	$7,694	$6,900	$4,085	$920

Overleaf is a graph I've drawn to illustrate the relationship between the cash down, cash back and the net profit percentage figures across each of the four financing options. Take a few moments to study the graph, and as you do, see if you can identify the following key trends:

⊃ the increase in the net profit percentage as the required cash down decreases, and

➲ despite the various financing options, the amount of interest paid remains relatively constant.

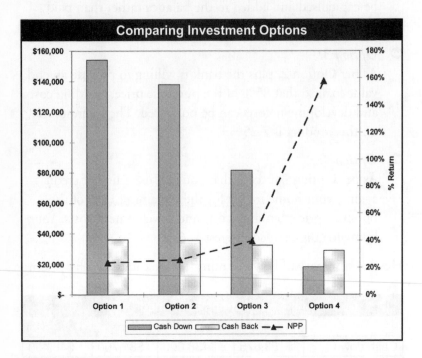

Note: The graph above and the numbers below were derived from an Excel spreadsheet I created. If you think it would be useful, you can download it from <www.PropertyInvesting.com/book3>.

Let's now see if any of the four financing options pass my three key deal evaluation benchmarks.

Financing Options — Three Second Solution Test				
	Option 1	Option 2	Option 3	Option 4
NPP	23.46%	25.75%	39.74%	157.76%
Required	21.00%	21.75%	21.75%	21.41%
	✓ Pass	✓ Pass	✓ Pass	✓ Pass

Financing Options — Two x Interest Paid Test				
	Option 1	Option 2	Option 3	Option 4
2 × Interest	$31,752	$32,886	$39,009	$45,893
Profit / cash back	$36,099	$35,532	$32,471	$29,092
	✓ Pass	✓ Pass	✗ Fail	✗ Fail

Danger Money Multiple for an Expert Investor				
	Option 1	Option 2	Option 3	Option 4
DMM	4.69	5.15	7.95	31.55
Required	5+	5+	5+	10+
	✗ Fail	✓ Pass	✓ Pass	✓ Pass

Overall				
	Option 1	Option 2	Option 3	Option 4
	✗ Fail	✓ Pass	✗ Fail	✗ Fail

The above table now reveals that Option 2 is the only way to get a return from this deal while also staying within my risk boundaries. As it's so close to the line, I might still accept Option 1 if I could somehow mitigate the interest rate risk. For example, one possibility might be to fix the interest so I was not left vulnerable to adverse movements. Alternatively, I could try to shop around for a cheaper interest rate which would increase the profitability and improve my Danger Money Multiple.

IT'S ALL UP TO YOU

This has been a pretty full-on chapter, so you might need to read it a few times in order for the concepts to fully sink in. If you need some help then you'll find plenty of fellow investors waiting and willing to assist at the PropertyInvesting.com forum boards.

Finally, I've designed a handy template to record all the required numbers to help you to easily calculate and interpret the information. I'd like to give you this as a free gift.

You can either download it right now at <www.PropertyInvesting. com/book3> or else I can send you a copy in the mail if you send a stamped self-addressed envelope to:

Free Template Offer
PropertyInvesting.com
PO Box 92
Blackburn Vic 3130
AUSTRALIA

Can you commit 10 minutes a day to practising? That's all you'll need and before long these three deal evaluation techniques will become second nature. Once you've mastered them then you'll join an exclusive club of sophisticated investors who can accurately evaluate a deal, at which point you'll sidestep marginal and dangerous opportunities and leave them for investors who buy on emotion rather than fact. Don't give up — if I can do it with my maths-challenged brain then you can too!

SUGGESTED SOLUTIONS FOR PROJECT X

Three Second Solution Test		
	Option 1	**Option 2**
Cash back	$8,125	$3,450
+ Desired annual growth	$20,000	$20,000
= Total profit	$28,125	$23,450
÷ Cash down	$62,500	$29,500
	× 100	× 100
Net profit percentage	45%	79.5%
	Option 1	**Option 2**
Average interest rate	7%	8.5%
	× 3	× 3
Three second solution	21%	25.5%
Net profit percentage	45%	79.5%
Pass / fail	Pass	Pass

Two × Interest Paid Test		
	Option 1	**Option 2**
Cash back	$8,125	$3,450
+ Desired annual growth	$20,000	$20,000
= Total profit	$28,125	$23,450
	Option 1	**Option 2**
Interest paid	$14,000	$20,200
	× 2	× 2
2 x Interest paid	$28,000	$40,400
Total profit	$28,125	$23,450
Pass / fail	Pass	Fail

Risk-Free Return		
	Option 1: 80% Borrowing	Option 2: 95% Borrowing
Cash down	$62,500	$29,500
Interest	5%	5%
Risk-free return	$3,125	$1,475

Danger Money Multiple Test		
	Option 1: 80% Borrowing	Option 2: 95% Borrowing
Cash back	$8,125	$3,450
+ Expected annual growth	$20,000	$20,000
= Profit	$28,125	$23,450
÷ Risk-free return	$3,125	$1,475
= Danger money multiple	9	15.9

SUGGESTED SOLUTIONS FOR BALLARAT SOUTH CASE

Ballarat Deal — Three Second Solution Test	
Net Profit Percentage	
Cash back	$36,099
÷ Cash down	$153,876
	× 100
Net profit percentage	23.5%
Pass or Fail	
Average interest rate	7%
	× 3
Three second solution	21%
Net profit percentage	23.5%
Pass / fail	Pass

Ballarat Deal — Two x Interest Paid Test	
Net Profit Percentage	
Interest paid	$15,876
	× 2
2 × Interest paid	$31,752
Cash back	$36,099
Pass / fail	Pass

Ballarat Deal — Danger Money Multiple Test		
Risk-free return		
Cash down	$153,876	
	× 5%	
Risk-free return	$7,694	
Calculate multiple		
Cash back	$36,099	
÷ Risk-free return	$7,694	
= Danger money multiple	4.69	
Borrowing risk	80% LVR so 'Medium'	
Skill and Experience	**DMM Needed**	**Pass/Fail**
Novice	>7+	Fail
Average	>6+	Fail
Expert	>5+	Fail

Chapter 15 Insights

Insight #1:

Success is no fluke. If you're not monitoring your investments then you shouldn't be surprised if you lose money.

Insight #2:

I think it's a good idea to set advance targets for each of the three benchmarks. That way, if you fail to achieve a pass then you'll quickly identify the need to take corrective action. The alternative is to live in ignorance and invest with your fingers crossed in the hope that everything will be okay.

Insight #3:

The best way to tackle a fear of numbers is head on. If your head is spinning then seek help — <www.PropertyInvesting.com> is a great place to start.

Insight #4:

Don't forget to accept my template gift! The quickest and easiest option is to download it at <www.PropertyInvesting.com/book3>. Alternatively, you can send a stamped self-addressed envelope. Do it now and start benefiting immediately!

PART III SUMMARY

Now, we've dealt with a lot of intensive theory in Part III so it's important to just quickly check over the ground we've covered and to make sure you're still following me. If needed, you might like to check back over any areas that you don't recall or any concepts that you don't feel comfortable with just yet.

We started the section with a broad discussion of how to begin building a portfolio from the ground up. We looked at focusing on your market rather than your product, and then examined a conceptual Property Tree, which can help you to put your strategy first, before your investment, and to decide whether you will seek cash or cashflow returns.

Strategies for taking small chunks (like the Cookie-Cutter Shark) of profits from multiple deals are very useful in the current market and we've also examined the different types of scarcity that can add real value to the way you market your deals.

The big question that many investors want answered is, 'Where can we find positive cashflow properties?' Of course, my response is to advocate that you ask a different question, and that is, 'How can we create positive cashflow situations by maximising our returns?'

There are many techniques available including reducing debt levels (possibly by subdividing and selling parts of a deal), negotiating creative terms to reduce interest or costs, or locking in above-average rents through various strategies.

Of course, there is more to creating long-term wealth than simply finding a deal or two. I have stressed the importance of automated profits — that is, the systematic reproduction of profitable actions.

PART III SUMMARY (CONT'D)

To this end, managing a portfolio and regularly reviewing investment returns, to avoid 'lazy money' is an important pastime. I've given you a detailed assessment of the five different profit return formulas in chapter 14 — each of these 'money-making' formulas is useful, but each lends itself to assessing returns from certain strategies so, again, your reviews should be in line with your goals.

Finally, we've just taken a significant look at the three tests I use to quickly evaluate potential deals in the current market. Before I allocate too much time to a potential deal I will check that it passes:

1. the Three Second Solution test

2. the Two × Interest Paid test

3. the Danger Money Multiple test.

Okay, if you're still with me then next we're going to put the theory aside and see how some real investors are using this knowledge to make great profits in today's market. Part IV has been written by some of the participants from my R.E.S.U.L.T.S. mentoring program. Let's see how they've gone putting this theory into practice!

Deal
Time

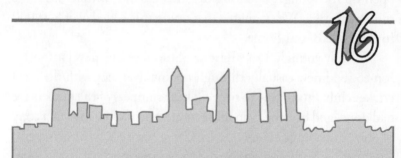

Troy and Bec
Aim for Reno Riches

Background:
Troy and Bec are young, married and passionate. These guys are as keen as mustard with their property investing, and they're also deeply interested in sharing their highs and lows with other investors. Troy has written this chapter to share their story.

TOY ISLAND!

Until recently, I (Troy) was the proud proprietor of a children's toy store called Toy Island and, as the owner, I'd regularly work 70-hour weeks. Some days I would be the first to arrive at 7am, and be the last to leave at 10pm. Bec and I had previously become interested in real estate after buying and renovating our home in 2000. We were keen to maximise the potential resale value and embarked on a small renovation project by knocking out a wall to open up the lounge, updating the kitchen and completing some minor painting. We estimated that doing this added over $50,000 to the value of our home.

Funnily enough, Dave Bradley (Steve's ex-business partner) is someone I knew casually through my involvement with the local cricket club. From time to time I'd hear snippets of the deals Dave had done, and became even more interested after he gave us a copy of Steve's first book, *From 0 to 130 Properties in 3.5 Years*, as a gift. I remember reading it and wondering how much of it was true. When Dave told me, 'All of it', I must admit I shook my head and thought, 'Wow, that would sure beat owning a toy store!'

When I read Steve's second book, *$1,000,000 in Property in One Year*, I walked away thinking how lucky those people were to have been mentored by Steve and Dave, and how I would jump at the chance to be a part of such an opportunity. So when Bec and I saw the R.E.S.U.L.T.S. mentoring program we joined up right away and not long afterwards we decided to sell the toy business. My plan was to become a full-time property investor while Bec would continue to earn money from her job to cover our lifestyle expenses and to keep the bank happy.

Finding Time

As you might expect, December is a very busy time for toy stores. Having started the R.E.S.U.L.T.S. program in October, I was becoming frustrated because I was receiving lots of information about investing, but was unable to apply most of it while I was working over 10 hours a day.

Things changed after the Christmas rush though, and we had more time to look for deals in the quieter January period. As we started looking, we hoped that there would still be one or two motivated sellers at a time when most buyers would be on holidays. One tactical idea that we'd implemented was to set up various email alerts on <www.RealEstate.com.au>, which would notify us whenever a property was listed that met our criteria. We had the following requirements:

➲ must be located in, or near, our preferred investing area

➲ must be less than $300,000 in price, and

➲ must feature three or more bedrooms.

An email arrived early in the new year advertising a three-bedroom homestead in North Blackburn with an asking price of $225,000 plus. We had to look twice because it seemed ridiculously cheap and we wondered what sort of awful condition it must have been in. We went along to the open house for a first inspection, and while the property wasn't exactly falling down, it was certainly in need of a massive revamp. Having had a little experience in renovating, Bec and I saw past the obvious visual handicaps and thought there was potential to give the home a face-lift and to make a tidy profit.

A Bargain in Blackburn

Negotiating the Deal

Despite being a real estate agent, the person handling the sale seemed to have very little idea about the value of the property.

Later I discovered that the property was an ex-rental and that the vendor was extremely keen to sell to be rid of the vacant and deteriorating investment.

Using the knowledge we'd gained from the R.E.S.U.L.T.S. program, we submitted the following two offers:

1. a low price offer of $207,000 with a shorter 30-day settlement, or

2. a higher price offer of $218,000, but with a longer settlement period of 150 days.

Both offers were subject to a satisfactory building and pest inspections. Our motivation was to flush out the price that the vendor really wanted. The result was that the vendor counter offered with:

➲ $222,000 on 30 days, or

➲ $223,000 on 60 days.

Enjoying the game, I counter offered again at $222,000 on 60 days and it was accepted.

PROFIT OPPORTUNITY

In becoming familiar with our chosen area, Bec and I had spent many hours searching the internet, going to countless open-for-inspections, attending auctions and reading the local papers. All our research caused us to conclude that there were simply no three-bedroom houses in Blackburn for less than $300,000. Our research suggested that any way you looked at it, this homestead deal on 380 square metres of land was an absolute bargain!

From a value-adding perspective, there was scarcity in that there weren't many (if any) 100-year-old homesteads left in Blackburn. If we could renovate it to its former glory then we expected to be able to sell it quickly to a buyer looking for a charming home.

Despite doing the numbers and coming to the conclusion that you'd have to do something remarkable not to make a good profit, the 'Mr Doubter' voice in my head said otherwise. When you add $250,000 of debt into the equation, there was still a lot of fear associated with buying. I'm told that although investing becomes easier, that internal fear never fully leaves you. The voice in your head becomes quieter but never silent.

After settling we immediately started completing the renovation. With an initial budget of $34,200 and a timeline of three months, we began by addressing the structural issues before tackling the cosmetic ugliness.

The Renovated Kitchen

Specifically we:

➲ fixed the cracked walls

➲ patched up holes in the floors

➲ extended the house by a fraction to give more room to the kitchen

➲ provided better access to a new deck that we built

➲ painted to convert the 1970's brown into a more modern white

- removed the timber wall panelling

- put in a new timber feature kitchen

- completed some basic landscaping (with lots of fresh looking mulch)

- added new carpet and floating timber floors

- produced a new bathroom — bath, shower, toilet and vanity

- plonked a nice picket fence at the front, and

- tidied up all the other fine points that come with doing the above (such as tiling, light switches, door handles, taps, and so on).

One of our concerns was that we needed to draw a line somewhere to ensure we didn't overcapitalise. In a nutshell we tried to restore the home and add a 'wow factor' in the mind of the purchaser in order to sell it quickly.

THE NUMBERS

Here's a summary of our budgeted and actual numbers:

A Summary of the Numbers		
	Original	Actual
Purchase price	$222,000	$222,000
+ Purchase costs (at 5%)	$11,100	$11,100
+ Reno costs	$34,200	$47,600
+Holding costs (interest, rates, etc.)	$8,190	$8,550
= Total cost	$275,490	$289,250
Selling price	$300,000	$374,000
– Sales costs	$9,000	$12,603
= Sales proceeds	$291,000	$361,397

A Summary of the Numbers *(cont'd)*		
	Original	Actual
Sales proceeds	$291,000	$361,397
– Total cost	$275,490	$289,250
= Profit	$15,510	$72,147

Time (settlement to settlement) was six months.

WHAT DIDN'T GO TO PLAN

Rather than tell you how smart we were and how well we did, you'll probably learn more from all the little mistakes we made that we'll definitely be avoiding next time. Here's a list of the bigger mini-disasters:

➲ When we did the inspection we noted that the light switches looked newish. We therefore assumed that the wiring behind the switches was also in good condition. We were wrong. Old wiring can be hidden by new switches. This set us back almost $3,000 in unbudgeted expenses as we needed to engage an electrician to rewire almost the entire house.

➲ In repairing the cracks we found that the internal rendered walls (the inside walls were concreted rather than plastered) were much harder to fix than we anticipated. We had to take out a tonne of gap filler and then start again from scratch. This added more time and money to the project.

➲ The agent we chose to sell the property refused to market it as we requested. We quickly learnt that many agents say what you want to hear to get your business and then do whatever they like afterwards. Specifically, the agent under-quoted the asking price and advertised at $290,000 plus when we specifically requested $300,000 plus as a minimum.

➲ Triple theft! During the renovation we had a couple of pot plants stolen. It was no big deal but we should have responded and thought more about how to secure the property rather than just ignoring it as a one off. Following our inaction, during an open-for-inspection we had a large orchid pot plant stolen, which was very disappointing, particularly as we'd borrowed it from Bec's mum. Finally, just after we'd signed the contracts, a thief kicked in the front door and stole some of the furniture that we'd hired to give the property that 'lived in' feeling. In summary, a vacant house is an easy target. This is why it's difficult to insure an unoccupied home.

What We Learned from the Experience

Where do we start? There were a thousand lessons, and we probably haven't even worked out half of them yet. Still, here are some of our insights:

- Something that worked well for us was listening to the suggestions of the tradespeople who we engaged for the renovation work. For example, 'Big Tim', our plasterer, warned us that patching the rendering would lead to an inferior result. Instead he suggested that we glued on the plaster. All up we spent an extra $1,200 but this dramatically improved the visual impact and gave a modern feeling to the hallway. It certainly added extra value and also helped to sell the property.

- When we bought it, we actually thought the property was advertised at $225,000, not $225,000 *plus*! Had we noticed the 'plus' then we probably would have offered more than we did. This mistake led to us offering a lower price and saving. Up until then we'd been influenced by the asking price but now we make our offers based on what each property would be worth to us as an investment.

- Beer is worth much more than its retail price. We actually took a spare fridge to the site and always kept it stocked with beer for the tradies. We believe that providing beer, and the occasional lunch, worked very well for us as happy workers are productive workers. We'll never know how much it saved us, but it certainly meant the tradespeople were looking for ways to help us in return for our generosity.

⮑ Finding tradespeople through the usual advertising channels will mean you run the risk of poor workmanship and reliability issues. If you're looking for tradies, seek recommendations from friends, other investors or other tradespeople that you've worked with before and who you trust. For example, ask a plumber for an electrician, and an electrician for a carpenter.

NEXT TIME

What will we be doing differently in our future projects? In a nutshell, we'll be doing less of the work ourselves, even if it means a lower profit. We found that the world passed us by while we completed the renovation works, to such an extent that when we came to the end we didn't have any future projects lined up to move on to. Also, as our lives became eating, sleeping and living the renovation in every spare second, we soon became quite sick of the project and couldn't wait to finish it. We've pledged to do more *thinking* and less *doing* on future projects.

If We Could Pass On One Tip ...

It would be that you should always ask lots of questions of lots of people! In order to understand the property market you have to spend time listening to what it has to say. We ask as many people for their opinions on as many topics as possible, to ensure that the work we do is appealing and attractive to our target audience.

It doesn't matter how good you are, you will not get it right all the time alone. Don't let your pride get in the way of making a profit — be prepared to ask questions even if you look silly. That's how we've learned.

A HAPPY ENDING

In case you're wondering, the toy store has finally now been sold and we're looking forward to continuing on with our property investing and learning more and more from each deal that we do. It's an exciting time!

TROY AND BEC

To find out more information about what Troy and Bec are up to, together with more photos of the deals they've done, visit:

<www.PropertyInvesting.com/TroyandBec>

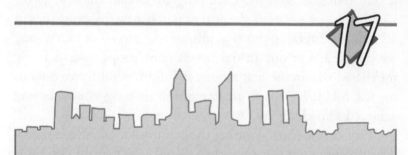

Tammy and Co. Go Mining for Cashflow Gold

Background:
As a mortgage broker, Tammy is used to thinking laterally to solve her clients' problems. She's able to use her nimble mind in her property investing too, where she joins forces with her business partners Andrew, Kylie and Geoff. In this chapter Tammy tells the story of how they came to own a positive cashflow property that will return an impressive $2,500 per month.

ACCOUNTABILITY LEADS TO ACTION AND ACTION LEADS TO SUCCESS

Having made the decision and the investment to join Steve's R.E.S.U.L.T.S. mentoring program, we were extremely keen to take full advantage of the information, coaching and support while it was available. Soon after the program began, Andrew, Kylie, Geoff and I set ourselves the goal of purchasing five properties in 12 months. Breaking this goal into smaller targets or milestones, we decided that our initial investment property had to be purchased within the first month as I didn't want to see Simon, my R.E.S.U.L.T.S. coach, at our monthly meeting without having achieved something serious.

I hit the internet, scouring the country for positive cashflow deals. Before long I was on <www.RealEstate.com.au> and was searching the Mount Isa region. I wasn't taking a guess that this would be a good region, I'd actually lived in the area for seven years and I still conduct business that sees me travel to that part of Queensland on a regular basis.

Approximately 100kms east of Mount Isa you'll find Cloncurry — a small town where about 3,000 people live. While the population is on the low side, our research indicated that rental returns were high. We'd also found out that there was strong demand for housing. In fact, there was a waiting list for rental properties.

Rather than buy something sight-unseen though, Kylie and I decided to take a week off work to explore potential deals.

DRIVING THE DUSTY STREETS OF CLONCURRY

Upon arriving in Cloncurry, Kylie and I immediately started driving around looking at houses we'd seen on the internet. The first house we inspected was an old Queenslander. Although it was vacant, the numbers revealed that once tenanted it would provide us with a net positive cashflow outcome (that is, our cash received would be higher than our cash paid). We didn't want to beat around the bush so we immediately made an offer of $175,000. (This was subsequently accepted and within a week of settlement we'd found a tenant willing to rent it for $350 a week.)

Encouraged by what we'd found, Kylie and I decided to see if the agent knew of any similar properties — good quality houses at the lower end of the price range. Happy for the inquiry, the agent smiled and made a few phone calls so that we could inspect another property later that afternoon.

With a few hours to kill until the inspection, Kylie and I decided to buy a sandwich and to visit the local council offices. This hadn't been part of our plan to begin with, but the real estate agent had mentioned that the town was poised to boom on the back of a new mine opening up. Rather than just believe what the agent had told us, we decided to seek independent confirmation from the council.

It was a good thing we did because after a five-minute conversation with a friendly council worker, we established that the new mine was only at the feasibility planning stage. However we also discovered that several smaller mines were more advanced in their planning and that the companies behind these mines wanted staff to live in the town rather than fly in and fly out.

It seemed the agent was right after all — new employees would add pressure to an already tight rental market, driving rental returns higher.

Another Red Hot Deal

Our afternoon appointment came around quickly and we met the agent out the front of the property that he'd arranged for us to inspect earlier that day. It was a rather humble looking three-bedroom, one-bathroom weatherboard house that was neat on the outside but required some internal renovations. Interestingly, for some reason, this deal was not advertised on the internet.

When we asked the agent why the vendors wanted to sell, we were told that they'd already purchased another property and were starting to get a little desperate as they had to leave town in the next five weeks. While the vendor's asking price was a little optimistic at $165,000, we didn't feel embarrassed about putting in an unconditional cash offer of $100,000 because we were offering a quick 28-day settlement.

After some counter-offering we eventually agreed on the price of $112,500. Our plan for this property was to renovate and subdivide, particularly because the property was located on a half-acre block that was zoned light industrial.

We allowed ourselves four weeks to do the renovation and had found a local builder to complete the works. As part of our purchase we made it a condition that we were allowed access to the property before settlement so the builder could measure up and provide a quote. This was a good idea as it meant that we could start planning the renovation during the settlement period and organise for the tradies to be ready to start work the day the property settled.

Before Renovations

After Renovations

It only took a week for the builder and his team to do the renovations and the final cost came in at $9,200, which included a new fence. The results (shown in the photographs above) speak for themselves.

Our momentum continued because the real estate agent had started telling prospective tenants about the work we were doing to the house, which led to a tenant contacting us and offering to pay $300 a week on a 12-month lease. When we told the tenant about our plans to build an industrial shed out the back he simply replied that it didn't bother him one bit.

THE NUMBERS

Cash Down	
20% deposit	$22,000
+ Closing costs	$5,500
+ Renovation costs	$9,200
= Cash required	$36,700

Cash Back	
Rental (95% occupied)	$14,820
– Finance costs	$7,133
– Ownership costs	$2,278
= Annual cashflow	$5,409

* The property is managed in-house so there is no rental management.

Cash-On-Cash Return	
Cash back	$5,409
÷ Cash down	$36,700
	× 100
= Cash-on-cash return	14.7%

AN INDUSTRIAL SHED

Our timeframe for subdividing and building the shed out the back of this property is 10 months and this fits perfectly with the expected start up of the new mine. We've contacted the mine's manager and are in regular communication with him to try to ensure that the shed is rented the second it's finished.

We estimate that the shed will cost $86,000 to build and that once completed it will easily rent for $24,000 (plus GST) per annum. As it will be an industrial lease, the tenant will pick up the outgoings, which means that our revised annual net cashflow will be $2,500 per month! The news just gets better and better because a valuation of the house alone (not including the industrial land) has just come back at $205,000!

HOW TO FIND DEALS

Steve constantly reinforces that it's unreasonable to expect good deals to just land in your lap. I'd agree, but I would also say that plenty of great deals are out there if you do the hard yards and become an area specialist.

Allocating the necessary time to analyse areas and to inspect houses will dramatically help to build your confidence. For example, once we were familiar with the town we didn't limit ourselves to properties that were for sale. Instead we drove around writing down the addresses of properties that we thought had potential, went to the local government department to find out who the owners were, and then cold called them offering to buy their properties. This rather direct approach has paid off as we've bought two more properties at very good prices. In fact, the vendors were willing to accept lower offers since there are no agent commissions payable on private sales. You might think this technique sounds quite gutsy, but once you've done it a few times your fears soon subside.

SUGGESTIONS FOR NEW STARTERS

The deal described in this chapter was no fluke. It was the result of a lot of hard work, much of which was challenging and uncomfortable. I guess that's why the opportunity was there in the first place — most investors didn't work quite as hard to find the deal or to see its potential.

If you're just starting out then I'd suggest that you:

⮑ Seriously consider joining Steve's mentoring program. Despite being a mortgage broker and understanding the industry, the information and accountability you get with the R.E.S.U.L.T.S. mentoring program will really open your eyes to a new way of investing that has worked well for me.

⮑ Make sure you learn how to crunch the numbers. Investments are financial decisions and you want to protect yourself from being over emotional. You should work out how much you can afford to borrow as this will help you to identify what sort of properties you should target.

Finally, I'd like to share the realisation that the only thing that stopped me from starting earlier was my fear and uncertainty about whether or not I could be an investing success. Having now bought 10 properties in three months, I'd encourage anyone with an ounce of inclination to face their fear and to give it a go. I did, and now my life has forever changed for the better.

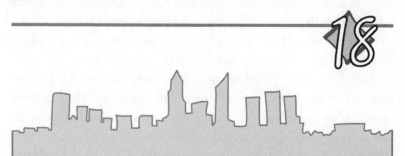

Suzanne and Katrina Do Their Block for a 322% Return!

Background:
Suzanne and Katrina are dynamic investors who also juggle the demands of raising young families. Their inspiring story shows what can happen when you get out of your comfort zone and commit yourself to achieving a result. It's been a pleasure working closely with them in the R.E.S.U.L.T.S. program, and I can confidently say that their success was no fluke, even if the outcome wasn't quite what they were anticipating.

FINDING THE DEAL

This is the true story of how Suzanne and I found, bought and then profited from the sale a block of land in outback Queensland. When we were looking for areas with potential deals, we both stumbled onto a town at the same time, but from separate sources. It was a town in regional Queensland that had positive cashflow properties advertised with potential for future growth an extra bonus.

After finding the town on a map, we immediately visited <www.RealEstate.com.au> to research the types of houses that were for sale and also the prices being asked. Going one step further, we used the phone numbers from the online ads to call a selection of agents to see how strong the rental demand was. We did this with words from Steve about strong rental demand indicating scarcity ringing in our ears. As strange as it sounds, after a couple of calls we concluded that there were virtually no houses available for rent. In fact, there was a waiting list!

HEADING NORTH

With growing excitement we decided to head north. Of course, it wasn't quite as simple as it sounds. Before we booked our plane tickets we needed to make arrangements for our families while we were away. While Suzanne's family could look after her children, due to my husband's work commitments, my only option was to take my son with us on the trip.

Our next hurdle was to find accommodation because, as we'd just discovered, rental accommodation was in huge demand. Most hotels were booked out for months in advance but, with persistence, Suzanne found and booked a room that became available at the last minute. While the lack of accommodation was frustrating at the time, it at least confirmed that the town was a hive of activity.

In the few days leading up to our trip north, we continued to do as much as we could to learn more about the area. This included broadening our research and crunching numbers on the potential outcome of building two units on vacant blocks of land. The numbers looked good so we secured the only seven available lots under contract, subject to inspection and further council investigation.

The day we flew out of Melbourne we were both out of bed before sunrise and as excited as children on Christmas morning. It wasn't all plain sailing though. Suzanne wasn't feeling well and I was struggling with the pressures of managing my luggage and a two year old — both seemed to want to go in separate directions.

It would have been easy at this point to wonder if our adventurous spirits had caused us to take leave of our senses, but the enthusiasm returned when we landed and packed ourselves into the hire car. As we travelled the 250 or so kilometres from the airport, we took the opportunity to explore the towns along the way and to become familiar with a part of Australia that neither of us had visited before. And, of course, as we stretched our legs we also took a passing interest in the type and styles of the houses.

One particular residential house looked promising as a positive cashflow opportunity, until we learnt that the land was not freehold. We noted that this was definitely an issue that we should add to our list of questions for our real estate agent.

It was mid-afternoon when we arrived and the first thing we did was find our accommodation. On opening the door we both immediately screwed up our noses — the room was filthy! Not to be discouraged though, we set out to have a look around and to find Bill, a friendly local real estate agent that we'd spoken with over the phone from Melbourne.

Bill was like a walking history book. He was very happy to answer all of our questions and we were quick to learn that he was a 'tell it like it is' person. It was also interesting to compare his laid back, 'it will happen soon enough' approach to the more aggressive style of the city real estate agents we were used to dealing with.

After getting the run-down of the local area from Bill, and once we'd inspected the seven blocks of land that we'd flown up to see, Suzanne and I were starting to feel like we had a much better understanding of the region. We knew this was important as Steve had told us about the need to know the area like a local. Our time on the ground certainly reinforced the importance of conducting personal inspections in the local area, especially where investors are inexperienced or unfamiliar with the local rules and ways of doing business.

As the afternoon progressed Suzanne visited the local council while I looked after my sick child. (It's amazing how quickly children can get sick. Fortunately they tend to recover equally as quickly.) During her visit, Suzanne discovered that the seven blocks we had earmarked were not suitable as sites for multiple dwellings due to density regulations. This was surprising as we'd been told on the phone that they were viable development sites. Again, it highlights the importance of independently confirming everything and not making assumptions.

Understandably disappointed, we contemplated packing up and heading home, however we quickly dismissed that option and instead headed back to the streets to see what else was available. Jumping back in the hire car we spent the next day exploring neighbouring towns. Changing our strategy, we consciously sought out the advice of local builders as to the potential of building single houses on the blocks (rather than multiple dwellings). The numbers still looked good, however the construction time was a big issue since demand for builders was high and waiting lists for their services were long.

Returning to our humble accommodation, we contemplated the hundreds of kilometres we'd travelled only to be left with the question of, 'What now?' As we went for a walk to clear our heads, we happened to pass by a notice in a local shop window advertising a government land auction scheduled for the next day. Since we were already in town, we made plans to attend as observers.

THE AUCTION

The auction was like no other we had ever attended. It was conducted in the hot sun, at the side of the road, and at an address on the opposite side of town from the actual block of land being auctioned. We quickly concluded that, if circumstances continued to go our way, we might even like to make a bid. Our research of the area was certainly comprehensive enough to confidently put in an offer.

The auctioneer sighed with disappointment when he realised that only two parties — us and another buyer — had turned up to the auction. Mustering all the energy he could, he started proceedings. The first bid was $23,000 followed by two increments of a further $5,000. Applying an effective auction technique we had learned, we attempted to slow the auction process down by offering $1,000 and then $500 increments. It worked. In the wash up we were the winning bid at the bargain price of $38,500! Here's a picture of the block of land:

An Auction Like No Other

The next few hours were filled with the administrative formalities of paying a deposit and signing contracts. Once all the paperwork was signed we went back to visit our newly purchased block and discovered that, due to the existing high-density accommodation adjoining the land, council might consider a multi-dwelling accommodation.

Potential profit-making strategies ranged from holding the block for six months before selling it, to building two units, each with two bedrooms, and holding them for five years as positive cashflow investments.

Even though our trip turned out nothing like we had planned, it had certainly been worthwhile. It provided a valuable lesson about the importance of getting out there on the road and meeting people, while looking for potential deals in unusual circumstances. We learnt that even though the first lead may come to nothing, it can take you to another opportunity that you wouldn't have otherwise found.

RETURNING HOME

We decided to build on the land, and when we arrived home we immediately started filling out planning application forms for the council and also contacting builders. After a few frustrating months of dealing with people over the phone, we quickly learnt how difficult it is to try to run a development project off-site. We either had to make the commitment to travel frequently during the development process or else decide to hold the block for a few more months and then sell it for a quick profit.

To help us we called Bill (the real estate agent we had met up in Queensland) to give us an idea of the current value of the block. 'I can't see why you couldn't get $70,000', he replied. There and then we asked him to list the block for us and we were encouraged when Bill concluded the conversation with the comment, 'I should have a buyer by the end of the week.'

It turned out that Bill was overly optimistic. After waiting two weeks we followed up with him again, which is when he told us about Nigel — a potential purchaser. Nigel had offered to purchase the block for $68,000 but with a condition attached. It was subject to him receiving council approval for his proposed development.

Knowing that these things can take months and months, our solicitor wisely advised us that if we accepted we should limit the amount of time he had to gain council approval (called a sunset clause). This is exactly what we did.

Two weeks later the only thing that had changed was our increased frustration! The contract was still going back and forth, so we told Bill to put the property back on the market. Fortunately, Bill said he'd received more inquiries for vacant land, and he promised he would follow them up and let us know how he went.

Yet another week passed and, rather than just accepting the status quo, we decided to phone Bill to tell him that we were going to give the property to another agent to sell. This propelled him into action, and he pleaded for us to give him until the following Monday — just three more days.

Sure enough, Bill called that Monday saying he had a signed unconditional contract at $70,000 with a 30-day settlement period. The rest of the transaction went smoothly, however we had learned another valuable lesson about the importance of being decisive and taking control of the sale process in order to achieve our desired outcome.

THE NUMBERS

Here is a summary of the numbers.

Total Cost			
	Paid in Cash	Borrowed	Total
Purchase price	—	$38,500	$38,500
+ Closing costs	$4,654	—	$4,654
+ Legals	$792	—	$792
+ Travel and accommodation	$1,290	—	$1,290
+ Interest costs	—	$1,426	$1,426
= Total cost	$6,736	$39,926	$46,662

Total Profit	
Sales price	$70,000
− Sales fees	$1,645
= Sales proceeds	$68,355
− Cost	$46,662
= Profit	$21,693

Cash-on-Cash Return (Annualised)	
Cash back	$21,693
÷ Cash down	÷ $6,736
	× 100
= Cash-on-cash return (for project)	322%
Project length	7 months
= Cash-on-cash return (annualised)	552%

LEARNING OUTCOMES

What did we learn from our adventure? Well, here's a list of the five most important lessons we took from this experience:

1. Opportunities for profitable deals are everywhere. While it takes effort to find the deals and to purchase them, the hardest part is the decision-making and management phase.

2. Flexibility is essential when looking at property. You just never know where your searches may take you.

3. Talk to the locals as much as possible. Most are more than happy to talk about their town and to help any way they can.

4. When starting out as business partners it was a good idea for Suzanne and I to test our joint venture agreement on one small deal before launching into a massive project.

5. The best deals are found by being out on the road. Sitting at your computer screen after work, it's unlikely that a great deal will jump out at you.

HOW TO FIND DEALS IN THE CURRENT MARKET

Set your goals, choose your area and get out on the road. Don't be afraid to pass up deals if you're not sure you are ready. While it can be disappointing at the time, the missed opportunities act as great yardsticks and can be used to compare circumstances, and profits, for future deals.

It's often said that the best teacher is experience. While we agree that experience is important, the best outcome possible is when you combine experience with education, because once we knew what to look for, all we had to do was find it.

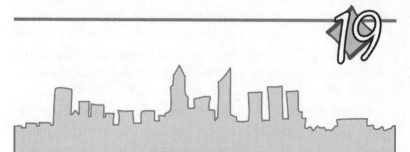

$65,974 in
Four Months and Two Days

Background:
Since beginning the R.E.S.U.L.T.S. program, the investing team of Anna, Mal, Rikki and Jodi have acquired an impressive $1.2 million worth of property that has a current market value of $1.9 million. Success hasn't just landed in their laps — they've worked extremely hard and thoroughly deserve the profits they've made. In this chapter Anna shares the story of how they made $65,974 in four months and two days.

DIAMOND IN THE ROUGH

It would be much more interesting to say that finding this deal required months of planning, weeks of training and days of searching. In reality, we simply identified an area and a price bracket for properties matching our criteria, and then registered for daily updates on <www.RealEstate.com.au>. The location we chose was an area in transition in southern Perth. There was a major new infrastructure project in progress to expand the local shopping centre. We expected this would help to give the area a fresh new look and vibe, but most of the typical houses looked a bit tired and were cheap by Perth standards.

Once we'd identified our area, the next step was to develop a plan to address the 'housing problem' by purchasing the worst house on the best street, and renovating it without overcapitalising. This was especially important given that our budget-conscious first home buyers would be our target market for onselling the deal.

Specifically, we were looking for a property under $250,000 on approximately 700 square metres of land, and with at least three bedrooms. In addition, we didn't want to be faced with any major structural repairs, and the property couldn't be located on a main road as this would limit the potential appeal for the next purchaser. An undercover carport was preferred, but not essential. Finally, there needed to be access to public transport nearby.

While it sounds like an extensive wish list, shortly after beginning our search we became aware of a deal that seemed to fit the bill. It was, to be frank, in a visually appalling condition, which explained why it had been on the market for several weeks without attracting a single offer.

WHEELING AND DEALING

From our initial discussions with the agent we learnt that he felt the vendor was highly optimistic in asking for $235,000. We asked the agent if he could estimate how much we should budget to renovate the property. We felt his reply was a little excessive, but it helped us to justify negotiations for a substantially lower asking price.

As we ran through the 'Questions to Ask Agents' that Steve had provided as part of his R.E.S.U.L.T.S. program, it became apparent that the owner wanted to sell in order to raise enough finance to purchase a business.

Based on our inspection of the property, together with the responses the agent gave to our questions, we wrote up and submitted an offer for $190,000. Within the hour the agent called back to say that the vendor was thinking it over, but that an additional $10,000 would clinch the deal. The manner in which the agent put this to us made us feel like the vendor was merely 'trying his luck' to see if he could increase the price. Our response was that we didn't think the property was worth any more, and that our original offer stood. Later that evening the agent called back to say the vendor was happy to proceed at the lower price.

Ugly is Another Word for Opportunity Knocking

An Ugly Opportunity

As you can see by the photo above, the home was brick veneer. It had three bedrooms, one bathroom, a large kitchen and a good-sized lounge. The backyard was quite spacious, but not big enough to be subdivided. There were no gardens.

Internally, the property was so disgusting that I couldn't bring myself to touch the door handle or light switches. It took all my strength just to sit at the kitchen table and to write up the offer

The Original Bedroom

The Original Kitchen

when I really wanted to rush home to take a shower! Still, others wouldn't even set foot inside the front door. Another couple that turned up to view the property at the same time took one look and drove off in a hurry.

You'll see some photos of the interior in its original condition on this page. All in all, despite the shoddy appearance and awful smell, I was actually starting to get very excited about the profit-making prospects of this property. Yes, there was more grime and more bugs, rodents and spiders than I had ever seen in a home before but, from what I could tell, the structural side of things was fine. In summary, the holes in the walls and the obscenely painted bedrooms really only added to our bargaining power since these problems could be easily and cost-effectively fixed.

Our Plan

Our plan was to buy, renovate, and to then put the property back on the market in order to make a quick and tidy profit. We had allowed four months from the date we settled our purchase to the date we would settle on our sale ('settlement to settlement' as Steve calls it).

The Bathroom

The appearance of the kitchen and bathroom can be a property's biggest asset or largest shortcoming. So we nearly always allocate the biggest part of our renovation budget to transforming these rooms. In this case, given their state of utter grunge, we assumed both would need to be fully stripped and replaced. Additional areas that we targeted for improvement were:

- ➲ floor coverings, in particular, polishing the floorboards and re-tiling the wet areas

- ➲ internal paint to modernise the colour and freshen up the appearance and smell

- ➲ external landscaping and painting, and

- ➲ potential replacement of the air conditioner if we couldn't fix the existing unit.

Crunching the numbers we came up with a total renovation budget of $17,000. This would have been more expensive if we had outsourced all the labour, however we decided to do as much of the work as possible to increase our profit margin and to improve the turnaround time. Some of the other measures we took to avoid over-capitalising were:

- ➲ Saving a lot of money by purchasing a near-new, good-quality second-hand kitchen (found in the local classifieds), which came with a sink, taps and an almost brand-new, stainless-steel oven.

- ➲ Buying a second-hand bathroom vanity that had been used as a display unit.

- ➲ Having the iron bath resprayed rather than removed. Removing the bath would have increased the plumbing cost dramatically.

- ➲ Only organising basic landscaping — a little mulch and a few basic plants. We did go a little further though by painting the rear fence and putting up privacy screens on the veranda because this really improved the visual appeal of the back yard.

THE NUMBERS

Here's a summary of the numbers:

A Summary of the Numbers	
Purchase price and closing costs	$199,000
+ Renovation costs	$13,296
+ Finance and holding costs	$5,190
= Total cost	$217,486
Actual sale price	$293,000
– Sales costs	$9,540
= Sales proceeds	$283,460
Sales proceeds	$283,460
– Total cost	$217,486
= Pre-tax profit	$65,974

While the numbers are great, I want to stress that this whole project was hard work. Some of the things that didn't go to plan include:

⮑ Finding out that the property next door was rented as government housing. Our fear was that the tenants would be rowdy and troublesome.

⮑ Discovering that the house across the road, and a couple of houses down the street, were like parking lots given the number of clapped out old cars that were parked on the nature-strip and in the front yard.

⮑ Losing a few days due to 'fumigation issues'. There was no way on this planet I was going to help renovate a property where you could see fleas jumping around — and I can tell you that they didn't die without a fight!

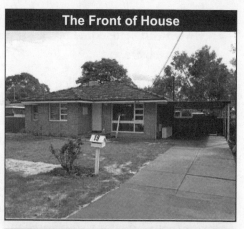
The Front of House

Luckily, none of these problems impacted on the sale, and the neighbours on either side turned out to be some of the loveliest people we've ever met. Above are a few post-renovation photos.

The Kitchen

LEARNING OUTCOMES

Learning as you go is one of the best parts of investing. This deal taught us to:

The Bathroom

➲ Make sure that we're very specific about what we want from a selling agent. For example, when the agents said they would place a 'For Sale' board out the front, we assumed that it would be big and bright. It wasn't. When the agents said they would list the property on the internet we assumed that it would be on <www.RealEstate.com.au> but it was only placed on their office's website.

◌ Get the floorboards sanded towards the end of the project rather than at the start. The advice we received and acted upon was to do it at the start, but we ended up tip-toeing around for weeks afterwards to avoid causing damage.

◌ To avoid delays and down time, be sure to book your tradies (such as carpet layers, electricians and plumbers) as far in advance as possible, and to make sure you follow up with them a day or two beforehand to remind them that you're counting on them to be there on time.

◌ A little trick a real estate agent brought to our attention was that fluorescent lights in the kitchen make a house (especially one with polished floorboards) look much better when you opt for a slightly warmer globe rather then the standard 'cool' globe.

◌ The main downfall of the house, and the reason it took us three weeks to sell, was that there wasn't a separate eating space away from the kitchen. This is something we will more carefully consider from now on.

FINAL THOUGHTS

Don't worry if you're not feeling supremely confident about your first, or perhaps first few, investment purchases. The only way to overcome the fears and doubts that endlessly run through your mind is to take continual action. Don't act blindly without carefully identifying and mitigating potential risks, but don't forego taking action. Rest assured, the growth in confidence and experience you'll gain from taking action will make the stress and worry well worthwhile.

Simon, Lynn and Tony Commercialise New Zealand

Background:
Simon, Lynn and Tony attended one of my investing events back in early 2004. Prior to the event, they'd done a lot of reading, attended a lot of seminars and done a lot of procrastinating. Like many others they wondered where all the positive cashflow properties were. Well, they must have found the answer because they'd bought their first deal within the next 24 hours! In fact, they went on to acquire 11 properties in the next four months. In this chapter Simon shares the story of a recent positive cashflow commercial property bought in sunny New Zealand.

HOW WE FOUND THIS DEAL

My wife Lynn and I, together with our business partner Tony, had been investing in New Zealand for about 18 months when we found this deal. During that time we'd built relationships with a number of Kiwi real estate agents. This particular opportunity was brought to our attention by an agent who was trying to sell a 'quiet listing' (a low-key listing — the vendor wanted minimal attention for personal reasons).

The deal consisted of a small shopping mall — eight retail and office premises on a main road, with a two-bedroom house and a large yard at the rear. This was spread over three titles that were being sold as one package. I must admit that the location had some emotional appeal to me — it was just 200 metres from my old primary school! It's funny that I seem to have gone full circle. I've been living in Australia now for several years, but I suddenly find myself having a presence right back where I spent the first years of my life.

Reservations

We actually didn't think much of the deal when we first looked at it (despite my fondness for the location). The agent emailed us a draft copy of the details, which we briefly looked over, but on first glance the numbers seemed less than ordinary.

When we didn't respond after three or four weeks, the agent came back to us a couple of times suggesting that we really should take a closer look. It was then that I actually took the time to go over the deal carefully and I started to see some real potential.

For starters, I noticed a formatting issue in the draft listing information, and when I fixed this a couple of leases that had somehow been hidden in the document suddenly became visible. (Ironically, I'd recently listened to a tape by Robert Kiyosaki where he talked about seasoned property investors developing a skill that he called 'seeing the invisible'!) Taking these new leases into account the numbers started to look a little more interesting. It also became obvious that there was some key information missing, such as figures for the lease of the house and for one of the shops.

We followed up with the agent and posed these questions, while also conducting some other due diligence tests.

It's amazing how simply asking intelligent, open-ended questions about a property can open up all sorts of possibilities. For example, we discovered that one of the leases was actually for an automatic teller machine, and that there was a currently vacant office attached to the machine that formed part of the deal!

Dealing With Agents

There were actually two selling agents involved in this deal — the one who introduced us to it and another who appeared to have a pre-existing personal relationship with the vendor. It became clear early on that this second agent was far less forthcoming and wasn't particularly well organised when it came to providing information that we requested. So we tended to liaise with the first agent (the one we had an existing relationship with) wherever possible, and we were very happy with her responsiveness.

We always submit any serious offer in writing (and generally, all of our offers are serious). In this case, the whole negotiation was handled by email, fax and telephone. We drafted up the special conditions that we wanted included (such as a builder's report, review of all leases to our satisfaction, and the offer being conditional on finance approval) and emailed these to our agent, who then drafted the contract and faxed it back to us for signing. There was a little more complexity in the contract due to the number of titles and commercial leases involved, but we were still able to submit the offer/contract by fax.

An advantage of negotiating from a distance like this is that it makes it easier to take the time to reflect on the process and to keep emotion out of it. Don't get me wrong, I've found that agents can be very adept at trying to create a false sense of urgency by phone or email as much as they can in person (using phrases such as, 'You'd better act quickly, there's another interested party!') but it's just easier to pause and to think when they're not breathing over your shoulder, applying the hard sell.

The vendors were asking for $550,000 plus for the properties. We took the time to carefully crunch the numbers on the deal, and opened with a written offer (contract) for around $510,000. The agents thought this would be a bit low, but agreed to submit the offer to the vendors. In response, the vendors dropped their asking price and we ended up (over a number of faxes, each more illegible than the last, with items crossed out, amended and initialled) agreeing to a purchase price of $535,000 with a longish settlement and an agreement by the vendors to lease-back the house and one of the shops for a fixed period. We agreed to a deposit amount that was sufficient to cover the agents' commissions, and I think they were pretty happy with that outcome.

We did experience a few communication issues with multiple agents involved in the process, and there were a couple of occasions during negotiations when it became necessary to bypass the agents and to speak directly with the vendors. I think this actually worked quite well, as we were able to exercise some 'relationship management' skills to overcome concerns that the vendors had about our offer.

THE NUMBERS

Here are the numbers associated with this deal.

Numbers on the Deal	
Vendor's asking price	$550,000+
Actual purchase price	$535,000
Valuation at settlement	$587,000
Loan amount	$321,000
Loan interest	8.4% interest only
Loan term	15 years

Cash Down	
Deposit	$214,000
+ Closing costs*	$5,000
= Total cash required	$219,000

* There is no stamp duty in New Zealand.

Cashflow Return	
Total gross rent (at settlement)	$66,005
– Finance	$26,964
– Property management	$3,960
– Non-reimbursed outgoings	$10,000
– Maintenance allowance	$1,000
= Cashflow	$24,081
Cash back	$24,081
÷ Cash down	$219,000
	× 100
= Cash-on-cash return	11%

All figures are GST exclusive and before tax.

Many investors might have stopped there and just been happy with an 11% cash-on-cash return. However, we've learned that buying a property is just the beginning, and that you make your real money in the management of the deal. Not the day-to-day management of the property, but the process of actively trying to optimise your investment. This means identifying, planning and taking actions to improve the returns, mitigate risks, and to prevent or quickly resolve issues.

Some of the actions we've already taken to improve the income and value of the properties are as follows:

➲ We renegotiated the automatic teller machine lease at renewal, to take into account inflation since the last review. This alone increased the rent by $500.

⊃ A new retail lease was negotiated to bring in an extra $2,100.

⊃ We created and leased a new storage area. It cost us under $100 to create and it allowed us to earn $1,040 per annum in extra rent.

In summary, in just a few months these combined actions have created an additional $3,640 in positive cashflow and, applying Steve's 'Rental Multiplier Theory', we've added an estimated $38,000 to the value of the property.

SEEING PROFIT

While this deal met Steve's old '11 Second Solution', what we really found attractive were the opportunities to improve the properties to increase the income streams. For starters, one of the premises was vacant. Naturally, a vacant commercial premise is a turn-off for a passive investor as it represents a lack of income. Yet applying Steve's 'Problem + Solution = Profit' formula, we figured that if we could solve the problem by finding a tenant, then we'd not only improve the cashflow, but we'd also increase the value of the property in the eyes of other commercial property investors.

It was clear to us that the properties could be managed a lot more professionally and proactively than they had been and that the rents were a little on the low side compared to other rents in the area. From what we could see, the properties had suffered from 'casual' management.

Physically, some parts of the properties were starting to show signs of neglect and were in need of maintenance. Looking at the leases, some tenants had not had any kind of rent review for several years, so inflation had eroded the value of the leases. A few of the existing tenants were on short-term periodic leases (paying month to month) which also represented a problem for a commercial property, where investors are often looking for the security of longer term contracts.

We could also see opportunities to develop new sources of income. For example, there was a large yard at the back of the shops. Part of this was being used by one of the tenants as a materials storage area, but another part was unused and could potentially be redeveloped.

In summary, while the property numbers were okay, we were confident they could be made a lot better.

Our Immediate Plans

Aside from finding a tenant for the vacant premises, our plan for the properties was to develop new income streams and to improve the existing income streams over the next four or so years. This would improve the cashflow, at the same time as improving the market value of the properties. We could then leverage the equity created to invest in other properties.

We've already added a storage area for one of the existing tenants, which provides a little more income. We're now looking at options for converting the unused space in the yard into garaging or self storage units, which we could then lease out as a further income stream.

We didn't want to be heavy handed in trying to jack the rents up as high as possible, so we started by working to help the tenants enhance their businesses by making improvements on the properties and contributing to fitouts for new tenants. We've taken an active interest in the local business association so that we can keep in touch with developments in the area and understand the needs of our tenants better.

Our approach is to create win–win situations where the tenants benefit from improvements to the properties, and we benefit through incremental increases in the rents, from new income streams, and from tenants on periodic leases moving up to longer-term agreements. We want our shops and offices to be the place that local businesses want to rent. For example, something out of left field is that we're using our computer knowledge to put together a website for the local business association — check it out at <www.homedale.co.nz>. Local businesses will be able to promote themselves on the site. Who knows, maybe there's another income stream for the future right there!?

NOT EVERYTHING WENT TO PLAN

Like many things in life, not everything with this investment went quite as planned. Just a month or so after settlement, our property manager informed us that one of the tenants was unable to sustain his business and would not be able to continue leasing from us. As the tenant was in real financial hardship and was going through some personal issues, we allowed him to break out of the lease. Of course, this put a dent in our cashflow for a few months while we found a new tenant!

Furthermore, while we'd had a building inspection done, it wasn't particularly thorough as it overlooked several obvious issues that have subsequently cost us money to repair. In retrospect we should have put in the legwork to find a building inspector with references, and carried out a more extensive physical inspection ourselves.

Learning Outcomes

What have we learned from the deal? For one thing we now have a much greater appreciation for how the income generated by a commercial property affects its value, based on market yields. That is, for the value of a commercial property to increase, either the income generated by the property needs to increase or the market yield accepted by property investors needs to fall. So if there are opportunities to improve the income streams of a commercial property, then this can represent a great opportunity to increase the overall value of the property too.

It's been a change in mindset to realise that the opportunities to improve an investment are only limited by your imagination.

For example, right now we're assessing the potential of using the wall at the end of the buildings for advertising space, to create another potential income stream. Or maybe we could make use of the airspace above the buildings — the sky's the limit, right?!

Multiple income streams are a great way to mitigate some of the risks inherent in commercial property. We know from first-hand experience that it can take a lot longer to retenant a commercial property, than it often does for a residential property, so it's good to have multiple leases that will offset any vacancy.

We now have a much better understanding of the differences in commercial versus residential lending such as lower loan-to-value ratios (typically 60% to 75%), shorter-term loans (10 to 15 years) and higher than residential interest rates. Each of these can have a significant bearing on the numbers in a deal, so you've got to be careful about your assumptions.

We've also learned how banks evaluate commercial properties and commercial leases for lending purposes. For example, location influences the loan-to-value ratio (higher LVRs for metropolitan or CBD locations, and lower LVRs for suburban locations). Rents are often discounted when assessing loan serviceability (periodic leases are discounted by a set percentage, but fixed-term leases may often be taken into account at full net value).

However, the biggest thing this deal has taught us is probably the importance of having solid relationships with people on the ground when investing overseas — especially if you want to make the most of those investments! Having a great team is always important, but it becomes so much more important when you are geographically separated from the investment. We've spent time in New Zealand getting to know solicitors, our accountant, bank manger, real estate agents, property managers, builders, tradespeople and other local bodies. I really have to credit John and Mel who represent us on the local business association and who have been such an amazing help in liaising with the tenants and managing the work that we've been doing on the properties!

It would be fair to say that without these relationships we wouldn't have been able to achieve the success we have with our New Zealand investments.

SHARED INSIGHTS

Lynn, Tony and I believe that the most important insight we can leave you with is this: make sure your investing decisions are always based on facts, not emotions or opinions.

This means learning to crunch the numbers on property deals, doing your due diligence, and always checking your assumptions. Figure out your likely profits, but also understand your worst-case scenario and make sure it's something you can live with before undertaking any investment.

A lot of people never get started in investing because they're afraid of making mistakes and of losing money. Risk can never be totally eliminated, but if you know the likely numbers in a deal, and understand your worst-case scenario, then you'll be a lot more confident in taking managed risks.

Oh, and don't forget to have some fun!

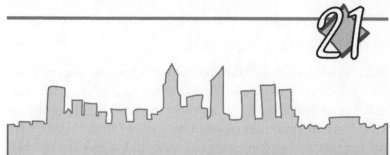

Melissa and Andrew Divide and Conquer

Background:
Melissa and Andrew live on acreage in regional New South Wales where they own and manage a lot of cattle. They have a real affinity with the land and are keen property investors. In this chapter, Melissa tells the story of a subdivision and construction deal.

FINDING DEALS

Having bought a reasonable amount of property over the last few years, when Andrew or I are asked how we find deals in the current market, our reply is almost always, 'It depends on your strategy'. We say this because we see a lot of people making the mistake of buying properties first and then applying strategies as afterthoughts.

In our case, we primarily use two strategies:

1. buy, renovate and sell, or

2. buy, subdivide, build and sell.

Since we stick to these strategies, we know the processes well and have some benchmarks and ideas as to the sorts of properties that make good investments. For example, we wouldn't generally buy a property that was prerenovated with the plan of holding it for the long term. We are more hands on than that and like to create our own profit rather than wait for it.

A good example to highlight our approach is the deal that we've chosen for this chapter. It came to our attention as a beautifully maintained solid-brick home that was located just 500 metres from the town centre, and positioned across the road from a leafy park with a walking track and beautiful views. The house was situated at the front of a 3,400 square metre block of land.

The Front — an Existing House

After buying the property our plan was to:

➲ Subdivide the existing house from the land at the rear.

➲ Sell the existing house and use profits to reduce the cost of holding the remaining land.

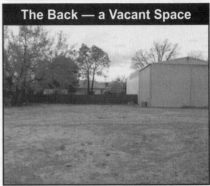

The Back — a Vacant Space

➲ Subdivide the remaining land again into eight smaller parcels and build townhouses or free-standing villa units.

⮑ Sell as many units as possible to repay the total debt and then hold the remaining properties debt-free for a positive cashflow return, or as an 'equity bank' that could be used to borrow against for future projects.

We started this project in 2004 and although it's taken longer than we first thought, it will be completed by the end of 2007.

THE NUMBERS

Here are the numbers relating to the existing brick house that we rented out for 18 months until the subdivision was approved.

Purchase Costs	
Purchase price	$279,000
+ Closing costs	$13,950
= Total purchase costs	$292,950

Holding Costs	
Interest costs	$39,843
+ Subdivision costs	$3,280
+ Rates	$2,380
= Total holding costs	$45,503

Income and Sale Proceeds	
Rent received	$9,360
+ Sale proceeds	$232,000
= Total sales proceeds	$241,360

Summary of House	
Income and sale proceeds	$241,360
− Purchase costs	$292,950
− Holding costs	$45,503
= Cost of remaining land	$97,903

Having worked out the cost of the remaining land, we can then work out the cost and profit of the eight units that we are building.

Land, Building and Other Costs	
Cost of land	$97,903
+ Subdivision costs	$4,200
+ Planning costs	$22,192
+ Construction costs	$1,358,160
+ Finance costs	$107,295
= Total costs	$1,589,750

Sale Proceeds (If All Are Sold)	
Expected sales price	$2,240,000
– Sales costs	$56,000
= Expected sales proceeds	$2,184,000

Profit Summary	
Expected sales proceeds	$2,184,000
– Land, building and other costs	$1,589,750
= Net sales proceeds	$594,250
– Estimated net GST payable	$73,300
= Expected profit	$520,950

Some people may be frightened by the size of these numbers, however, if you're going to build eight units then you're going to be investing millions of dollars.

WHAT WENT WRONG

Actually, the deal has been very successful for us overall, but we're not going to tell you about all the things that went right, and how clever we were. Instead, you'll probably learn more from a short list of some of the things that went wrong:

- ➲ We didn't think to do a property inspection on the day of settlement, which is a pity because we would have noticed that the front gates to the property were missing.

- ➲ The subdivision has taken an astounding amount of time. This was partly due to another major property acquisition that soaked up all our available funds. We also used our own 'out of town' surveyor rather than the only local consultant. Next time we'd be sure to engage the local surveyor to begin work immediately after the property became unconditional so we could lodge plans with council the day after we settled.

- ➲ Instead of waiting for subdivision of the existing home, for the sake of getting a sale we could have sold or given an option to buy 'subject to council approval' of the new title.

- ➲ Overall, our preliminary planning was very basic and too optimistic. We have learned to hope for the best-case scenario, but to expect and budget for the worst.

- ➲ We procrastinated for too long with some of our other investments, which took our focus away from getting our systems in place for the development of these units. There was more profit in this deal than our other investments, so we should have prioritised our time accordingly.

In summary, the biggest learning outcome we gained from this deal was to realise that our management style needed to change. Now we set strict deadlines for time management and use a simple system to keep all of our deals in place so that they progress consistently in line with our strategies.

FINAL THOUGHTS

We've come to understand and appreciate that you need many skills to be a successful property investor, and that while reading books and attending seminars can make you aware of the skills you lack or need to improve, it's the experience you gain from real-world investing that provides the best learning opportunities.

Finally, before you buy anything, make sure that you know your market, know your area and, most of all, know your strategy.

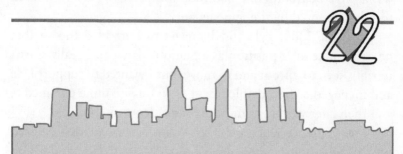

Kate and Lyle's Positive Cashflow Executive Gem

Background:
Over the years I've met and chatted with thousands of investors, and from time to time you meet the most incredible people who you know are going to set the world alight with their enthusiasm. Kate and Lyle certainly fall into this category. Both paramedics, they chased down their unusual dreams by moving from sunny Perth to the dusty outback roads of north-west WA and, once there, snapped up a positive cashflow gem.

PROPERTY INVESTING PARAMEDICS

Lyle and I (Kate) met in May 2002 through our jobs working as St John's Ambulance paramedics. Actually, to share a secret, he was my tutor! As property investors, we bought our first deal — a block of land — in 2003. Our second purchase came in 2004. It was a three-bedroom, one-bathroom property in Perth, which to this day is rented by the same tenant.

In April 2004, Lyle and I moved to Port Hedland so that he could take up a position as a Station Manager. I really wasn't terribly keen to uproot and to move, but I wanted to support Lyle and managed to find employment as an on-site mine paramedic, and then later working out of the same depot as Lyle.

The hours we work are crazy — in fact, we've even clocked up the ridiculous figure of 96 hours straight! Lyle and I also regularly work cross shifts, which means I sleep when he works and vice versa. This can make for lonely living as we don't get much quality time together.

To fill in the hours apart I'll often read literature about how to use property to make money. That's how I came across Steve McKnight's two books. Reading *From 0 To 130 Properties in 3.5 Years* left me feeling fired up and in the space of two weeks I'd found and bought two properties in Port Hedland. I had negotiated long settlement dates with a view to earning capital gains since the town had been buzzing and the news of a major port expansion had led to a severe housing shortage.

A technique that's worked well for me is using online search criteria. For example, the deal that I have showcased in this chapter was found after looking for an 'executive-style' three or four bedroom house that could be marketed to company executives being relocated to manage the expansion of the port.

DEALING DIRECTLY WITH A VENDOR

Using <www.owner.com.au>, my search revealed a potential property that I had at first dismissed because I thought it was extremely over priced. It was on the market at $370,000, which was about $40,000 more than I thought it was worth.

Sure, the pictures looked lovely, but I thought the owner was just being too greedy. Nevertheless, a few days later I had cause to be in the area so I decided to drive by for a street inspection. Feeling a little more optimistic I called the contact listed on the internet who actually turned out to be the owner! From our discussions I discovered that the property was overpriced because the owner had renovated it himself and was extremely proud of its lovely condition.

I also discovered that he needed a sale so he could build another home.

Executive Accommodation

From further conversations and research, Lyle and I discovered that the property had been on the market for two weeks but that no-one else had called and that the owner was becoming anxious to make a sale. We discussed this with him, and eventually we mutually agreed on a price of $360,000 with a longish settlement

A Quality Finish Inside

of four and a half months. At the same time we negotiated for him to rent back the property on an open lease at $600 per week.

In the end we paid a little more than we really wanted to, but the longer settlement time allowed us to market the property during the peak time of year when companies were looking for executive accommodation.

SEEING THE PROFIT OPPORTUNITY

As the property was completely renovated inside and out, it was clear that the vendor had contributed a lot of blood, sweat, tears and money to facilitate its fantastic condition. It really was a complete package, and very nicely presented as an executive home. It's not an overstatement to say that it was one of the best properties in South Hedland. Some of the many features included:

➲ a fully fenced plot in a quiet cul-de-sac

➲ 640 square metres of land

➲ four good-sized bedrooms with full-length, built-in robes

➲ one large bathroom with a separate toilet

➲ a lovely kitchen with great built-in cupboards and lots of space

➲ an outdoor patio and entertaining area, and

➲ low-maintenance gardens (they looked almost Japanese style with all the pebbles) and water fountains in the back yard with three large shade sails.

Since most of the value-add work to the physical property had been done, we concentrated on marketing it in such a way as to command a premium rent.

South Hedland was a town in transition since the wharf was being upgraded to allow for the shipping of bulk iron ore. Our strategy was to offer the property as an executive residence to one of the CEOs of the many consulting companies that had set up as a spin off to the major infrastructure works. We expected to own the property for one or two years and to then sell it for a tidy capital gain on the back of increasing home values.

I decided to enrol in a property management correspondence course run by the Real Estate Institute of Western Australia. Aside from what I learned, it also allowed me to self-manage the property, thereby avoiding the need to pay exorbitant property management fees (which were sometimes as much as 9% of rent collected — an amount between $4,000 and $5,000 for this property).

TRANSACTION TROUBLES

You'll recall that we purchased the property with a four-and-a-half-month settlement period. About eight weeks before settlement was due, the vendor asked us to visit him to discuss a problem. He wanted us to delay settlement further or to reduce the rent to $500 a week on a lease where he could walk away when it suited them.

We explained that the purchase was an investment and we required some level of certainty (as we did not want to miss out on the company wanting to rent such a great quality home). We were prepared to help the vendor out if he committed to a short-term lease.

Sadly, at this point the vendor became very angry and emotional, and decided to cancel his potential rental agreement. Worse, despite it being a condition of our purchase, the vendor made it difficult for us by playing hard-ball when we wanted to show potential renters through the property prior to settling.

Nevertheless, in hindsight it probably worked in our favour as we had a new signed lease within two hours of settling, at $650 per week. Already the current tenant has contacted us asking if we are interested in a renegotiating a longer five-year lease with another five-year option.

THE NUMBERS

The numbers for this deal are summarised in the table overleaf.

Good News!

Two months after settlement, the property was conservatively valued at between $420,000 and $430,000. That's an increase of between $60,000 and $70,000! This confirms our strategy to buy scarce, good-quality properties in a market experiencing jobs growth on the back of booming infrastructure improvements.

A Summary of the Numbers	
Purchase price	$360,000
Deposit	$—
+ Closing costs	$15,300
= Total cash required	$15,300
Annual rent at $650 per week	$33,800
− Finance costs*	$23,400
− Rates	$2,000
− Insurance	$2,400
− Repairs and other costs	$764
= Budgeted cashflow	$5,236
Cash back	$5,236
÷ Cash down	$15,300
	× 100
= Cash-on-cash return	34.22%

* Repaying the $360,000 borrowed at 6.5% interest-only. We borrowed 100% of the purchase price by using equity in our home and two other investment properties.

THE BIGGEST LESSON LEARNED

While it seemed new and exciting at the time, the decision to deal directly with the vendor to make this transaction created a lot of extremely hard work.

I often had to act like a counsellor as much as I did an investor, and that wasn't much fun. In the future, unless there's a compelling reason for doing otherwise, we'll stick to buying and selling property through real estate agents.

FINAL INSIGHTS

It's a mistake to run out and to buy just anything. Instead, think about, research and find a niche market, and then know it better than the average investor or homeowner. In particular, assess where growth is likely to occur before buying. If the right circumstances don't currently exist, try to create them!

PART IV SUMMARY

Wow! What an inspiring collection of stories!

The aim of the chapters you've just read has been to remind you that, for all the dangers we discussed in the early sections of this book, and all the fears and doubts that you may be feeling, real success is out there and there are real people enjoying it. Right now. In today's market.

Each of the investors you have heard from has been part of my R.E.S.U.L.T.S. mentoring program and has had to be accountable to an investment coach and other participants. Now, you don't have to join such a group to ensure success but you do need to be accountable for the actions you're taking to reach your goals and a strong support network can be vital to help you do this.

As the participants shared some of the keys to their successes, did you notice any common themes? If you were reading carefully there were many clues as to the ingredients you need to create a successful investing recipe.

One of the key elements in each of the stories was a willingness to take on and to solve a problem that other investors had been keen to walk past. This approach allowed R.E.S.U.L.T.S. participants to see 'invisible' profit potential where others saw none.

Another of the common traits was an ability to manage the numbers and the shape of each deal. Many would-be investors are still wondering where all the positive cashflow deals are, but if you've read all the previous pages in this book you should be starting to realise that successful investors are *making* their deals rather than *waiting* to find them.

PART IV SUMMARY (CONT'D)

This means trying to add value and to examine creative ways to vary settlement time, rental amounts, and leases in order to mould the numbers into the right shape.

Rarely will a perfectly-shaped and convenient profit fall into your lap. Instead profits are being made by taking awkward situations and actively changing them into more attractive deals.

Well, the bulk of this intensive property tutorial is now behind us. So where does that leave you, as a reader? It's been nice having your attention for a while but you now have to ask yourself a question. Does it end here?

My tutorial is fast approaching it's finish, but in the final section I'm going to present you with a plan to help you implement some of the strategies we've discussed for yourself.

When you turn the page and start reading the final chapters, be sure that you're fully focused and ready to start taking action. If you do, you'll find that this tutorial is not finishing after all. In fact, it's just starting and while I can't do the investing for you, if you're ready to take action your learning journey is only just about to begin!

PART V:

What Next?

23

Your Step-By-Step Implementation Plan

Let me warn you that writing a book can be a real pain in the neck — literally! In the course of typing this manuscript I've been to my physiotherapist at least six times, and I've also had a dozen or so massages to ease stiff and sore areas in my back, neck and shoulders. Lena — my friendly physio — seems to take particular delight in hearing me squeal as she mobilises muscles, tendons and joints that have become worse for wear after hours hunched over a keyboard. When I cry out, Lena chuckles like a playful masochist and explains that some degree of pain is necessary to get the joints moving properly again. Strangely enough, the mild agony soon feels almost nice and before long all the pain has gone and I'm back at the computer like nothing was ever wrong.

Investing is not dissimilar in that making a start is often the most difficult, challenging and painful stage of the entire process. Just as I am mobilising joints that have become stuck in a rut, new investors are effectively trying to mobilise a part of their lives that may have been previously stuck.

For instance, it will take a lot of time and effort to overcome the difficulties of sourcing trustworthy and knowledgeable advisers, sorting through conflicting information and finding the courage to eventually bite the bullet and to take action.

STEVE'S 24-DAY 'PATH TO PROGRESS' PROGRAM

I'm told it takes 21 days to make or to break a habit. With this in mind I've devised a 24-day (I added a few extra just for good measure) program to help you gain momentum as you work your way through the challenging start-up period.

Furthermore, it's my sincerest desire that this book does not become just another volume gathering dust on your shelf once you've had a quick read. I want it to be the catalyst that inspires you to take action to change your circumstances. I can say with complete certainty that, provided you follow the program as written, then in just 24 days you'll be in a much more knowledgeable and confident investing position.

While it doesn't really matter what day you begin, for simplicity's sake I've assumed that you'll begin on a Monday. There are several factors that will influence how long it will take you to complete each day's activities. However, as a guide, allow around 40 minutes.

WEEK 1

Week 1 begins at a gentle pace as we do some financial warming up in preparation for the sessions ahead.

Day 1 (Monday)

Reading: Re-read chapter 1.

Essential Principle: Sometimes you need to reach rock bottom before you find the motivation to change to your life.

Actions:

1. In the table below:

   A. List in the left-hand column the top five things that you would like to change in your life.

   B. In the middle column rate your desire to change between 10 (must do it immediately) and 1 (not urgent at all).

   C. In the column to the right, identify how investing can help you to achieve the life change you'd like to make.

How Investing Can Help Achieve Your Goals		
Need for Change	Desire	How Investing Helps
1.		
2.		
3.		
4.		
5.		

2. Using the space below write down something you've been putting off (a task, conversation, phone call, or anything) that you'd like to address within the next 24 hours.

_____

_____

_____

Day 2 (Tuesday)

Reading: Re-read chapter 2.

Essential Principle: We do the things we do for a combination of selfish (to gain a greater feeling of significance about ourselves), and selfless (to contribute to the lives of others) reasons.

Actions:

1. Start by taking care of the task you listed yesterday as one that you'd been putting off.

2. In the space below, list the areas in your life that provide significance, and also the various ways you contribute to the lives of others.

Increase Your Significance	Contribute To Others

Looking at your list, is there an equal mix of significance and contribution? If not, is that a sign that your life is not correctly balanced?

3. Using the space below write down something you've been putting off (a task, conversation, phone call, or anything) that you'd like to address within the next 24 hours.

_____

_____

_____

_____

Day 3 (Wednesday)

Reading: Re-read chapter 3.

Essential Principle: It's up to you to take control and responsibility for building the financial future you desire.

Actions:

1. Start by taking care of the task you listed yesterday as one that you'd been putting off.

2. Provide an estimate of the following figures:

    ➲ How much employment income do you earn each year? $_____

    ➲ How much money do you currently owe others? $_____

    ➲ What is the total current value of all your investments, excluding your home (cash, property and shares)? $_____

3. Using the space below write down something you've been putting off (a task, conversation, phone call, or anything) that you'd like to address within the next 24 hours.

_____

_____

_____

Day 4 (Thursday)

Reading: Re-read chapter 4.

Essential Principle: Your current financial position is no fluke — it's the result of the way you've been managing your money. A better outcome can only be created by improving the way you handle your investments.

Actions:

1. Start by taking care of the task you listed yesterday as one that you'd been putting off.

2. Work through the Steve McKnight challenge (see chapter 4).

3. What has completing the challenge highlighted as an area in your investing that needs immediate attention? Use the space below to make a list of changes that you want to make.

Changes	Deadline for Changing

Day 5 (Friday)

Reading: Re-read chapter 5.

Essential Principle: Debt represents a drawdown of future income. The more money you borrow, the harder and longer you'll have to work to repay it.

Actions:

1. Complete the 'Keys To Financial Freedom' exercise (page 81).

2. If you are committed to a brighter financial future then take action by signing up for the 33:30 Challenge at: <www.PropertyInvesting.com/book3>.

3. Test your knowledge and understanding of the 'Y − E = S' formula by explaining it to a family member or friend.

4. What action have you taken today to bring about the changes you identified on Day 4? Be accountable to your goals and list the steps you've taken to achieve them.

_____

_____

_____

Day 6 (Saturday)

Reading: Re-read chapter 6.

Essential Principle: If you're planning to get into debt, make sure you also have a plan for how you are going to get out of debt.

Actions:

1. Complete the table on page 102.

2. Start a 'Property Journal' — you can use something as simple as an A4 exercise book in which you paste real estate ads that you've cut out. Write down your thoughts and observations about the market.

   Make your first two entries about two auctions or open house inspections that you've attended. Collect the advertising brochures and paste them into your journal. Also include comments about the following:

   ➲ conduct of the real estate agent

   ➲ nature of the property (layout, style, features)

   ➲ what had been done to make the property visually appealing

   ➲ who you think is the 'target market' that the sellers are trying to attract

   ➲ your thoughts about the asking price.

3. What action have you taken today to bring about the changes you identified on Day 4?

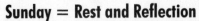

Sunday = Rest and Reflection

Have a rest — you deserve it! As you put your feet up and enjoy a cup of coffee, take a few moments to reflect on what you've accomplished over the past week.

WEEK 2

Week two is about picking up the pace and improving your knowledge of the property market. The tasks may start to become a little more difficult and they might also start to take you slightly more time to complete.

Day 7 (Monday)

Reading: Re-read chapter 7.

Essential Principle: The property market moves in cycles. It's unwise to invest against market momentum.

Actions:

1. In regards to the Steve McKnight Property Clock, what 'time' do you think it currently is in the real estate market in which you're investing?

2. What is the appropriate approach suggested for these conditions?

3. What inconsistencies exist between the way you're investing and the method outlined in the Property Clock?

4. What actions have you taken today to bring about the changes you identified on Day 4?

_____

_____

_____

_____

_____

_____

Day 8 (Tuesday)

Reading: Re-read chapter 8.

Essential Principle: The secret to building massive wealth is to grow your equity faster than you grow your debt.

Actions:

1. Use the table below to make a list of all the properties you currently own. Make an estimate of their current market values, the current debt owing on each, and the equity you have in each investment.

Properties You Currently Own			
Now	A	B	C
Address	CMV	Debt owing	Equity (A – B)
Total	$	$	$

2. Use the table overleaf to make a 'budget' of how you'd like the situation to look in six months' time:

Properties You Currently Own			
6 Months' Time	**A**	**B**	**C**
Address	CMV	Debt owing	Equity (A – B)
Total	$	$	$

3. What action have you taken today to bring about the changes you identified on Day 4?

_____

_____

_____

Day 9 (Wednesday)

Reading: Re-read chapter 9.

Essential Principle: Buying properties in your own name provides little asset protection and poor tax planning opportunities.

Actions:

1. Complete the survey on page 155.

2. What observations have you made as a result of completing the survey?

3. *WealthGuardian* is an excellent product that comprehensively explains the ins and outs of asset protection and tax planning. It's been specifically written for Australian property investors who need help or further ideas about how to improve their asset protection at the same

time as legally minimising their income tax. Find out more by visiting <www.PropertyInvesting.com/wealthguardian>.

4. Call the real estate agents who you met at the properties you inspected on the weekend. Ask them if they have any properties on their books that have been listed for longer than three months. Make an appointment to inspect them.

5. What action have you taken today to bring about the changes you identified on Day 4?

    _____

    _____

    _____

Day 10 (Thursday)

Reading: Re-read chapter 10.

Essential Principle: Beware of investing based on best-case scenarios.

Actions:

1. What are the nine ways I provide to help investors to survive and to thrive in a property market downturn?

    1. _____

    2. _____

    3. _____

    4. _____

    5. _____

    6. _____

    7. _____

    8. _____

    9. _____

2. Circle which of the nine areas you need to work harder at mastering.

3. Consider booking into the next one-day '0 to 260+ Facilitation Seminar' (see www.PropertyInvesting.com/book3). Bring along a copy of your book and receive up to a 150% credit against any other education materials purchased that day.

4. Make a list of three things that you've accomplished over the past 10 days?

_____

_____

_____

_____

Day 11 (Friday)

Reading: Re-read chapter 11.

Essential Principle: Automatic profits cannot be expected at all stages of the property market. On the other hand, automated profits are within your power to create, but you must solve people and housing problems in a cost-effective manner.

Actions:

1. Looking back over the table you completed on Day 8, how much of your current equity is 'Automatic', and how much of it has been 'Automated'?

2. Over the next three years, what is going to provide the majority of the 'growth' in your property portfolio?

3. Identify three suburbs or areas that you think are primed for exceptional growth. Why do you think these places are poised to earn above-market returns?

4. Try to explain the Property Tree model (page 190) to a friend or relative.

5. Visit <www.PropertyInvesting.com/forum> and spend at least 10 minutes surfing the community forum boards to see what sort of issues are being debated.

Day 12 (Saturday)

Reading: Re-read chapter 12.

Essential Principle: In flat markets that lack momentum, it's easier and less risky to make smaller profits more often, than to look to invest for huge once-off windfall gains.

Actions:

1. Complete the tables in chapter 12 to practise crunching numbers.

2. In the table below, use the left-hand column to summarise (in one sentence) the tip for accelerated growth, and in the right-hand column identify an area where you feel that opportunity is available.

| Tips for Accelerated Growth ||
Summary of Tip	Area / Suburb
1.	
2.	
3.	
4.	
5.	
6.	
7.	
8.	
9.	

Tips for Accelerated Growth *(cont'd)*	
Summary of Tip	**Area / Suburb**
10.	
11.	
12.	
13.	
14.	
15.	

3. Inspect two 'Open House' properties and make a note of all the problems you see. If you'd like to use the same Property Inspection Templates that I do then these are for sale at <www.PropertyInvesting.com/BuyerBeware>. Be sure to write down your observations in your Property Journal.

Sunday = Rest and Reflection

Wow! Two weeks down and look at all you've accomplished! If you're happy with what you've achieved then treat yourself to something special (of course, don't go and blow the budget!)

WEEK 3

Okay, I've given you two weeks to build up some momentum, but now it's time to pick up the pace a little. After starting with a look at how you can find positive cashflow properties, we'll turn our attention to deal evaluation and then finish off with some case studies.

Day 13 (Monday)

Reading: Re-read chapter 13.

Essential Principle: While positive cashflow outcomes can be bought, the best opportunities are made by solving problems.

Actions:

1. Write down seven tasks that you want to have accomplished by this time next week.

    1. _____
    2. _____
    3. _____
    4. _____
    5. _____
    6. _____
    7. _____

2. In the table below, use the left-hand column to summarise (in one sentence) each of the 12 ways (as outlined throughout chapter 13) that you can find or make a positive cashflow outcome. In the right-hand column identify how you might apply each method.

| How Will You Find or Create Positive Cashflow Properties? ||
Method	Area / Application
1.	
2.	
3.	
4.	
5.	
6.	
7.	
8.	
9.	
10.	
11.	
12.	

3.   Identify which of the methods listed in the previous table is the one that you want to start investigating immediately.

Day 14 (Tuesday)

Reading: Re-read chapter 14.

Essential Principle: Avoid being a property buyer who dabbles in investing. Be an investor who uses real estate to maximise your returns. Having changed your mindset, track your success with some or all of the five money-making formulas.

Actions:

1.   Complete all the number crunching examples included in chapter 14.

2.   Use the free template at <www.PropertyInvesting.com/book3> to calculate the five returns for each property in your portfolio. If you don't own any properties then use a deal that you've previously inspected.

3.   Complete one of the seven tasks that you'd set yourself to finish by next Monday.

Day 15 (Wednesday)

Reading: Re-read chapter 15.

Essential Principle: Unsophisticated investors buy on emotion or gut feeling and therefore hope for a profit. Smart investors allocate time and money to completing their homework before buying and they can expect a profit. Are you hoping for or expecting a profit?

Actions:

1.   Work through all the number crunching examples in chapter 15.

2. Use the free template at <www.PropertyInvesting.com/ book3> to perform the three quick tests to evaluate a property that you've previously purchased or inspected. What does your analysis reveal?

3. Complete another two of the seven tasks that you'd set yourself to finish by next Monday.

Day 16 (Thursday)

Reading: Re-read chapter 16.

Essential Principle: Golden opportunities rarely land in your lap. You need to position yourself to gain a slice of the profit pie.

Actions:

1. What are five things you have gleaned from reading Troy and Bec's case study?

   1. _____
   2. _____
   3. _____
   4. _____
   5. _____

2. Complete two more tasks from the 'To-Do' list you set on Monday.

3. What has been the outcome from the two inspections you attended on Day 9? What have you learned? Record your thoughts in your Property Journal.

Day 17 (Friday)

Reading: Re-read chapter 17.

Essential Principle: Good deals are not location specific — they exist wherever you can find people and/or property problems that are within your power and budget to solve.

Actions:

1. What are five things you have gleaned from reading Tammy and her crew's case study?

1. _____
2. _____
3. _____
4. _____
5. _____

2. Complete another task from the 'To-Do' list you set on Monday.

Day 18 (Saturday)

Reading: Re-read chapter 18.

Essential Principle: Good opportunities exist in unusual places and circumstances.

Actions:

1. What are five things you have gleaned from reading Suzanne and Katrina's case study?

1. _____
2. _____
3. _____
4. _____
5. _____

2. There should only be one task left to do on the list you set last Monday. Finish off the week well by completing it now.

3. Attend another two open houses. Write down your observations (in your Property Journal) about potential problems, and also gather enough information to crunch all the deal-evaluation numbers.

If you'd prefer to save time and effort by automating the number crunching then a purpose-written software program called *Investment Detective* can be a tremendously powerful tool. Download a free trial version now from: <www.PropertyInvesting.com/InvestmentDetective>.

Sunday = Rest and Reflection

If you've been faithfully following the daily program then you should be congratulated and you will have achieved considerable momentum. You might feel like you've accomplished more in this short time than in the previous few months or even years.

WEEK FOUR

This week we'll starting wrapping up and, in doing so, we'll look at ways to ensure that you don't lose your momentum.

Day 19 (Monday)

Reading: Re-read chapter 19.

Essential Principle: Minimise the potential for losses by knowing your target market and by avoiding over-capitalising.

Actions:

1. What are five things you have gleaned from reading the case study provided by Anna and her team?

    1. _____

    2. _____

3. _____

4. _____

5. _____

2. Write down seven tasks that you want to have accomplished by this time next week.

1. _____

2. _____

3. _____

4. _____

5. _____

6. _____

7. _____

Day 20 (Tuesday)

Reading: Re-read chapter 20.

Essential Principle: There are good commercial properties and offshore opportunities, but make sure the profit is worth the additional risk.

Actions:

1. What are five things you have gleaned from reading Simon, Lynn and Tony's case study?

1. _____

2. _____

3. _____

4. _____

5. _____

2. If you haven't already done so, consider signing up for the next one-day facilitation session. Details are available online at <www.PropertyInvesting.com/book3>.

3. Complete one of the seven tasks that you'd set yourself to finish by next Monday.

Day 21 (Wednesday)

Reading: Re-read chapter 21.

Essential Principle: There are many ways to profit from property. The more ways you can master, the more money-making opportunities there will be that you can take advantage of.

Actions:

1. What are five things you have gleaned from reading Melissa and Andrew's case study?

    1. _____
    2. _____
    3. _____
    4. _____
    5. _____

2. Complete two of the seven tasks that you had set yourself to have finished by next Monday.

Day 22 (Thursday)

Reading: Re-read chapter 22.

Essential Principle: Great deals exist in all price ranges. You just have to think laterally!

Actions:

1. What are five things you have gleaned from reading Kate and Lyle's case study?

1. _____
2. _____
3. _____
4. _____
5. _____

2. Complete two of the seven tasks that you'd set yourself to have finished by next Monday.

Day 23 (Friday)

Reading: Source some more property related books from a library or bookstore to further your knowledge. I have written two other books if you're stuck for a place to start!

Essential Principle: Momentum requires discipline and dedication. As you practise your investing you'll become more skilled and better able to identify opportunities that others pass over.

Actions:

1. Make a list of ten accomplishments that you've achieved over the past 23 days.

1. _____
2. _____
3. _____
4. _____
5. _____
6. _____
7. _____
8. _____
9. _____
10. _____

3.   Complete the second last task that you had set yourself to have finished by next Monday.

Day 24 (Saturday)

Reading: Continue to explore new property books, magazines, and websites that will help you to keep up with current trends.

Essential Principle: Watch out for people who try to protect you as you move forward but end up just holding you back!

Actions:

1.   Attend another two open houses. In your Property Journal, write down the potential problems, and also gather enough information to be able to crunch the numbers using the formulas and 3-2-1 deal analysis framework identified in this book.

2.   Make a list of three other people (friends, family or colleagues) who you feel would benefit from reading this book.

1. _____

2. _____

3. _____

Only begrudgingly lend them your prized copy. If possible, be generous and invest the $30 or so dollars needed for them to buy their own, and give them the gift of financial knowledge!

Sunday = Rest and Reflection

If you've faithfully followed the program then congratulations, you will have an excellent chance of success in reaching your goals.

My final task for you is to look back on all you've achieved. Well done on your accomplishments. Keep up the good work!

WHAT NEXT?

If you like the idea of a structured program that encompasses education and continual action then, like those featured in the case studies section, you're extremely likely to gain massive benefit from joining my R.E.S.U.L.T.S. mentoring program.

R.E.S.U.L.T.S. participants are assigned a dedicated coach, receive regular mentoring folders that include audio, video and written components, and attend regular mini-seminars to network and to learn from like-minded investors.

Given it's a 12-month program, and considering the personal nature of the program, only a strictly limited number of mentoring participants can be accepted. To find out more visit:

<www.PropertyInvesting.com/Results>

Final Thoughts

On a recent family vacation to the Whitsunday Islands my young daughter and I shared a special moment as we searched for hermit crabs while the tide went out. As she danced and skipped across the beach I was reminded of a story I'd read on the internet a short while beforehand. It went something like this.

THE BUCKET STORY

A boy was walking along the beach one afternoon when he came across a fisherman. He was an old man with huge hands that had become weather-worn after years of exposure to the sun and wind. Sitting next to the fisherman was a slightly dented and rusted steel bucket. Peering inside the boy saw six or so crabs, all alive, that he presumed the fisherman had caught earlier. Puzzled that there was no lid on the bucket, the boy couldn't help but ask, 'Excuse me sir ...'

'Yes', the fisherman said with an aged but friendly voice.

'Aren't you worried that the crabs might escape?'

'Escape?' the fisherman wondered. A half smile came across his lips as he replied, 'Perhaps I might be if there was only one'. Pausing for a few seconds in thought, the fisherman continued, 'But when you put lots of crabs in a bucket together then those that try to scurry away are dragged back in by their friends. It seems the crabs' only concern is that they all suffer the same fate'.

THE PAINFUL DIFFERENCE

If you aspire to be financially free then you're making a choice to be different. Sadly, instead of being supported in your decision, you may find that your family, your friends and your work colleagues all try to drag you back to their way of thinking. Don't allow that! Be strong. Hold on to your dreams and don't permit other people to steal them from you.

Yes, there will be an amount of pain associated with leaving some previously close friends and associates behind, but that is, unfortunately, inevitable.

Steve's Investing Tip

Make sure you seek the support of people who share your passion — don't waste energy trying to convert others to your different way of thinking.

Here's an interesting exercise. In the space provided opposite write down the names of five people that you currently spend a lot of time with (children excluded). Then, in the next column to the right, note down whether that person is currently financially worse off, the same, or in a better monetary position than you.

Your Friends and Their Financial Positions	
1.	
2.	
3.	
4.	
5.	

When I did this exercise a few years ago I discovered that I'd surrounded myself with people who were in a similar financial position to my own. I didn't consciously do this, but on reflection it seemed that I'd conspired to be in the same bucket as others who shared comparable life and money goals.

Are you in the same boat? Are you seeking wealth-creation answers from people who are no more enlightened than you? How can you search out and apply the wisdom of those who have already done what you aspire to achieve?

Sowing and Reaping

Let me share with you a favourite popular saying that's been attributed to Samuel Smiles (a Scottish-born political reformer from the 1800s):

```
Sow a thought, reap an act.
Sow an act, reap a habit.
Sow a habit, reap your character.
Sow your character, reap your destiny.
```

In summary, it seems that the first step to carving out a new destiny is to change the way you think. Next, you must apply your new money mindset by changing the way you act, and over time, your new actions will form habits that will result in increasing 'money attractiveness'.

Finally, the way you use your money will reveal to others your true nature. Financial success brings out the worst in people more often than the best because greed is an appetite that can never be fully satisfied. Watch out then to ensure that your character isn't adversely shaped by your money and that, instead, the way you choose to spend your money allows others to see your true nature positively shine.

CAN YOU DO IT?

Three years ago I was approached by a cynic who asked, 'Do you misleadingly claim that anyone can replicate your success?'

'No', I replied, 'all I say is that the opportunity is open to all. Of course, not all are open to the opportunity'.

If you're open to the opportunity and are willing to undertake years of hard work, then I'm confident that you too will carve out a superior financial destiny. Surely you owe it to yourself to at least try.

Well, I think that's enough for now. I hope you've enjoyed this book and that it's provided you with many new investing insights, together with the motivation to try something new.

Thank you for giving me this opportunity to share my ideas with you. Until we next meet, remember that success comes from doing things differently!

Warmest regards,
Steve McKnight

PS — Go on, give it a go! There's a much better life on offer outside the bucket!

Appendix A

Definitions Behind the Sustainable Debt Levels Matrix

In chapter 6 we looked at sustainable debt levels and just how to decide on the right mix of cash and debt for your investing. Obviously everyone's circumstances are different, but I'm asked this question so often I've come up with a matrix (see below) that can be useful as a guide.

Guide to Sustainable Debt Levels					
Skill and Experience	Property Market				
	Crash	Down	Flat	Up	Boom
Novice	<50%	50% to 70%	60% to 75%	70% to 85%	75% to 90%
Average	<50%	50% to 75%	65% to 80%	75% to 90%	80% to 95%
Expert	<60%	60% to 80%	70% to 85%	80% to 95%	85% to 100%+

Early feedback from those who have seen the matrix indicated that it would be easier to use as a tool, if I could provide clearer definitions as to just what I meant by a 'market crash' and an 'average investor'. Obviously these are quite subjective, and it doesn't matter if you agree with them, the important thing is that you understand how your own investing abilities and chosen markets fit into the grid provided.

SKILL AND EXPERIENCE

Here's a guide for how I'd gauge investing ability:

➲ *Novice Investors*
You're new to property investing, or alternatively you have invested before but have made significant losses.

➲ *Average Investors*
You've been investing for a while now, however you've only completed a handful of deals. You feel you have some confidence, but you don't yet feel completely in control. You'll also need quite good personal money habits to qualify for this category, in order to prove that you can handle being in a moderate amount of debt. This includes budgeting and record keeping.

➲ *Expert Investors*
You have both the knowledge and also the proven experience to complete this investment. You've made significant profits in the past. You need strong personal money habits to qualify for this category, as solid debt management will be essential to your success.

PROPERTY MARKET

All property markets are cyclical, and this means that they'll experience seasons of growth and decline. Here are my definitions for each stage of the property market used in my matrix. As you read, have a think about how you would categorise the current market.

Crash

Front page headlines trumpet the news of property value declines, with home values falling by 50% or more from their peaks across multiple suburbs. There will also be many loan defaults, and a large number of mortgagee auctions. Typically, weaker institutional lenders start to fold as their bad debts increase.

Down

There's a general downturn in the property market, and this is underpinned by consumer pessimism about real estate opportunities. Home values are falling as there is more supply than demand, and it is taking a lot longer to sell a piece of real estate — perhaps several months. Furthermore, sellers are receiving offers of significantly less (say 20% or more) than their asking prices. Financiers start to tighten their lending policies and pay more attention to the quality of the assets being put up as security. Valuers become more conservative with their estimations. The press report stories of homeowners doing it tough rather than tales of quick fortunes being made.

Flat

Some suburbs may be increasing in value, while at the same time others are going down or remaining flat. The papers often contain conflicting accounts of positive and negative stories.

Up

Consumer sentiment is buoyant and prices are bobbing along. There's an expectation that money can be made through property investing, and this is enticing speculators to undertake riskier projects. Houses are selling quickly, and sellers are receiving near or slightly more than their asking prices. The media contains stories of inflated values being achieved. Most properties are selling within a month of being listed.

Boom

The moon has turned blue and crazy things are happening in the market. Sellers are receiving offers far in excess of their asking price as buyers clamber to get into the property market or else face missing out. Properties are selling within hours of being listed. Financiers have relaxed their lending policies so that anything with a front door and a roof gets approved, and the papers are full of ads from people running seminars on how to use real estate to make a fortune.

SUGGESTED DEBT LEVELS EXPLAINED

With the skill and market conditions outlined, let's now look at the logic behind why I've assigned the percentage debt values the way I have.

Novice Investor in a Crashing Market
(Debt Levels Less than 50% of Portfolio Value)

While profits exist in all markets, the combination of low skill and a climate of falling property prices mean that the risk of making a loss can be quite high. One of the ways to protect yourself will be to keep borrowings to a minimal level, as this will reduce your interest costs and also provide an equity buffer should you need more cash in an emergency.

Novice Investor in a Downturn
(Debt Levels Between 50% and 70% of Portfolio Value)

There is a tendency for unskilled investors to buy in a downtrending market because they believe that bargains exist when current values are compared with prices achieved in better times. The price someone paid for a property several years ago is only relevant if the same market conditions exist. If times have changed then historical data may be interesting, but I wouldn't use it as a basis for gauging today's value.

Novice Investor in a Flat Market
(Debt Levels Between 60% and 75% of Portfolio Value)

In researching my second book, *$1,000,000 in Property in One Year*, I came to the conclusion that the average property cycle in Australia sees prices rise for one third of the time, and prices stagnating or down for two thirds of the time. Therefore, given the recent boom lasted for roughly five years, I'd expect the next flat or down phase to last for 10 years.

Does this mean that we should lock up our chequebooks or take up ostrich farming? No. It means that we need to be more selective about the investing strategy we adopt, and also our timing as we get into and out of the real estate market. A debt to current property value ratio of up to 75% is a good guideline to apply since it should keep you under most bank's risk-assessment radar screens.

Novice Investor in an Uptrending Market
(Debt Levels Between 70% and 85% of Portfolio Value)

Investors with little skill can start to be slightly more aggressive with their borrowings since an uptrending market compensates for their lack of experience. That is, most mistakes will be covered by the general trend of rising prices.

Novice Investor in a Booming Market
(Debt Levels Between 75% and 90% of Portfolio Value)

When the property market's booming, I'd do whatever's necessary to jump on the real estate bandwagon. This is the only situation in which you might consider aggressive debt holdings as a novice, but even then you wouldn't ever want to borrow more than you could comfortably afford to repay.

Average Investor in a Crashing Market
(Debt Levels Less than 50% of Portfolio Value)

Despite an average investor having more skill than a newbie, there's still a significant amount of risk when investing during a crash. Carrying less than 50% of your portfolio's value in debt will give you a safety buffer against dramatically falling values and also mean that you have access to money if you find an exceptional deal.

Average Investor in a Downturn
(Debt Levels Between 50% and 75% of Portfolio Value)

Debt reduction is sometimes the best strategy in a down market. Therefore, as the property market experiences a downturn, an average investor might like to sell poorer performing assets and use the profits to reduce debt.

Average Investor in a Flat Market
(Debt Levels Between 65% and 80% of Portfolio Value)

Flat markets lend themselves to quick-turnaround property deals, in which you get in and out of the property market within a matter of months and make a fast profit for your troubles. Unless you are coming out of a downturn, it's generally unwise to be investing in long-term projects (anything greater than 18 months), since you run the risk of having to sell the project in far less hospitable times.

This point was well illustrated by investors who bought properties off the plan during the latter stages of the recent boom, only to find that when construction finished the values had dropped because market conditions had softened.

Average Investor in an Uptrending Market
(Debt Levels Between 75% and 90% of Portfolio Value)

An upwards trending market carries with it enough momentum to sustain higher debt levels since growth should outpace negative cashflow. Until investors have more experience, they'd be wise to stick to 'normal' deals rather than creative options. Again, it's unsafe to ever borrow more than you can afford to repay!

Average Investor in a Booming Market
(Debt Levels of Between 80% and 95% of Portfolio Value)

A booming market is the safest time to take greater risks, so holding a higher percentage debt allows you to own more property and therefore be positioned to profit from greater exposure to rapidly rising prices. Be careful that you don't borrow too much and become a slave to your debt.

Expert Investor in a Crashing Market
(Debt Levels Less than 60% of Portfolio Value)

Experienced investors are better equipped to handle unforeseen circumstances, and so they're able to maintain higher debt levels even when the property market is crashing.

Expert Investor in a Downturn
(Debt Levels Between 60% and 80% of Portfolio Value)

Investors with substantial skills will see plenty of opportunities in a property downturn and will know how to buy and sell in order to make money. Nevertheless, opting to contribute more cash to each deal will help to mitigate the risks, so a good strategy in these times is to be more selective and take on less deals in order to retain purchasing power should an amazing opportunity come knocking.

Expert Investor in a Flat Market
(Debt Levels Between 70% and 85% of Portfolio Value)

Skilled investors trade rather than hoard property in flat markets, and maintaining a debt to property portfolio level of between 70% and 85% provides a sustainable situation for this to occur.

Expert Investor in an Uptrending Market
(Debt Levels Between 80% and 95% of Portfolio Value)

Investors who know what they're doing will want to use debt to buy more property, thereby increasing their exposure to potential price gains.

Expert Investor in a Booming Market
(Debt Levels Between 85% and 100% or more of Portfolio Value)

Boom times will present skilled investors with amazing opportunities. Accordingly, they will want to own as much property as possible and will accept greater debt risk for the potential to earn higher profits. Investors need to be mindful to reduce debt once the party stops or else they may be left with a killer financial hangover.

Appendix B

Definitions Behind the Danger Money Multiples Matrix

Back in chapter 15 we got stuck into some tools for evaluating potential deals. As we discussed, there are three core tests that I use and these were explained in detail in chapter 15. The third test involves the Danger Money Multiple matrix (see below), which requires further explanation.

Suggested Minimum Danger Money Multiples				
		Your Skill and Experience with the Strategy Being Implemented		
Debt risk	% LCMVR[1]	Novice	Average	Expert
Low	<70%	5+	9+	8+
Medium	70% to 85%	8+	7+	6+
High	>85%	12+	11+	10+

[1] LCMVR stands for Loan-to-Current Market Value Ratio and represents the percentage of debt to the property's current market value.

Specifically, early feedback from people who read this chapter, suggested that it would be easier to use this tool if I could better define my categories. For example, my idea of a novice investor and a crashing market may differ to somebody else's, and this has the potential to create misunderstandings and poor results when using the Danger Money Multiple matrix as an evaluation tool. To address this issue I've defined these categories below.

INVESTING SKILL AND EXPERIENCE

➲ *Novice Investor*
You are either just starting out as an investor or else you are trying a new investing strategy that is substantially different to, or more complicated than, what you're used to.

➲ *Average Investor*
You are not new to investing, but you still lack the confidence to feel like you have complete control. Alternatively, you're expanding on an investing strategy that you already know and understand.

➲ *Expert Investor*
You have both the knowledge and also the proven experience to complete this investment. You have done multiple similar projects that have also been profitable.

SCENARIOS EXPLAINED

Let's spend some time looking at each of the scenarios represented in the matrix and explaining them in more detail to help you to recognise each situation.

Novice Investor and Low Debt Risk
(Danger Money Multiple: 5+)
Since you're not borrowing much money, the amount of cash or equity you need to contribute to cover the deposit and closing costs

will be quite high. This means that your Danger Money Multiple will be at the lower end of the scale.

While possible, I wouldn't expect to hit the profit jackpot on your first few property deals, so a project that falls into this risk-assessment category may be a good entry level deal for investors who are looking to gain practical knowledge and experience in the marketplace.

Novice Investor and Medium Debt Risk
(Danger Money Multiple: 7+)

As you start to borrow more money, the required Danger Money Multiple will begin to increase given the additional risk associated with carrying more debt.

Novice Investor and High Debt Risk
(Danger Money Multiple: 12+)

This is a very risky category as you're carrying a high percentage of the property's value in debt at the same time as having little investing skill and experience.

If a serious problem were to arise then it would be easy to make a significant loss. I'd strongly caution everyone who falls into this category to think twice about whether or not they want to be so heavily leveraged in the property market, especially at a time when conditions are so uncertain and home values are sliding.

Average Investor and Low Debt Risk
(Danger Money Multiple: 9+)

Given your increased investment skill level, combined with the lower borrowing, you may decide to accept deals with a lowish Danger Money Multiple of 9 or more. These deals won't be the best ones you'll ever do, but they can be good little money earners in an uncertain market.

Average Investor and Medium Debt Risk
(Danger Money Multiple: 6+)

This is the most common mix of skill and debt, and lenders are usually happy to keep financing such projects so long as investors:

➲ keep contributing around 20% of their own money, and

➲ demonstrate an ability to afford to repayments.

Given that less investing capital is needed, the required DMM actually drops from nine plus in the previous category to seven plus.

Average Investor and High Debt Risk
(Danger Money Multiple: 11+)

While it's good that you have some skills as an investor, carrying debt of more than 85% of the property's value adds to the danger of investment and therefore raises the required DMM to make the investment risk acceptable.

Expert Investor and Low Debt Risk
(Danger Money Multiple: 8+)

Highly skilled investors want to make their limited capital stretch as far as possible, so the Danger Money Multiple will need to be high enough to entice them to buy into the investment. In this circumstance, if it's a quick-turnaround deal then the project may be undertaken for the sake of bringing in some fast and easy money.

Expert Investor and Medium Debt Risk
(Danger Money Multiple: 5+)

The Danger Money Multiple actually drops in this area because less precious investing capital is needed to buy into the deal, and debt is at a safe enough level so as not to add any excessive risk.

Expert Investor and High Debt Risk
(Danger Money Multiple: 10+)

Highly specialised projects require a significant profit margin to justify the time and risk involved. For example, I doubt Bill Gates would get too excited by the prospect of making $50,000 on a property deal — it wouldn't be worth his time.

Many projects in this category will be rejected as either too high risk, or too much trouble for the return on offer. With the combination of greater skill and higher risk from borrowing such a large percentage of the value of the property, the Danger Money Multiple will need to be 10 or more for projects to make it past the casual observation stage.

Index